PELICAN BOOKS

A383

WINES AND SPIRITS

L. W. MARRISON

L. W. MARRISON

Wines and Spirits

✡

PENGUIN BOOKS

Penguin Books Ltd, Harmondsworth, Middlesex

U.S.A.: Penguin Books Inc., 3300 Clipper Mill Road, Baltimore 11, Md

AUSTRALIA: Penguin Books Pty Ltd, 762 Whitehorse Road,
Mitcham, Victoria

—

First published 1957

Reprinted with revisions 1958

Made and printed in Great Britain
by Spottiswoode, Ballantyne & Co. Ltd
London & Colchester
Gravure plates by
Harrison and Sons, Ltd.

CONTENTS

Part One
WINES

CONTENTS

LIST OF PLATES

7

LIST OF TEXT FIGURES

LIST OF MAPS

The text figures and maps were specially drawn
for this book by Mr John Woodcock

PREFACE

The author's intention in this book has been to give a purely factual account of wines and spirits. It is well known that facts are rarely pure, however, and in addition, it is all but impossible to write of wines or spirits without obtruding one's own opinions. If any unusually percipient reader happens to detect any of the author's personal views, he is advised to distrust them, for on this subject only one's own opinions are worthy of respect.

ACKNOWLEDGEMENTS

I AM very grateful to Dr Rieu for permission to reprint the lines from his translation of *The Odyssey* (Penguin Books) which appear on page 30, to Mr. T. F. Higham and the Clarendon Press for the passage on page 30 from Mr Higham's translations from Hesiod in *The Oxford Book of Greek Verse in Translation*; and to Mr. P. Oyler and Messrs Hodder and Stoughton for the extract which appears on page 63 from *The Generous Earth*.

I should like to acknowledge the special debt of gratitude I owe to M. Jean Calvet of Bordeaux, M. Pierre Poupon of Beaune, and M. Serge Jacquet of Azay-le-Rideau, and to Mr Bryce Rankine of Adelaide and Mr H. L. Manuel of Sydney. I should also like to thank the following, who have helped me in various ways in supplying information: Messrs W. E. Andrews, B. C. Denby, P. Gee, C. C. Gordon, A. P. Hasslacher, Colin Mackay, H. Marzagelli, S. B. Metaxas, R. Teltscher, Mrs S. M. Tritton, and Gonzalez Byass and G. G. Sandeman; Messrs K. G. Armstrong of Toronto and Joseph F. Wright of Detroit; M. J. Batier of Ampius, Bouideuser of Saumur, F. Calassor of Nîmes, Jean Dubois-Challon of Saint-Émilion, Bernard Ginestet of Bordeaux, P. Mengaud of Perpignan, Jacques Moreau of Chablis, H.-P. Verger of Tournon; Prof. Dr N. Arntz of Bonn, Herr Cornelssen of Mainz, H. Fahrnschon of Frankfurt-on-Main, W. Wasum, junior, of Bacharach, and the Vereinshaus Treviris of Trier; Dr Jennerwein and Herr Johann Kattus of Vienna; MM. Cachin of Sion, Campiche, and J.-P. Gintzburger of Lausanne, Juvet of Neuchatel, and Ryf of Zurich; the Senior Trade Commissioner at South Africa House and Mr G. E. de Bruyn of Zuider Paarl; the High Commissioner for New Zealand and the Director-General, the Administration of Monopolies, Istanbul.

To Tom Carline, Bill Orrell, Dorothea Johnson, and Joe Lowe I owe a more personal debt for their help. And the thing would never have been finished at all if it had not been for my wife's secretarial and critical activities and her attitude towards procrastination.

Part One

WINES

CHAPTER I

INTRODUCTION

IT is necessary at the outset to be quite clear as to what is meant by the word 'wine'. Properly speaking, wine is the fermented juice of the grape. Nevertheless, the word is used quite commonly for fermented drinks made from other fruits and even from vegetables: 'elderberry wine', 'parsnip wine', and so on. Like true wine, all of these consist of a flavoured mixture of alcohol and water: there is quite a variety of other things present, but these are the essentials.

In making wine from grapes, it is the sugar of the grape which ferments to form the alcohol, but when other fruits are fermented there is so little sugar naturally present that the result is undrinkable. In these cases, sugar is added to the juice before fermentation.

'Wine' in ordinary speech means grape-wine, and 'wines' made by fermenting flavoured sugar-water are relegated to chapter 16 of the present book. The word 'wine' comes quite certainly from the Greek word *oinos* (οἶνος), and the Greek usage is similar to our own: alone, it meant grape-wine, but when qualified, it could mean the fermented juice of other fruits. They went further than we do, for they spoke of barley-wine when we should say beer, and of pear- and apple-wine when we say perry and cider. In most modern languages, wines and fruit wines are distinguished from beer and other drinks made from cereals, and it seems reasonable enough to do so, for the raw materials and the processes differ quite considerably, and so do the tastes of the products. In making beer, the starch of the grain is first converted to sugar. Then this is fermented. Also, of course, beer is flavoured with hops; no flavours are added to wine, which, as any Frenchman, Italian, or Spaniard will very promptly tell you, is the un-adulterated juice of the grape, merely allowed to ferment. The most placid Latin can usually be inspired to fierce argument if this proposition is doubted ever so slightly.

Beer, cider, and perry have been excluded from consideration in this book, but in chapter 15 some mention is made of alcoholic drinks derived from the sap of trees which take the place of wine in such places as Mexico and India.

Before proceeding to consider the sorts of wine there are, it is necessary to see what further limitations are usually set in practice to the dictionary definition of wine which has been given, and which for many purposes is really rather broad in its scope.

In France, which produces much more wine than any other country, the law has been obliged to specify exactly what is meant by wine. A good many frauds have been attempted, and practised, at one time or another by wine-merchants, and the present decree defining wine, first passed in 1905 and since modified in details, stands as follows: 'No drink may be kept or transported with a view to selling it, held for sale, or sold, under the name of *Vin*, which is not exclusively produced from the fermentation of fresh grapes or of the juice of fresh grapes.'

One of the most important words in this definition is 'fresh'. At one time there was a good deal of trouble in France because dried grapes, that is, raisins, were imported and used to make wine, either alone or mixed with fresh grapes (see page 90).

In Italy, the second largest producer of wines, the law of 1925 runs: 'The name of *Vino* is reserved for the product of the alcoholic fermentation of the juice of grapes, either fresh or slightly dried, in presence or absence of their skins.' This is intended to exclude the use of raisins, but to allow grapes which have been allowed to dry up a little on the stem: 'passulated'. The French law takes this last point for granted. Some of the well-known and most cherished wines of France, the so-called 'straw-wines', are made from passulated grapes, and in the decrees governing the descriptions of district wines, the methods of making these *vins de paille* are specified (see pages 62 and 90).

The German Wine Law of 1930 reads, '*Wein* is the drink obtained by the alcoholic fermentation of the juice of fresh wine-grapes.'

The other wine countries all follow these definitions with the exception of Greece. The Greek laws quite cheerfully allow the use of dried grapes for vinification; it is probably felt that Greek wine has been made in this way for three thousand years or more and that it is a little hard to have to change after all that time. So Greek wines are allowed into France only if they are described as 'Greek wines'. This appears to satisfy everyone, and would certainly appeal to the Marx brothers.

Each country producing wine has passed laws, which differ in details, specifying the treatments that may be given to wines. These are considered incidentally in chapter 5.

In fermenting a sugar solution, either grape juice, or simply a solution of cane- or beet-sugar in water, it is found that the yeasts which carry out the fermentation cannot make a wine containing more than acertain amount of alcohol. This amount varies somewhat with the yeast, but is generally about 15 per cent. Like every other organism, yeast cannot stand more than a certain amount of alcohol. Wines from straight fermentation in practice contain up to about 12 or 14 per cent alcohol at the most, and some locally-made wines often have as little as 7 per cent. These are the table-wines or beverage wines, such as claret, burgundy, hock, Mosel, and so on.

However, there is a considerable demand for stronger wines than these – stronger than yeasts can live in. Some wines are therefore raised in alcoholic strength to about 18 or 20 per cent, or even more. Such are sherry, port, madeira, etc., the fortified wines (see chapter 7). Alcohol is added to them at the end of the fermentation, or when the fermentation has proceeded part way. In the latter case, some sugar is left unfermented, for of course fermentation cannot continue once the alcohol has been added, and so the wine is sweet. Vermouth is also a fortified wine, but is usually considered separately, as it is in this book (see chapter 16).

There is another type of wine, sparkling wine, of which champagne is the king and the father. This is a wine which, after the normal fermentation is over, is cleared and bottled, and then a second fermentation is carried out *in the bottle* by adding extra sugar and yeast. At least, that is the way the best sparkling wines are made. Second-grade and really inferior ones are made a little differently, in ways described in chapter 6.

Apart from these there are the oddments of the wine trade. There are the medicinal wines, that is, wines to which something has been added which is intended to do the drinker good. There are several opinions about these, one of which is that if the wine was good wine before, it seems a pity to spoil it by putting things in it, and if the wine was originally a poor wine, no addition will help it much. However, medical men recommend these wines and even prescribe them, though perhaps not so eagerly as once; but then the modern doctor is a little more sceptical than his forerunners.

Medical wines, such as ipecacuanha wine, are not commodities of the wine trade at all, but alcoholic extracts of drugs, like tinctures, and belong to the druggist's.

The 20 per cent alcohol content of the fortified wines is insufficient for some drinkers. For them there are spirits. These have an alcohol content which is 40 per cent in Great Britain, though higher in some other countries. They are made by taking a fermented liquid, which is sometimes wine, sometimes a fruit wine, sometimes an alcoholic mash from grain or molasses, and separating off some of the water, so as to increase the alcohol content. This is carried out by distillation, described in chapter 11.

Finally, there are the liqueurs. These are made from spirits of various sources, flavoured with herbs, usually sweetened heavily with syrup, and sometimes coloured.

Let us summarize the main wines and spirits so as to see the whole range at a glance.

	Alcohol per cent	Made from
Table-Wines	about 10	grapes
Fortified Wines, Vermouth, Aperitifs	about 20	wine and brandy (or other spirit)
Spirits		
Brandy	40 or more	wine
Whisky	40 or more	grain
Rum	40 or more	molasses from sugar-cane
Gin	40 or more	maize (or potatoes or molasses)
Calvados } Applejack }	40 or more	cider
Schnapps	40 or more	potatoes
Aquavit, Akvavit	40 or more	grain or potatoes
Vodka	40 or more	grain
Arrack	40 or more	palm-sap, rice, etc.
Liqueurs	40 or more	spirits from various sources

The Beverage Wines

A few words about the table-wines before proceeding further may avoid some misunderstandings. These beverage wines are drunk with meals, just as fortified wines are normally drunk before and after meals: dry before and sweet after. (In wines, dry and sweet are opposites, and dry wines are those in which all of the sugar has been fermented out.)

Beverage wines may be red, white, or pink. The difference between red and white wines is not that they are respectively made from black and white grapes; red wines are made from black grapes by fermenting the juice with the skins, the pips, and often the stems all together. The colouring matter is in the skins and the fermentation extracts it and so red wine is the result. White wines are made from either black or white grapes, but if black grapes are employed, the skins are separated before fermentation takes place, so that the colouring matter does not pass into the wine. It happens that, except in one or two varieties, the juice of black grapes is almost devoid of colour. White wines are not water-white, but always have a pale yellow or yellowish-green tint.

Pink wines, known as *rosé* wines, are not very common (see page 73).

There are certain table-wines which have a reputation so widespread that it may be well to list them at once.

Claret is the red wine of the Bordeaux district of South-West France.

Burgundy comes from the old French province of Bourgogne in eastern France. There are white burgundies, but most are red.

Sauternes and *Graves* are white wines. They are made in the Bordeaux district also. Sauternes is a sweet wine and Graves usually somewhat dry, although some Graves is quite sweetish (and some is red).

Hock is the white wine of the Rhineland of Germany. It may be quite lusciously sweet, or dry.

Moselle (or Mosel) is a white wine which comes from the German part of the valley of the River Mosel, which flows into the Rhine at Coblenz.

Champagne is a white effervescent wine which is made in the limestone area around Rheims and Épernay, just east of Paris.

The Quality of Wines

When one comes to the classification of wines by quality, considerable difficulties arise at once. A fuller discussion of these is deferred to a later stage, after we have seen how wine is made and what connexion there is between taste and composition of wine.

The subject will, I believe, be clarified, if we consider wines as roughly divisible into four classes. The division is merely a matter of convenience, but does correspond to generally accepted standards of quality and, to a considerable degree, to price. The four classes are:

Great Wines
Fine Wines
Standard Wines
Ordinary Wines

GREAT WINES

There are some vineyards in the Bordeaux and Burgundy regions of France, and the Rhineland of Germany, which give wine by general consent classed as quite outstanding. These wines are made by a judicious mingling of experience and science, and they have the inestimable luck of coming from vineyards which are in the best positions and on the most suitable soil, and from vines which are tended by experts, while the wine is made and treated with the sort of loyal care which the reputation of the wine inspires. These wines sell at much higher prices than those from adjacent vineyards, and the greatest care is taken that their reputation is maintained: so much so that in years when the weather is bad, no wine is sold under the name of the vineyard.

The great (beverage) wines are as follows:

Clarets	Château Lafite
	Château Margaux
	Château Latour
	Château Haut Brion
	Château Mouton Rothschild
Sauternes	Château d'Yquem
Burgundies, Red	Richebourg
	La Tâche
	Chambertin (and Clos de Bèze)
	Musigny
	Romanée
	Clos de Tart
	Clos de Vougeot
	Grands-Echezeaux

Burgundies, White	Le Montrachet	
Hocks	Schloss Johannisberg	only those with the
	Steinberger	qualification Auslese,
	Marcobrunn	Spätlese, or Kabinett
Mosels	Bernkasteler Doktor	

In some years, Rauenthaler (Hock) and Wehlener Sonnenuhr (Mosel) may qualify. Some people would demote Bernkasteler to the status of a very fine wine. At one time Chablis from some vineyards (see plate 12) was ranked as great.

It may be added as a footnote to this list that in favourable years vineyards not cited sometimes give wines of quality comparable to these. In each year a slightly different list might be made, excluding some of those given and including others. To make the final choice is a task for the expert who has been drinking judiciously for many years, and experts never agree.

Fine Wines

There are twenty wines which are classed as great. Lower than these is a large army of wines which are very good indeed. These are the wines one can buy and drink fairly frequently without involving oneself in bankruptcy. They vary in quality from those which are candidates for inclusion in the category of great wines to others which narrowly escape relegation to the 'ordinary wines' of the fourth division.

Standard Wines

The classification of wines into great, fine, and ordinary does very well for European wine, but when one considers the wines produced in Australia, the U.S.A., Canada, and South Africa, one finds them to be 'fine' wines with a difference. European wines are at the mercy of the weather of the year in which they were produced, and vary from year to year, so that in 1945 and 1947, for instance, a great many wines could be classed as great, or very nearly great. In climates which are more equable (and where scientific control is paramount) the wines produced vary very little from year to year. They can always be relied upon to be good, but it is equally certain that they will not have the outstanding quality of the great European wines, or of the near-great fine wines of Bordeaux, Burgundy, and the Rhine. Such are the wines of Australia, the U.S.A., Canada, and the Cape. A fairly reliable climate makes for little variation in the ripe grapes and any differences that do take place from year to year are rectified at once by the experts in Melbourne and Adelaide, in Berkeley, California, in Ontario, and at Stellenbosch, Cape Province. For this reason, I have separated the wines of these four countries from those of the rest of the world and described them as 'standard' wines, that is, wines of unvarying quality.

To drink one of the fine French or German wines is to some extent an adventure: it will not be poor, if it is chosen properly, and it may be magnificent. To drink an Australian or South African wine holds no hope of a surprise: it will be a good, sound wine, no more, no less. A bottle of good Dominion table-wine costs seven or eight shillings; a quite good burgundy or Bordeaux is ten or twelve shillings; hock and Mosel are rather more – twelve or fourteen.

ORDINARY WINES

In this class, we include all the other wines, from the French soldier's *pinard* and the coarse red or white liquids sold in Continental bars and *estaminets*, which are as much an acquired taste as Caporal cigarettes, to the cheapest wines imported into Great Britain as 'Bordeaux wine', or 'burgundy'. They are drinks, no more.

Let us consider the great wines and many of the fine wines as hand-made articles, shaped by craftsmen and bearing the stamp of individuality upon them. Let us think of the standard wines as resembling mass-produced commodities, admirable and with their own elegance, reputable and reliable, but in no way showing the marks of *individual* attention. Then the ordinary wines have the virtues of neither. Roughly knocked into shape, shoddy; like furniture which shows the occasional mark of the rasp, on which you may get caught by a projecting nail, from which a scrap of putty may fall out to reveal knot-holes.

The appreciation of wine is a purely psychological phenomenon, one must remember, and like falling in love and the appreciation of art may be much affected by the adventitious circumstance.

CHAPTER 2

THE WINE COUNTRIES

I SUPPOSE that when one thinks of wine, France naturally occurs to one's mind first, and indeed more than one-quarter of the wine of the world is made in France. Next, one probably considers Germany, Portugal, and Spain. Italy is in fact the second largest producer, with Spain next, and then, rather surprisingly, Algeria. Germany takes fifteenth place: German wines have a reputation based on their quality, not on their quantity. After Algeria comes the Argentine, then the U.S.A. and Portugal. Next there is a long drop to Yugoslavia, Russia, Rumania, and the medium producers, not one of which produces half as much as the Argentine or a tenth of the Italian production.

	Millions of gallons (in round figures)
1 – France	1,340
2 – Italy	1,300
3 – Spain	350
4 – Algeria	315
5 – Argentina	300
6 – U.S.A.	240
7 – Portugal	220
8 – Yugoslavia	115
9 – Russia	105
10 – Romania	90
11 – Greece	80
12 – Hungary	80
13 – Chile	80
14 – South Africa	60
15 – West Germany	50
16 – Bulgaria	50
17 – Morocco	45
18 – Tunisia	24
19 – Australia	22

		Millions of gallons (in round figures)
20 – Austria	22
21 – Uruguay	18
22 – Brazil	15
23 – Switzerland	15
24 – Poland	15
25 – Czechoslovakia	9

The world's total annual production is about 4,900 million gallons, which, when one considers it, is almost two gallons a head, man, woman, and child, black, white, yellow, and brown. A popular drink.

The present world output is not far from the record of 1935, when the five thousand million gallon figure was approached. During the war years 1940 to 1945 production was less than two-thirds of the peak: just over three thousand million gallons. One does not feel that the available statistics are sufficiently accurate to warrant stating them more precisely.

Of course Europe makes most of the wine of the world: nearly four-fifths. Africa, floated up on the deluge from Algeria, contributes 11 per cent and South America 8 per cent.

French wine comes from six or seven main areas, although vine-yards are scattered about the whole country south of Paris, and one in six of the population is said to be engaged in the industry in one way or another. The principal *vignobles* of France are the Bordeaux region – the Aquitaine of the Middle Ages; Burgundy in the east; Touraine, which includes all the valley of the Loire and its tributaries, in the west; the Rhône valley from Lyons to Avignon; the Champagne area some eighty miles north-east of Paris, centring around Rheims and Épernay; Alsace, along the left bank of the Rhine, where moderate quantities of white wines are made; the slopes of the Jura mountains; and the Midi, the Languedoc region, which includes the departments of Aude, Hérault, and Gard, the home of the *vin ordinaire*, where wine of sorts almost oozes from the ground.

Bordeaux – and to make the distinction with the city of Bordeaux it is convenient to refer to the area as the Bordelais – the Bordelais makes six of the great wines of the world (see page 20), and a very large proportion of the fine wines. The region extends on both sides of the river Garonne; to the west, the area of the Médoc contains all but one of the great, and many of the fine, claret vineyards, while south of it lie the white Bordeaux vineyards: Sauternes, Barsac, and Graves are the principal districts. On the right bank of the river, to the east, are the two communes where very fine wines are made, but no great ones: Saint-Émilion and Pomerol, which lie back from the Garonne, on the other side of the Dordogne, its tributary. Between the two rivers, which join just below Bordeaux city, is the area known as *Entre-deux-Mers*, where much of the minor fine wine is produced: wine without great qualities, but very good of its kind. Nearby (see map 3) others of the lesser wines of the Bordelais are made: Blaye, Fronsac, and Bourg.

Burgundy is an elongated area (so far as the *vignoble* is concerned) stretching from Dijon south almost to Chalon-sur-Saône, with outliers to the north-west (Chablis) and to the south (the Mâconnais and the Beaujolais). The northern area is the Côte d'Or, the Slope of Gold, and on these eastward-facing slopes are the vineyards, almost all giving fine wines and several great wines, red and white.

The Touraine *vignoble* is strung almost east to west along the Loire and extends up the side valleys. There are no great vineyards, but a number of fine wines are produced. Vouvray, Saumur, and Angers are the main centres. Most of the wines are white.

Rhône wines once had a reputation second to none. Hermitage a century ago was a great wine, from all accounts. Nowadays, the reputation is for good, full wines like Châteauneuf-du-Pape. The Rhône vineyard area lies along both sides of the river and perhaps gets too much of the Mediterranean sun to produce great table-wines. Tavel is the best *rosé* wine.

The Champagne region is the fifth and last of the fine-wine regions of France. It is unique in several ways. Champagne does not sell by the names of vineyards but by the name of the firm which makes it. It is almost a 'standard' wine, for although it has its great years and its not-so-great years, it is a blended wine and more depends on the method of making than with any other table-wine. It is for this reason that a special chapter has been devoted to it (page 99).

Of the Midi wine little can be said. Vast amounts are produced. After mixing with Algerian wine, and wines from Spain and Italy, it is sold by the million gallons to men with dry throats.

There are smaller vineyard areas in France, such as the Savoy and the Jura, and Alsace, to the east and south of Burgundy.

Italy makes wine in every one of its provinces, from the Alpine valleys of the Trentino to Sicily. A great variety of light and fortified wine is made. Chianti and the fortified Marsala are those principally imported into Britain.

Spain is well known for one wine in particular, and that a fortified wine, sherry. Malaga, a sweet fortified wine, is also imported. As in all the countries of the northern Mediterranean littoral, grapes are grown in every part of the land.

Portugal's reputation rests firmly on port wine, but a certain amount of beverage wine also comes to Britain.

Germany, with its comparatively small production, yet exports a larger amount of fine wines than any other country except France. Although much red wine is made, very little leaves the country, and although vineyards are found all over the southern part of Germany, it is only the white wines of the western part which reach England and have any reputation here. That reputation is of the highest.

Luxembourg wines from the upper reaches of the Mosel are rather acid, but fresh and pleasant.

Swiss wines, as crisp as Alpine air, are made all over the country, although exports are very small. The best Austrian wines are made in the south-east of the country, but some comes from western Austria.

In Central Europe and further east there are vineyards on sunny slopes south of the Polish border, or thereabouts. The wines of Hungary, Romania, Bulgaria, and Yugoslavia are from these vineyards. Some are good, some less good, and of many, next to nothing is known in the West. It is highly probable that none is a fine wine. Tokay of Hungary has a somewhat legendary fame and is sweet and luscious; perhaps some would class it as great.

To the south, in Greece and the islands of Ionia and the Aegean, are wines known since the dawn of civilization. In fact, toasts to that dawn were doubtless drunk with their aid.

Russian wines once had some reputation and probably they are still good, for there is much activity in experiment, and many claims for improvement in grapes and wine.

To the south of the oases of Uzbek, Iran grows wine-grapes near the ancient town of Shiraz.

Further east still, among the Himalayas in Kashmir, wine is still made as it has been since the days of Akbar the Great in the sixteenth century, although from a different grape.

Returning to the Mediterranean, besides the well-known wine of Cyprus, there is a small production from the coastal plains of the Levantine mainland in Israel.

The wines of North Africa, Algeria, Tunisia, and Morocco come from the slopes of the foothills of the Atlas mountains and from a few oases to the west, at last reaching to within sight of the Atlantic at Mogador. A couple of hundred miles offshore is the island of Madeira, far-famed for its dessert wines.

The remainder of the vineyards of the world are in the old colonies of Spain, Portugal, and Great Britain. The vineyards of Australia, mostly in the eastern part of the continent, are unique in being founded by Englishmen.

The wines of Cape Province, South Africa, first made by Dutch settlers in the seventeenth century, all come from within a hundred and fifty miles or so of Cape Town.

The United States, which has nearly every climate within its borders, makes 90 per cent of its wine in California, on the inland slopes of the San Joaquin and Central Valleys. A little, and that chiefly sparkling wine, comes from the shores of Lake Erie, not far from the Canadian vineyards.

South America, more than half as large again as Europe, has an even greater variety of climatic conditions. In Bolivia the vineyards are far higher than those of Kashmir, and more than twice as high as the Valais of Switzerland. In the northern vineyards of Peru the rainfall is less than two inches a year. In Chile, between a region where no rain has ever fallen and another where it rarely stops, wine is produced in considerable amount – nearly 100 million gallons a year: twice as much as Germany and three times as much as Australia. The Argentine vineyards are on pleasant inland slopes, where the rainfall is usually between seven and eight inches a year, and irrigation trenches are run between the vines. Here, huge areas are sown with vines and more than 5 per cent of the world's wine is made. Brazil, Uruguay, and Paraguay all make enough wine for their own needs, with slight supplements from their neighbours, especially Argentina and Chile. All have to battle continuously with drought, late frosts, and the locust.

CHAPTER 3

THE HISTORY OF WINE

WHEN Noah left the ark, he promptly planted a vineyard, it is recorded, and this, according to the once-popular chronology of Archbishop Ussher, was a mere fifty generations after the Creation. Doubtless there were vineyards in antediluvian times, even if Biblical history does not mention them. Certainly Milton, who described the Garden of Eden at a much later period, had no doubt that the vine flourished at that time.

Archaeologists, unable to be as precise as archbishops, find evidence that wine-making was practised in Mesolithic times, some ten or twelve thousand years ago. The fermentation of honey may be even earlier. Certainly, when graphical history began, the fermentation of fruit juices, and presumably of grape juice, was already being practised in Egypt. Palm-wine is at least as old as the pyramids; from wall-paintings of the beginning of the second millennium B.C., date-wine seems to have been even more popular.

The first definite mention of grape-wine occurs in writings of the reign of Gudea of Mesopotamia: that is, about 2100 B.C. Both in the valley of the Nile and in Mesopotamia, wine was being made well before 2000 B.C., it is certain. Neither region supports vineyards nowadays. In Egypt the Pharaohs and the hierarchy of priests seem to have kept viticulture as a monopoly of church and state (which were one). Vines were trained on pergolas, much as they are in some parts of the world today.

The kings of Assyria, from the eighth century before Christ onwards, including Sennacherib and Nebuchadrezzar, were enthusiastic oenologists, and by their orders extensive vineyards were cultivated; some contained twenty or thirty thousand vines. The royal palace had extensive wine-cellars, and lists of the best wines were compiled; one list is still in existence, although the names are of course meaningless. It was customary to add spices to the wine.

Early Egyptian wall-paintings give a complete series of pictures, in the strip-drawings which were then so popular, of all the operations of making wine: it seems that there is nothing new under the sun Men, women, and children are seen gathering the grapes with sickle-shaped knives identical in shape with those used around the Mediterranean to this day. Singing and music accompanied the vintage and the treading of the grapes.

The climate of Egypt and Mesopotamia is not well suited to the vine and, long before Homeric times, the Mediterranean was seen to be the natural home of wine-making. By the time of Herodotus (fifth century B.C.) grape-wine was being imported into Egypt from Greece, for it was no longer being made in the Nile Valley.

By the time the Mycenean civilization had established itself in the second millennium B.C., wine was used not only for sacrifices to the gods in the way described in the first book of the *Iliad*, but generally as a drink. Always among the Greeks wine was drunk mixed with water. Only barbarians, like the savage, the 'insolent and oppressive' Scythians, took their wine neat. At an Aegean feast or symposium a *krater*, or mixing bowl, full of watered wine was brought in.

Economically, the Mediterranean civilization was based on wheat, the olive, and wine: the so-called 'Mediterranean triad'. Meat was not commonly eaten, for it was too scarce, as it still is in parts of the Balkans and the Levant. Wine was the only alternative to water, and the water was often untrustworthy, although as water was added to the wine, there was little gain from the point of view of hygiene, for wine has only a mild bactericidal action. There were no conscientious tee-totallers in classical times and the literature of ancient Greece and Rome is drenched with references to wine. One of the most mysterious of Homer's cliché-epithets is the description of the colour of the sea as 'wine-dark'. Far more than wheat or the olive, wine is a recurrent motif, especially in the *Odyssey*. In Calypso's bower,

> A Vine did all the hollow Cave embrace;
> Still green, yet still ripe bunches gave it grace.
>
> (Chapman's translation)

And to enchant the sailors of Odysseus, Circe

> . . . led them in and set them on bench and lordly seat,
> And a mess of cheese, and meal and honey pale and sweet
> With Pramnian wine she mingled; and she blended therewithal
> Ill herbs, that the land of their fathers might clean from their memories fall.
>
> (Morris's translation)

When Odysseus returns at last to his kingdom of Ithaca after nineteen years' absence, he identifies himself to old Laertes, his father, whom he finds in the terraced vineyard, by reminding him,

I was only a little boy at the time, trotting after you through the orchard, begging for this and that, and as we wound our way through these very trees, you told me all the names. You gave me thirteen pear-, ten apple-, and forty fig-trees, and at the same time you pointed out the fifty rows of vines that were to be mine.

(Dr E. V. Rieu's translation: Penguin edition)

A century or so later than Homer, in the eighth century before Christ, Hesiod already looks forward two thousand years to Omar Khayyam the Persian poet, in his vivid description of the hot days of June in the Mediterranean:

When the cardoon flowers, and the loud cicada sings
perched on a tree, pouring from under his wings
a flood of shrillest music time and again:
when summer is ripe, and the heat a burden of pain,
then are the she-goats fattest, and wine is best,
and women most fain; but men are languidest,
for Sirius parches the heads and the knees of men
and burns their bodies with drouth. O give me then
the shade of a rock, with Biblis' wine set by,
and bread of the best, and the milk of goats drained dry!

(Mr T. F. Higham's translation)

To Homer, the nectar of the gods of Olympus seems to be no more than a special sort of wine; for it too is mixed in a *krater*. Perhaps the first drinking-song extant is a paraphrase by Alcaeus, in the seventh century B.C., of the passage already quoted from Hesiod. Drinking-songs were always popular from this time onwards, until Greek literature petered out some ten centuries later.

Although for the West the Greeks secularized and democratized wine, in the Far East it remained a drink restricted to religious observances, or for the use of the privileged. In ancient times, Indra, the warrior god and the most popular deity of the Hindu pantheon, was in some mystic sense identified with or symbolized by *soma*, an intoxicating drink. *Soma* was poured as a libation and drunk at religious ceremonies:

The heavens and earth themselves have not grown equal to one half of
    me:
Have I not drunk of soma-juice?
I in my grandeur have surpassed the heavens and all this spacious earth:
Have I not drunk of soma-juice?
I, greatest of the mighty ones, am lifted to the firmaments:
Have I not drunk of soma-juice?

Soma is thought to have been fermented honey, or perhaps a beer-
like drink, but it seems at least as likely that it was fermented grape-
juice.

Except for a few centuries under Mogul rule in India (sixteenth to
eighteenth centuries A.D.), wine seems never to have been drunk much
in the Middle and Far East. Date- and palm-wine in the Middle East
and rice wine in the Far East were much more popular. There are few
parts of Asia suited to the cultivation of the vine.

Wherever the Greeks went, they took the vine with them; where-
ever they founded a colony, they immediately planted a vineyard.
The merchants of Tyre and Sidon in some cases were before them; it
was they who introduced the vine to Cadiz and Malaga (Cadir and
Malaca) perhaps before 1000 B.C. The Greeks have the credit for the
vineyards of Southern France, through the colony they founded in
600 B.C. at Marseilles (Massalia), and in Magna Graecia (Sicily and
Southern Italy) a century or two earlier. The Greeks colonized east
at the same time and took their vinestocks with them into the
Euxine (the Black Sea); they are believed to have founded the
famous vineyards of the Crimea. Long before the Christian era
there were vineyards all around the Mediterranean, from beyond the
Pillars of Hercules in the west, to the land of the Massagetae, on the
shores of the Caspian.

During the period of Roman domination of the Mediterranean
and beyond, the picture changed very considerably. Rome's economy
was calculated and organized. Latium, Campania, and Lombardy,
together with Spain and Syria, would supply wine for the Empire.
Sicily and (North) Africa would be responsible for sending home
wheat and barley; vines in those regions were uprooted and grain
laid down. In the case of North Africa this was partly spitefulness,
since it was only in 146 B.C. that Carthage was destroyed. Viticulture
languished for centuries in these two areas; the wine of Messina

was protected, for it was classed as a *grand cru* in Rome; the rest of Sicily went under cereals.

On the other hand, Andalusia flourished exceedingly. Baetica, the Roman name for the province, supplied not only wine, but other commodities, such as jars for wine and oil. In the great mound of shattered *amphorae* (Monte Testaccio) near Rome, fragments of no less than forty million jars have been found – narrow-mouthed jars for wine, wide-mouthed ones for olive oil. Each jar held eleven gallons or so. Rome had about a million inhabitants at this time (the second century A.D.).

Southern Spain had always been one of the advanced parts of the world: advanced but not aggressive, rich, civilized, densely populated. It had always supplied wine and fruits and metals; it still does: sherry, Almería grapes, and Rio Tinto copper nowadays. Spain is a conservative country; what was good enough for his grandfather ninety times removed is good enough for the modern Andalusian.

The armies quartered in the northern provinces of the Empire, on the Rhine and the Danube, were supplied with wine from Italy. They consumed a good deal, as soldiers do, and it was soon found that wine from Hungary could be more easily transported to the legion on the Danube. In the second century A.D. it was discovered that grapes could be grown in the Mosel valley and in Alsace and that a very pleasant wine could be made from them. In this way the thirst of the army on the Rhine was quenched. Soon vines were being planted in Flanders, Mecklenburg, and Pomerania, although the climate of none of these was at all suitable for viticulture.

As the Roman Empire wore on to its predestined fall, Western Europe became independent of the East in all the essential commodities, and the eastern trade concerned itself more and more with luxuries, although special wines still formed a fair proportion. Moreover, the Empire split into regions which began to fall apart in the third century A.D., each capable of supplying its own needs, though the home province, consisting of Italy and its near islands, became more and more parasitical upon the others; that is, upon the western block, Spain, Gaul, Germany, and Britain, the southern block of North Africa from Mauretania to Cyrenaica, and the north-eastern, which was more or less Central Europe, the Danube basin and South Russia.

By the end of the fourth century, the Eastern Empire left to set up business for itself, first as the Eastern Roman Empire and then as Byzantium. Here viticulture flourished with great vigour, but in the Western Empire agriculture and all else declined. In the fourth century brigands infested main roads of the once-so-well-policed Roman Empire, and poverty spread over the West. When the barbarian hordes came showering down from the north there was little spirit to resist them.

However, like all conquerors who pause too long, the Goths and the Vandals were subdued and absorbed, and by the fifth century the barbarian kingdoms were 'essentially Mediterranean in character' says Pirenne, the eminent Belgian economic historian. That is, the land returned to normal, although the invaders, who were converted nomads, had to learn viticulture from their subjects, and there was no vigour in Western Europe: the Dark Ages had descended. Syrian merchants still passed between East and West and linked up the West with the caravan routes from Constantinople, Trebizond, Antioch, and Damascus, but trade was bad, very bad. To a Syrian, trade is always bad, but now it was truly no more than a trickle, and soon it worsened.

In the seventh century the remarkable advance to the west of the Muslim armies began. By 703 they had conquered Tunisia, and by 711 their leader Tarik had landed at Gibraltar (Jabel Tarik, or Tarik's Hill). By 720 they were over the Pyrenees and at Narbonne. In 732 they reached Burgundy and Lyons. This was their furthest. After their defeat by Charles Martel they drew back over the Pyrenees and settled down in Spain, which they did not leave for another 760 years.

Northern Europe remained shut in on itself until early in the eleventh century. The activity of trade with the Baltic, to which wine had been taken by the vigorous Frisian merchants, was checked and then destroyed by the Norse marauders of the ninth century. The Frisians had carried wine across the North Sea, then known in fact as the Frisian Sea, to Britain, from which they returned with a most heterogeneous collection – wheat, iron, hides, hunting-dogs, slaves, oysters, and brooches. It took time – a century or more – to convert Norsemen to a liking for trade, although eventually that was their destiny.

With the Arabs settled in Spain and Africa, in command of the Mediterranean, in control of the seaports of the Levant, with Italian merchants depending on a furtive coastwise traffic only in the Adriatic as far as the western Peloponnese, Southern Europe had a deserted look. The Arabs at first hugged their own southern coasts, and the middle of the Mediterranean was almost empty. They had a raiding outpost at Garde-Freinet in the Alps, which discouraged merchants for many miles around and vastly increased the insurance rates in Northern Italy.

It might be thought that this was a bad time for viticulture. On the contrary, in Spain and North Africa and Sicily (which the Arabs held from the ninth until the very end of the eleventh century) the whole science of agriculture took a new lease of life. The Arabs were experienced husbandmen. The fighters, the 'strong-arm men', were certainly the wild nomads of the desert who never planted but lived on the fruits of other men's planting. But the brains of the Saracen armies were from Baghdad, the Yemen, and the populated oases of the Hejaz. They introduced scientific irrigation into Andalusia and North Africa, and no countries needed it more. These two regions, as well as Sicily, became the only places in the world where agriculture, and viticulture in particular, really flourished. Córdoba, Palermo, Baghdad were the great thriving cities of the world in the ninth and tenth centuries; Rome was moribund, Byzantium static and hidebound, London, Paris, and Cologne no more than swollen villages.

Vineyards in Western and Central Europe were attached to the abbeys or to ducal manors, or were little village plots giving enough only for local needs. Trade had dwindled to the barest necessities; every village was self-supporting in all but a few oddments like salt, millstones, fine cloth. A weekly village market sufficed for the restricted needs of the rural population. Government was in the hands of the Church, where were the only men who could write, or had the wealth and the energy to maintain large estates.

In the ninth century the Italian traders of Venice, Bari, Naples, and Amalfi, who would have traded with the devil had they known his address, began to establish contacts with the Arabs and sold them Slav slaves for the harems of Baghdad and Damascus, and timber and iron for building ships and forging arms the better to fight the West. This trade was confined to the Mediterranean. Meanwhile the Swedes fought their way across the steppes to South Russia, turned traders and brought back Eastern luxuries from the bazaars of Tashkent and Ferghana, and wines from the Crimea, the Caspian, and the Caucasus. Western Europe remained isolated still.

The revival was slow, but gathered force. In 1052 Pisa cleared Sicily of the Arabs, and by the end of the century Genoa was trading freely with the Syrian ports once more. The Alpine routes were opened up: the St Bernard leading to Burgundy and the Rhine, the Mont Cenis to the Rhône valley. In the north the merchants of the German Hansa towns joined hands with the Venetians, the Genoese, and the Milanese, and the stream of traffic started. France took the leading part, for by this time she had much to supply: wine 'unquestionably occupied the first place', says Pirenne.

All through the medieval period, wine, with salt, occupied the key position in trade. Wool for a time was of equal importance and in the eastern trade spice was paramount, but in Western Europe the trade in wine or salt made or broke a port or a market town.

Vineyards increased all over the West in these centuries from 1000 A.D. onwards. Population grew everywhere, agriculture spread rapidly, mining took a fresh lease of life. It was as if someone had shouted and the West had awakened. River traffic increased greatly, the roads which had become lost in undergrowth were cleared or made anew, bridges were built to replace the age-old fords, seaborne shipping took a great leap forward. In 1237 the formidable Schöllenen gorge in the St Gotthard was crossed with the first suspension bridge. Before this time ships had travelled east from Cadiz and north from La Rochelle and Bordeaux – all three ports depending for much of their prosperity and even existence on the wine trade. Never had there been regular sailings around from the Mediterranean and through the Bay of Biscay. Now large galleys were built at Genoa to make this passage as a regular trip. They went to Northern France, Flanders, and England, and took wine, spices, alum, and grain in exchange for cloth from Flanders and wool from England. Newcastle and Sluys, the port of Bruges, were their farthest north, for the Hansa merchants jealously guarded their Baltic and North German trade. It was in the thirteenth century that the rudder was perfected, and the mariner's compass came into general use in Mediterranean ships a century later.

The amount of wine consumed at this time was surprisingly large. For rural districts there are no statistics, it is true, but in Florence six million gallons were drunk each year, and in Milan and Venice much more. Certain districts became well known as suppliers of wine: Burgundy, Gascony, Provence, the Rhine. Andalusia, Latium and Campania, Sicily, Cyprus, and the coastlands of Asia Minor had long been famous. Trade was largely carried on at the great fairs which were started, probably in the eleventh century, at Champagne, at Troyes, Provins, Châlons-sur-Marne, and Château-Thierry in France, at Bruges, Ypres, Lille, Thourout, and Messines in Flanders. These towns grew with the prosperity brought by the fairs and had separate quarters for the wine-merchants from Spain, Italy, Montpellier, Montauban, Germany, and so on. Each town was sited on the junction of two or three or more of the great land routes. The Flemish towns rose to great importance because of their key position between the northern trade circuit, and the roads from the Mediterranean and the French wine districts.

The chief buyers of wine were England and the Low Countries. England had a considerable proportion of the wine regions in her own domain, for Prince Henry of England in 1152 married Eleanor of Guienne and she brought all the West of France to the English crown: Normandy, Brittany, Anjou, Poitou, Aquitaine, and Gascony, all covered with vineyards. The area includes the present-day wine-making districts of Bordeaux, the Loire, and the Charente, as well as the more northerly parts, which were then almost as prolific. The English drank a considerable amount of wine: three times as much per head as at present. For three centuries, until 1451, the Bordeaux region was in English hands and the wine trade grew so that at the end of the period it accounted for nearly a third of England's imports. In the 1448-9 season over three million gallons left Bordeaux for this country. Most of it was brought over by Gascons in their own ships, and they travelled through the more nearly civilized parts of the land selling it to the manor-houses, the retail merchants, and the inns. Bordeaux itself doubled in population.

The ships used in those days were of up to 480 tons; there were a few on the seas of 600 tons, but these were very exceptional. Salt, which took second place to wine, was made by evaporation at the bay of Bourgneuf, only just north of Bordeaux, and was shipped from

Blaye, across the Gironde. 'Bay salt' was well known throughout Europe, though in the north it had to compete with the Luneburg salt shipped from Lübeck.

At the beginning of the fourteenth century a strange decline overtook Europe, a slackening of trade which has not been completely explained. It would presumably have been no more than a small trough in the graph of progress, but a series of happenings intensified it. It has been suggested that the population of Western Europe had reached the maximum number which could be supported by the agricultural methods in use at the time, and that mines were reaching the limits of the veins which could be worked economically. A number of small wars and economic conflicts thwarted recovery. In 1315 famine spread all over Europe: the important trading centre Ypres lost one in ten of its inhabitants in six months. Between 1327 and 1343 seven of the leading Italian bankers failed, and this put a severe strain on the whole credit system of the West. Then, in 1347, the Black Death came to Europe. Starting in the Far East, it came with the Tartars who besieged Caffa (Theodosia), the Genoese trading port on the Crimea. Incensed by the resistance of the city, the Mongols catapulted over the walls the corpses of men who had died of the plague. Italian ships taking wine to the port and returning with fish, skins, wheat, and furs from the Volga basin also brought the plague westwards. It spread through Sicily, Tuscany, Genoa, Ragusa, Venice, and like a fire across central, northern, and western Europe, killing one in three of the population. The further scourge of war which raged across France from 1338 to 1453 multiplied the devastation.

Nevertheless, life continued, if at a lower level of vigour, and by the middle of the fifteenth century recovery was on the way. England lost Guienne, and the wine trade with France diminished, but Spanish wines began to come over. Rouen, the shipping port for the wines of Burgundy and the Paris basin, took a larger portion of the wine trade to England. England herself, which had had forty vineyards at the time of the Domesday record, now stopped wine-making, for although there had been fresh plantings in the twelfth century, the deluge of cheap, good Gascon wine made it clear that the wine-grape in England was an exotic.

The discovery of the sea route to India and the East in 1492 and of

America in 1497 profoundly affected Europe in almost every conceivable way, yet the wine trade did not change very greatly. The new lands which appeared so magically beyond the bounds of the Mediterranean produced no wine, nor were they customers for wine. The sea-traders of the coasts of Europe found far richer cargoes outside their home waters, and the Baltic and the Mediterranean were seen to be of considerably less importance than formerly. But wine was still demanded and still made.

Spirits appeared, and that strange drink, champagne. Schnapps, a grain or potato spirit from the Low Countries, became popular on the rise of the trade with Holland in the seventeenth century, together with French brandy from Nantes. Rum, from West Indian molasses, followed soon, and arrack from Batavia.

Meanwhile the wine position altered, so far as Britain was concerned. During the seventeenth century Italian wines shipped from Florence, which had been increasing in volume, began to deteriorate in quality and suffered a set-back at the same time as the French influence of the Stuarts was replaced by that of the compatriots of William III. A heavy duty was put on French wines and spirits, and Portuguese wine became popular, more because of its relative cheapness than by virtue of any outstanding superiority in quality.

It was at the beginning of the eighteenth century that the sale of gin increased so enormously (see page 250). When this died down, in the middle of the century, small beer was the usual drink, and tea, although very expensive, was becoming popular. It was Portuguese and Spanish wines which were the mainstay of the wine-importer. In 1786, of the total of four million gallons of wine imported, two-thirds was from Portugal and the rest more or less equally from Spain and France. A popular fashion among the upper classes at this time was for sillabubs (or cillabubs): one-third Spanish wine and two-thirds fresh milk. In St James's Park and at Bath they were all the rage. The country squire, the backbone of the country, however, 'eats nothing but salt beef, cold mutton, cabbage, carrots, and pudding, which last is his favourite dish; and that which is heaviest he likes best. His drink is ale, coarse Portugal wine, and now and then a little of the coarsest brandy.' This refers to Fielding's Squire Western and his cronies, of course. The rise of the shopkeeper class led to a continuous increase in the imports of wine from the Continent. By 1790, nearly seven million gallons came in, by 1795 approaching ten million. Portuguese wine was still about two-thirds of the total and French wine very creditably maintained itself, considering the internal troubles of France, at between a half and three-quarters of a million gallons.

At the opening of the nineteenth century the wines from the Cape began to be imported, chiefly Constantia at first. Constantia, like the Commendary of Cyprus, was a 'class' wine. Spanish wines increased in volume and drew level with Portuguese in 1829 for the first time; it was not until the 1840s that they outdistanced them. By this time whisky had added itself to the spirits repertoire and in 1854 Australian wine came on to the English market.

A fashion of the early nineteenth century was to drink hock with soda-water, 'Hock and seltzer', a curious mixture. Burgundy was more popular than claret; Hermitage was one of the great wines. In the 1860s French wines once more began to be imported in quantities comparable with the wines of Spain and Portugal.

In the earlier part of the century, the drink of the poorer classes was still small beer, as in fact it always has been. Nevertheless, although the days of 'Gin Lane' were two generations past, spirits were largely drunk. Gin was still popular (an account of the effect of hot gin on wooden legs may be found in chapter thirty-two of *Pickwick Papers*, an invaluable source-book on the subject of drinking). Rum, alone or with hot water, sometimes flavoured with pineapple, was drunk by almost everyone. Rum seems to have been the favourite drink of Quilp, that mighty drinker, and of Mr Stiggins, although the celebrated discourse on the vice of intoxication delivered by Mr Stiggins was prompted by port wine, warmed with a little water, spice, and sugar: this is described as 'negus'. 'Shrub', a mixture of rum or other spirit, fruit juice, and sugar, had been popular from the middle of the eighteenth century.

In 1876 French wine imports into Britain reached the record figure of seven million gallons, which has never since been attained. In fact the two million gallons total has never been reached since 1931. The much larger amounts of Spanish and Portuguese wines which come into the country do not represent at all accurately the amount of sherry and port which is drunk, for a considerable proportion goes for making 'English wines'. Australia sends between one and two million gallons to Britain, and South Africa rather less.

During the present century the most striking facts have been the great over-production in France, especially in Languedoc, the large increase in the amount of sherry and cocktails drunk, and in the few years since the war, the gradual rise in interest in 'quality' table-wines, particularly claret and burgundy, in Britain.

CHAPTER 4

THE MAKING OF WINE

IN the making of wine there are three distinct steps: there are the growing of the grapes, the fermentation of the grape juice, and the treatment of the wine so that it shall be sound and remain sound.

The main outlines, at least of the first two stages, are simple and have scarcely changed except in details since the most ancient times. It is true that new types of wine have been invented, in particular the fortified wines, and the sparkling wines of which champagne is the type; the invention of distillation led to the introduction of spirits, a drink which would have surprised classical man. Table-wines, however, are still made in much the same way as that employed by the Assyrians, the Greeks, and the Romans.

Numerous improvements have been made in all the three basic stages, some dating back many centuries, some quite recent, and to ignore these would be to give an erroneous notion of the process of making wine.

Nowadays, wine is a sound, dependable drink, for the wine-laws of the various countries insist that it shall be faithful to its type, keeping for long periods, indeed in many cases improving considerably on being kept. Wine can be bought cheaply, and in that case is notably inferior to that which costs more, but whether cheap or expensive, it complies with the three basic requirements of good wine: soundness, comformability to its type, and good keeping qualities. The excise charges in this country are so high that it is not worth while importing inferior wines.

In the Middle Ages, wine was sweetened with honey and flavoured with spices in order to hide its deficiencies. In the eighteenth century, Smollett says of the merchants of France, 'when the grapes are of a bad, meagre kind the wine-dealers mix the juice with pigeons'-dung . . . in order to give it a spirit which nature has denied.' There is no doubt that at that time worse sophistications were practised than those Smollett heard of. A writer even as recently as 1864 admits that nitric acid was added to wines to improve their colour, and 'spirits of nitre' to aid their bouquet.

All of these sophistications are forbidden by the wine-laws of all the producing countries.

In considering the account of wine-making which is given in the next few pages, the reader should bear in mind the great differences in the attitudes of those who make wine. There are the small farmers, from Anjou to Anatolia, who make wine merely as a minor adjunct to their main business, in the way their ancestors made it: the little vineyard is often under the charge of the farmer's wife, as bread-making and beer-brewing were in England not so long ago. There are also the large manufacturers of Southern France and Algeria, who make the maximum quantity from the minimum area of a product which shall duplicate exactly the liquid they produced last year. They expect 3,000 gallons or more from every acre of their vineyards. These two classes of producers make most of the wine of the world. Nevertheless, the best wines, which are those which are bottled or barrelled for export, are made by neither, but by the owners of the classed vineyards of the Bordelais, like the Baron de Rothschild and the Marquis de Lur-Saluces, and the *vignerons* of Burgundy and the Rhineland. They are satisfied with 120 gallons of wine from each acre, so long as it is good.

Growing the Grapes

CLIMATE AND WEATHER

Grapes suitable for making wine, drinkable wine that is, will only grow in certain parts of the world. In Western Europe, the most northerly vineyards are those near Bonn, on the banks of the Rhine and the slopes of the Seven Mountains, although there is at least one enthusiastic amateur *vigneron* at Maidstone, which is 51° 17′ north. From Bonn south as far as Marrakesh and Mogador in Western Morocco there are vines from which wine is made. This is a north-to-south range of some 1,500 miles.

Wines from the colder limits of this zone tend to be somewhat acid; those from the southern parts are flabby and dull, useful only for blending, unless indeed they are fortified. It is noteworthy that the wines of the Mosel and the Rhine, and of Alsace, all on the northern edge, are in general slightly lower in alcohol than the wines of the south. This is because the grapes have rather less sugar than the Mediterranean berries, and it is the sugar which gives the alcohol. They keep well, for they are rather high in acid, and acid in wines, so long as it comes from the grapes, makes for longevity.

The vine needs a warm spring to form the flowers, and as the year goes on there must be that nice balance of rain and heat to set the grapes and then to fill and mature them. Cold and rainy summers give poor, acid wines, but summers of great heat – and 1921 is the classical instance – are not welcomed by all *vignerons*. For the makers of the sweet white wines, such as Sauternes and Johannisberger, these are the great years, certainly, but on the Médoc, and in fact in all red vineyards, the wines are found to have a burnt taste, foreign to their usual nature. Heat at the time of vintage and fermentation means that more than the usual amount of attention must be paid to the problem of keeping the vats at the correct temperature, for, as will be seen in a moment, overheating in the vats leads to disease in the wine. The grapes must not be allowed to linger on their way to the vats, either, or premature fermentation will set in.

Frost spells which come in the summer on the unripe fruit can do much damage. Even if they only last overnight they may result in as much as 20 per cent loss. The slowly ripening grapes are checked, the leaves wither, and the formation of sugar is halted. At this stage the acid in the grapes is much higher than it will be later on, and the condition known as 'acid rot', which the German growers call *Rohfäule*, may set in. The wine will then have an off-taste, the *Frostgeschmack*.

Even less extreme conditions than frost and a sub-tropical summer can do much harm to the vintage: certain years are marked out as bad and others as good by the rainfall and the range of temperature during critical periods. Wine merchants publish little cards showing in tabular form which are the 'good years' and which the bad in the various wine-districts of Europe. It is an infallible sign of the amateur wine-connoisseur that he will immediately produce one of these from his waistcoat pocket when the conversation turns to wine. These tables should be used with discretion, however, for two vineyards only a few miles apart, but separated by a fold in the hills or by a strip of forest, may give wines of widely differing qualities, perhaps because one has missed a hailstorm which set the other back for weeks, or had a shower of rain while the other remained parched. This question of 'good' and 'bad' years will be dealt with again later on (see chapter 9).

SOIL

Good wine is a delicately poised combination of fullness, vinosity, acidity, sweetness, 'bite', and a good many other, less easily specified, qualities. It might be supposed that wine-grapes would need a very special soil to produce this complex balance, and that only where it was found would they grow well. On the contrary, the vine is by no means exacting. In the Champagne country around Épernay, the ground is as chalky as the Sussex Downs; on the Mosel, it is uncompromising slate. The fine wines of Bordeaux are grown on gravel overlying sands and clays; the peasants of the Douro, where the great vintage ports come from, are obliged to use crowbars and explosives to plant their vinestocks in the adamantine schist.

Perhaps, especially in the Médoc, one vineyard will produce the finest of growths, while another, adjacent, gives a most undistinguished tipple. Although there is usually some reasonable explanation for this – differences in the care and attention given to the cultivation, a band of acid soil or cold clay – there are anomalies which are still unexplained.

It has often been pointed out that a great many of the vineyards of the world are on slopes. The best hocks come from the steep hillsides of the Rhine valley. The country behind Jerez de la Frontera, which produces sherry, is made up of an unending series of spurs of the mountains of Cabras and Aljibe; the vineyards of Burgundy are on the so-called Golden Slope (Côte d'Or); in the Douro vineyards the ground is in many parts too steep for wheeled vehicles. The Graves district in the Bordelais is one of the few quality *vignobles* which is flat. Perhaps it is only a coincidence that many of the best judges of wine find all but a very few Graves to be dull and uninteresting.

On the steep hillsides of the Mediterranean region, terraces are cut to form level patches on which the vines are planted. In fact these form one of the most characteristic features of the South European landscape.

It is particularly obvious in the Côte d'Or that the best vineyards are neither too high on the hillside nor too far down in the valley, and in fact are often flanked on their upper and lower sides by inferior estates. It is best not to be too near the summit of the hill, so as to have some shelter from a sudden inrush of cold air, yet not to be down on the lower ground, which tends to be too rich in humus, so that the wine is undisciplined and lacks quality. To be successful, wine needs some opposition, but not too much.

VARIETIES OF GRAPE

Wild grapes are found all over the wine zones of the world, but, with a trifling exception, only vines derived from a single species, *Vitis vinifera*, are used for making wine. (In the eastern United States some native varieties are used.) The original home of *Vitis vinifera* is usually taken to be the area between Samarkand and the Caucasus, in Russian Turkestan, where Humboldt found it growing in the greatest profusion, like blackberries in England.

The genus *Vitis* has been common enough in Europe since long before the advent of man. Fossilized grape-stones, and in some cases leaves, have been found in the Miocene shale deposits of Bovey Tracey, in Devon (now being mined for open-cast coal), as well as in a number of contemporary sites in France and Germany. It is the European scions which supply the vineyards of Australia, South Africa, California, Peru, Chile, Argentina, Brazil, Palestine, and North Africa, if frequently on American *Vitis vulpina* or *Vitis rupestris* root-stocks.

The distinction between the different varieties of *Vitis vinifera* used in the various vineyards is in many cases very fine, and even obscure. Grapes used for the table are rarely used for fermenting, for they do not give good wine. On the other hand, some of the wine-grape varieties are quite pleasant to eat, but they are usually too small to be commercially attractive, and some have large pips and thick skins. In various parts of the Mediterranean the same grapes are used for drying to raisins or fermenting to wine. The raisins are good, but the wine is poor.

The number of varieties quite commonly used for wine-making is very large indeed. Over a hundred are conservatively listed for France alone, and thirty-seven for Spain. How many of these are the same varieties under other names it is impossible to say, for on transplanting a vine to another locality, it is often found to have changed its characteristics rather confusingly in the course of time.

The selection mentioned below includes almost all of those which account for the world's best wines. The greatest light wines are, as already mentioned, Bordeaux, burgundy, and hock. Each of these is largely or wholly produced from a single variety of grape, and the three great wine-grapes are, accordingly the CABERNET-SAUVIGNON, the PINOT NOÏR, and the RIESLING.

VARIETIES OF WINE-GRAPES

(B and W indicate respectively black and white grapes).

Aligote (w). This is a large grape, which grows in large bunches, so that the wine-yield is high. It is grown extensively in Burgundy to give a mediocre wine.

Aramon (B) (Aramon of the Plain). An extremely prolific grape, giving as much as 3,500 gallons per acre of a wine which is poor in colour and alcohol and uninteresting in taste; it is used for blending for *ordinaires*.

Cabernet-Sauvignon: see *Sauvignon.*

Carignane (B). A rather coarse, thin-skinned grape giving a wine which usually goes for blending.

Chasselas (B and W) (Gutedel; Fendent). A grape which ripens early and is dependable. Its wine lacks acidity and so does not keep well, though it has a delicate bouquet; it is low in alcohol. It has been grown as a table-grape since the sixteenth century at least. It is fairly prolific.

Corinth (B and W) (Apyrena). Grown only in Italy and the Levant, and there largely for drying to currants. Small stoneless grapes with a thin skin. Gives a very inferior wine. Sometimes considered as a different species from *Vitis vinifera* – *Vitis corinthiaca.*

Dégoutant (B). A black shining grape, giving a coarse wine. Grown only in the Charente.

Elbling: see *Pedro Ximenez.*

Folle Blanche (w). The cognac grape. Its wine is very poor indeed for drinking. (See page 215).

Furmint (w). A fine grape from which Hungarian Tokay is made (but not Californian Tokay, see page 187), and also some local superior wines of Germany.

Gamay (B). A large black grape from a vine on which the bunches ripen unevenly. A hardy plant, capable of giving as much as 1,700 gallons of wine per acre in good years. In Burgundy, all but the finest wines are wholly or in part from the Gamay. Well known since medieval times (Gamez, Gaamez).

Gewürtztraminer (B). A grape grown chiefly in Germany. It is a sub-variety of the Traminer and gives an even more scented, spicy wine.

Grenache (B). A fine, sweet grape with a strong bloom. The berries vary considerably in size on the same bunch. It gives a wine with a fine perfume and a fairly high alcohol content. It ripens early and is much grown in Spain and Southern France.

Malbec (B) (Noir de Pressac; Gourdeaux; Estrangey; Côt rouge; Pied de Perdrix; Jacobin). An abundant producer, ripening early and giving a light wine. Malbec, like Merlot, is used with Sauvignon in producing some of the fine clarets.

Malvasia (w). A very sweet and juicy grape, much grown for dessert wines in the Mediterranean area and Madeira. There are several sub-varieties (see *Trollinger*).

Merlot (B) (Gros doux). A bluish-black, rather flabby grape with a thick skin. It is grown in the Médoc as assistant to Cabernet-Sauvignon in giving the fine clarets. It ripens a little before the Sauvignon and soon rots.

Meunier (B). A grape much grown in the Loire basin for second-rate wines.

Müller-Thurgau (w). A cross between Riesling and Silvaner, produced by the eminent Swiss oenologist whose name it bears. It ripens early and is very prolific; in Switzerland and the German vineyards, where it is grown principally, its yield of 750 to 1,400 gallons of wine per acre is high for those regions. Its wine is pleasant and mild, rather low in acid, so that it does not keep very well.

Muscadels (w). A number of sub-varieties of this grape are grown in all but the best vineyards. Its wine has a pronounced flavour and is usually blended off. It is high in acid and so bestows some measure of longevity on other wines, but is poor in body. Sub-varieties are also used for table-grapes.

Palomino (B) (Napa Golden Chasselas). The principal grape of sherry, and otherwise grown fairly widely in Spain to give a rather ordinary wine, low in alcohol.

Pedro Ximenez (w) (P.X.; Elbling; Weissalbe; Kleinberger; Albuelis). A medium-sized white grape much grown in Andalusia and further north in Spain. It gives a fairly sweet must of rather low acidity, and a wine of good flavour and aroma. It is very largely used, not for wine as such, but in the form of a boiled-down *arrope* for sweetening and flavouring sherries (see page 116).

Legend says it is identical with the Elbling of the Mosel and was brought to Spain in the sixteenth century by a soldier in the army of Charles V named Pieter Siemens, hispanified as Pedro Ximenez. Spanish legend tends to improve on this by adding that it was taken at an earlier date still (anonymously) to the Mosel from the Canary Isles.

Pinot blanc (w) (White Burgundy; Chardonnay; Chardenay; Auxerrois blanc; Pineau blanc). A fine white grape, not hardy, but giving some of the best white wines in the world: the white burgundies, and in admixture with the black sub-variety, Pinot noir, the finest champagnes.

Pinot noir (B) (Blue Burgundy; Noirien; La Dôle). The grape of the great burgundies (Chambertin, Romanée, Vougeot). A delicate plant which gives a low yield, only a third of that of its plebeian neighbour, the Gamay. The berries are small and dark blue. They have a fine aroma and grow densely in the bunch. It has been much transplanted to other parts of the world to give tone to otherwise undistinguished growths.

Riesling (w) (Gentil aromatique). Like the Pinot and the Cabernet-Sauvignon, the Riesling is one of the aristocrats among wine-grapes. It forms rather small, irregular bunches of light-yellow, rounded grapes which become reddish as they ripen and are not very juicy. The yield is medium: 350 to 450 gallons an acre. Its wine is the most expensive in the world: the great hocks.

Rühlander (w) (Gray Burgundy; in Alsace and Switzerland, the Tokayer). The berries are small, somewhat elongated, and of a greyish-red colour. Its yield is medium: 350 to 500 gallons per acre, although specially bred sub-varieties will give nearly double this.

It was introduced from Burgundy into Germany by the merchant Ruhland.

Sauvignon (B) (Cabernet; Cabernet-Sauvignon; Petite Verdure). The aristocrat of the Médoc. The small, bluish-black, thin-skinned grapes have a heavy bloom. They are very juicy and ripen earlier than any other of the Bordeaux grapes. The vine flourishes in heavy soil. Its wine is long-lived and usually continues to improve until it is about twenty years old, sometimes for much longer. It has a fine colour and a magnificent bouquet. The clarets are made from 60 to 80 per cent Sauvignon grapes together with Merlot, Malbec, and the sub-variety of Sauvignon, Cabernet-franc (or Cabernet-gris).

Sirrah (B) (Shiraz; Hermitage; Syrah). The Sirrah vines are grown on the hillsides of the Rhône valley and bear rather narrow, elongated bunches of slightly oval grapes which are very sweet and juicy, thin-skinned, and ripen early. They have been widely adopted in South Africa, California, and elsewhere, for they are well suited to hotter climatic conditions. In California, wine from Sirrah grapes is sold as burgundy (for an unknown reason).

Sylvaner (W) (Östricher; Franconian). A heavily-cropping grape which, alone, gives mild wines and when blended with Riesling produces many of the good, but not first-class, wines of Germany.

Traminer (W) (Gentil duret). The berries of the Traminer are reddish and veined, with a thick tough skin. Their juice is very sweet and has a peculiar taste. The grapes ripen early and are unusually sensitive to early frosts. The wine tends to have a thick, fat taste, for it has too much pectin and insufficient acid. It is used to blend with wines of neutral taste to give them its distinctive flavour. It has no connexion with Tramin, in the Tyrol.

Trollinger (B) (Blue Malvasia; Frankentaler; Gross Vernatsch; Blue or Black Hambro'). This grape is much grown everywhere for table-grapes, and in Austria, Italy, South Germany, and Yugoslavia for making a wine of undistinguished quality. It may be indigenous to the Tyrol (Trollinger = Tirolinger = Tyrolean). The great vines of Hampton Court and Windsor, planted in 1768 and 1775 respectively, are Trollingers.

Verdot (B). Small, soft, uneven, reddish-black grape with a thin skin and a strong bloom. It ripens late and is much used for the ordinary red wines of the Bordeaux.

In the United States, almost all the wine is made from European varieties of *Vitis vinifera* grafted onto native stocks, but, especially east of the Rockies, a few indigenous species are cultivated, varieties of *Vitis labrusca*, *V. riparia*, *V. rupestris*, and *V. berlandieri*, such as Catawba, Concord, and Delaware. Wines from Catawba grapes in particular have a foxy taste which is very persistent and, to European taste, unpleasant. They are often blended off; ageing tends to ameliorate the taste. It is *Vitis riparia* (known also as *V. vulpina*, or the riverbank grape) which is chiefly used to supply root-stocks for European grafting, although many French vineyards have used *Vitis rupestris*, the Sand Grape. These American varieties of *Vitis* are sometimes classed separately by botanists as *Euvitis*.

CULTIVATING THE VINE

Grapes grown too far from the soil tend to be watery and acid, and to have little flavour. The closer they grow to the ground, the better they will mature, for in the day the reflection of the sun's rays from the warm earth adds to the direct sunlight, and during the night the ground radiates its absorbed warmth back to the grape. Nevertheless, in the hotter, more southerly climates, it is necessary to ensure that the grapes do not get scorched, and in Madeira, for instance, the method of cultivation has always been on horizontal trellises raised six or so feet from the ground. The pickers gather the grapes from the inside of these erections.

In spite of traditional methods which still linger on in all parts of the Continent, the training of vines is more or less uniform in the well-run French and German vineyards. They are planted in straight lines, a metre or more apart, and pruned severely. The general idea is to leave two branches, one to bear, and one to make wood for the following year. The fruiting branch is taken along a horizontal wire some four or six inches from the ground, and the grapes grow between this and another wire some nine inches or a foot higher. The branch to make wood is sometimes taken vertically and attached to a stake about four feet high, or is bent down again to the height of the upper horizontal wire. In the Médoc, the whole vine tends to be kept low as it always has been. Oxen were once used, and still are to some extent, for ploughing, and the yoke of the twin oxen and the plough they drew had to clear the young vines.

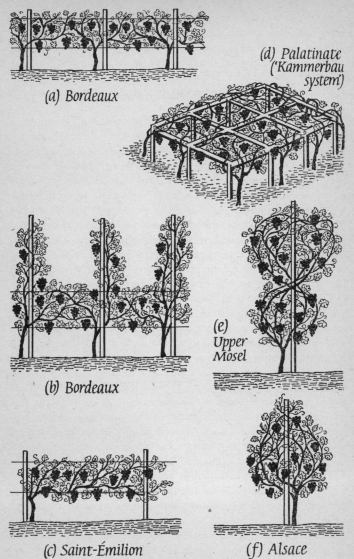

(a) Bordeaux

(d) Palatinate ('Kammerbau system')

(b) Bordeaux

(e) Upper Mosel

(c) Saint-Émilion

(f) Alsace

FIG. 1. Methods of Training Vines

In California and the southern hemisphere (Australia and the Cape) wider spacing is invariable, even where hoeing and ploughing are horse-drawn. Even in the older Australian vineyards, where the vines are still trained as bushes, the spacing is five or six feet each way. In the newer vineyards of Australia, where cultivation is, of course, mechanized, the rows are thirteen or fourteen feet apart, and the tendency is for even wider spacing.

In the Bordelais, the first ploughing takes place in March, and a special plough (the *cabat*) is used to uncover the foot of the vine. A month later, with a *courbe* plough-fitting, the vine foot is covered again and a furrow left for the spring rains to escape. When these are over, the *cabat* is again used, so that the roots are uncovered for fruiting. In the middle of June, the blossom forms and pruning is started. The Cabernet, a tender plant, must be pruned gently, but the other Médoc vines, the Verdot, the Malbec, and the Merlot, may be pruned severely. Later, when the berries are well formed, a fourth ploughing covers the foot of the vines and the green canes are pruned back to strengthen the fruit. At this stage, it is the Cabernet which stands heavy pruning and the others which are treated less severely.

This is the routine in the best vineyards of the Médoc. In the Saint-Émilion, to the east, the tendency is to train five or six canes from each stock along the lower wire and to lead them from there to the upper.

Various traditional methods survive, as already mentioned. The French small farmer will often take his vines up trellises or stakes in much the same way and to the same height as runner-beans are grown in England. In the Upper Mosel, the vine is grown as a tall bush and the runners brought down and secured to the supporting stakes a foot or two below the point at which they left the main stem. In the Tyrol a method on a pergola, somewhat like the Madeira system, is used, and in rural parts of the Palatinate, the old *Kammerbau* system lingers on. In this arrangement, a horizontal frame is supported a couple of feet from the ground and ten or twelve vines trained over it. The foliage shades the roots, which get insufficient sun and are difficult to get at to hoe or weed. In some places, indeed, mangolds are planted underneath.

It is in Italy that traditional methods have their full freedom. In 1765, Smollett found that 'the trees which form the hedge-rows serve as so many props to the vines, which are twisted around them, and continued from one to the other.' There has been little change in the past two centuries. In the plain of Lombardy, maple or mulberry trees are planted as supports, often at the same time as the vines. The mulberries supply food for the silkworms, whose product goes to the nearby factories of Milan, an ingenious method of double-cropping.

In Tuscany, vines are encouraged to clamber up wooden frames so constructed that the plants form a sort of top-heavy bush. Further south, the general principle followed is that any projection above the surface of the earth is suitable to support the vine, which can be seen trailing over houses, up, around, and through bushes of all sorts, down into ravines, anywhere at will. Much the same method was employed in the Garden of Eden, it seems (*Paradise Lost*, iv. 258; v. 215). In the past thirty years or so, especially in Northern Italy, there has been a certain leisurely change towards less happy-go-lucky methods.

PESTS AND DISEASES OF THE VINE

Like all horticulturists, those who grow vines carry on a continuous war against insect, mould, and virus pests: so much may be taken for granted. The *vigneron* has had a harder time than most, however. In the past century and a half he has escaped being driven out of existence only by the narrowest margin, on two occasions. The sequel to one of these crises profoundly revolutionized the whole wine-growing industry. For this reason, as well as because of the light thrown on the *vigneron*'s problems, a short account will be given of the three great crises in the industry.

About 1852, a powdery white mildew appeared in the vineyards and spread rapidly over Europe. The leaves of the vines withered and the wine made from the grapes was poor in taste and was peculiarly subject to diseases itself. It did not keep and no treatment seemed to improve it: it was profoundly 'sick'. Vineyards which were badly attacked by *oïdeum* gave no crop at all. No cure was known at that time and yields dropped catastrophically. The scourge spread beyond Europe, to Madeira and the Canary Islands. In Bordeaux the production of wine dropped to less than three-quarters of the normal. (See the graph, Fig. 2.) Just in time to prevent complete destruction of the industry, the expedient of dusting the plants with finely-powdered sulphur was discovered and the pest was slowly conquered. Nowadays it is normal practice to dust some sixteen pounds of sulphur over each acre of the vineyards in the spring, certainly in all areas which seem to have special susceptibility to *oïdeum*.

The remedy was discovered too late to save Madeira and the Canaries. The wine of Madeira was, at that time, very popular and about two million gallons were being produced annually in the 1840s; in good years three millions were made. In the spring of 1852, just as the blossom was out, *oïdeum* appeared in the island and in a few weeks completely wiped out the crop. There is no such thing as an 1852 Madeira, nor of any of the following years, for the *vignerons*, in order to recover their losses to some degree, planted sugar-cane and pumpkins. It was the end of Madeira's great days; by the time replanting began, the market had gone and men were drinking other wines at dessert. Canary wine had never had the popularity of Madeira, but before 1852 it had a good sale, being sold to the innocent drinker as Madeira. *Oïdeum* reduced production to one-tenth, and by 1870 or so, when it again came on the market, it was usually modestly labelled sherry.

Oïdeum is still a very destructive pest in spite of sulphur treatment, and especially in hotter climates, such as those of California and Australia, it is a recurrent danger during humid periods.

Dusting with sulphur had saved the vineyards of France, and by 1870 almost twice as much wine was produced as in the forties. The relief of the *vignerons* did not last long. An even more powerful enemy was gathering its forces. In 1854, the American entomologist Asa Fitch had discovered an aphid on the wild vines of the Mississippi valley. It was a small yellow louse, resembling that well-known English pest, the greenfly, and in fact it belongs to the same family of insects. It is far more formidable, however.

The aphid, *Phylloxera vastatrix* (Greek: *phyllon*, leaf; *xeros*, dry), had from time immemorial led a placid and somewhat humdrum existence between the Rocky Mountains and the Appalachians, sometimes, one may presume, a little short of food, and not without an occasional spasm of anxiety about the continuance of its race. Suddenly, in the 1860s, a few individuals were given the chance of a millennium. Perhaps on vine-scions, perhaps on table-grapes, they were brought across the Atlantic and in 1863 were seen both in

England and in the department of Gard, in Languedoc. The Gard vineyards are extensive, and border the great *vignoble* of Hérault, and also the vineyards of Vaucluse. In 1866, Phylloxera had reached Orange, in Vaucluse, and two years later had extended northwards to Drôme. These insects were lucky: they had established themselves in the most extensive vineyard area in the world. By 1868, the vines of Portugal and of Bordeaux had been attacked.

The symptoms of attack were unmistakable. The vines became stunted, and the leaves turned yellow and withered. On them, galls formed. The grapes, when they did appear, and this became rarer as the insects settled down, were hard and quite useless for making wine. Below ground, swellings on the roots took grotesque forms. Spraying with anything whatever was useless.

By 1870 the invasion north had reached the Beaujolais and the Rhône valley. Vineyards were being destroyed by the thousand. This was the date of the war with Prussia, when Bismarck exacted an indemnity of five thousand million francs from France; Phylloxera is said to have cost the country twice this.

When the life-story of the aphid was examined, it could be seen how very difficult it would be to get rid of it. The home of the insect is the gall which forms on the underside of the leaf, or the root-nodule. Here the aphids hatch out and then may migrate to another part of the plant, those from the roots flying up to the leaves, those from the leaf-galls dropping to the roots. Sometimes several generations are passed on the leaves, or, alternatively, on the roots. Eight generations a season is the usual routine, and the egg-laying capacity of the aphid is high, even among insects. There are four distinct forms of the adult, besides several immature stages. All live on the sap of the vine.

Even if the leaf-dwellers could be destroyed by spraying, it is clear that the denizens of the root-nodules would not be incommoded; not that a spray was known at that time which would kill the leaf-insects. In despair, owners of vineyards flooded the whole area to drown the Phylloxera. This heroic expedient was not very efficacious; even submersion for five weeks killed only two of every three insects. Afterwards, the ground was found to be so impoverished that very heavy manuring and intensive cultivation were necessary to restore it.

In 1873 the entomologists Planchon and Riley had high hopes of a new method of dealing with the scourge. A mite was known in America which preyed on Phylloxera. It was brought to Europe in the hope that it would fight the *vigneron*'s battle for him. Acclimatization of an organism in a strange land is not always successful, although Phylloxera itself had settled down very comfortably in Europe. However, *Tyroglyphus phylloxera*, the mite, took kindly to France and was successfully established there. Unfortunately, in this luxurious Latin air, it was found to have lost its enmity for Phylloxera, and the two lived side by side in amity. Meanwhile the French *vignerons* were losing £50 millions a year, it was calculated.

At about this time (1874) Phylloxera crossed the Rocky Mountains and began colonizing the vineyards of California, which dated from the times of the Jesuit missions. The following year it was at Geelong, Australia. In 1878 Burgundy was invaded in force. By 1884, sixty-seven departments of France were under the scourge, and there was still no way known of combating it.

An expedient which had a limited success in France was to treat the ground with carbon disulphide. This liquid, which is somewhat poisonous to human beings as well as to aphids, is not pleasant to handle, for it is extremely inflammable, besides having a foul odour. It was inserted into the ground in holes between the vines; up to two ounces were used in each hole. The method was very expensive, but at least caused some amelioration of the attack. By 1887, about 160,000 acres of vineyards had been treated in France.

By 1887 also, the Algerian and South African vineyards had been attacked. In the following year the aphids reached Italy. Not until 1891 were the champagne vineyards of Ay and Épernay affected. By this time, the solution of the problem was at hand.

The remedy was nothing short of tearing up every vine and replanting with vinestocks from the eastern United States. Californian stocks were no more resistant than European; in some respects, less, for the Phylloxera did not always appear in its leaf form in Europe, while in California it attacked above and below ground. The eastern stocks, *Vitis ruparia* and *V. rupestris*, are resistant. Alone, these vines would give wine which would by no means appeal to European tastes, but when European *vinifera* scions are grafted on to them, the grapes and the wines take on the characteristics of the scions. To replant three or four million acres is a formidable undertaking, but there was no alternative. As a matter of fact, this expedient of grafting on to resistant stocks had been suggested much earlier in an effort to combat *oïdeum*, and attempts at grafting were made then, but the technique had not been mastered, and the experiment was unsuccessful.

Replanting with American *porte-greffes* is not a complete solution to the problem, for the American stocks are not completely resistant, and the war against Phylloxera continues. By 1948, for instance, it was calculated that over half – $2\frac{1}{2}$ out of 4 million acres – of the Italian vineyards had Phylloxera in them, and in 1953 it was announced that two acres out of three in the West German vineyards were affected, and the cost of ridding the German vines of Phylloxera was put at over £100 millions.

There are those who say that pre-Phylloxera wines were certainly superior to those from grafted vines. With them it is difficult to argue, but the general opinion is that they are prejudiced. It seems clear that modern sherries at least are rather superior to those made before 1894, when Phylloxera hit Jerez.

The third war in which the vine-grower was engaged started about 1884, when a blue mildew, *Peronospera viticola*, was found to be spreading over the vines. The leaves drop, and the grape is deprived of its source of sugar and never matures properly. It becomes soft and flabby and is sour, with high acid content, rich in gums and pectins. It makes a poor wine, which has a strong tendency to turn yellowish, and has a musty taste – *mildewsé*. Fortunately, Millardet of Bordeaux found that spraying with copper salts ('Bordeaux Mixture') kept the pest in check. Bordeaux Mixture is nowadays used for protecting other fruits than grapes against mildew, of course. It is generally effective. Nevertheless, German scientists carried out an intensive search for resistant varieties of vine by inoculating between five and ten million seedlings with Peronospera and then selecting insusceptible varieties for propagation.

The graph (Fig. 2) shows the effect of the three attacks on the vine on the wine production in the Bordeaux area.

Apart from the perennial Phylloxera, the chief menace in European vineyards at present is probably that presented by three species of moths. One of these, a tortricid, *Polychrosis botrana*, has steadily increased since it first appeared in 1890, and is considered the most serious of the three. It goes through three generations in the course of

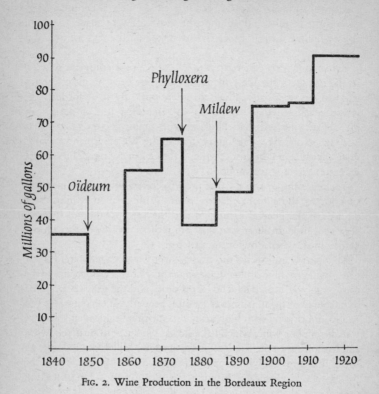

FIG. 2. Wine Production in the Bordeaux Region

the year, the third appearing just when the fruit is ripening. Spraying is often inadequate to hold it in check, and the parasites which might be encouraged to destroy it also attack parasites of that other pest, the cabbage white butterfly.

Even after this very superficial account of the difficulties attending the cultivation of the vine, it will be agreed that the punctilious precautions taken in the great German vineyards, for instance (page 158), are not unjustified.

THE RIPENING OF THE GRAPE

If not too seriously interfered with by *oïdeum*, Phylloxera, Peronospera, and the tortricids, in June the yellowish-green clusters of flowers appear on the vines, and soon the grapes set and fill. It would be interesting to trace exactly what happens in the grape as it ripens, but unfortunately, although a vast amount of work has been carried out to elucidate the matter, so much remains obscure that it is not yet possible to give a lucid and accurate account of the process.

It is certain that carbon dioxide is taken from the atmosphere into the plant, especially through the leaves, and that there it is changed into starch. Just how this takes place is the difficult part. Carbon dioxide contains a single carbon atom in its molecule, while the molecule of starch contains many thousands. It is true that the carbon atoms in the starch molecule are arranged in a repeating pattern and we are fairly sure that we know the pattern. Shorn of details, it is:

oxygen bridge   oxygen bridge   oxygen bridge   oxygen bridge

However, it is quite certain that the molecules of carbon dioxide do not arrange themselves straight away into this complex pattern without going through some preliminary associations into simpler molecules. It would be satisfying if these molecules were known. Then the even more interesting subject of where the energy comes from to carry out the changes could be tackled.

Quite recently (September 1954), Calvin, the well-known American chemist, has announced that it is now certain that among the intermediate products formed in the leaves of plants is glycerophosphoric acid; that is, a substance rather like glycerine, with a tail of phosphoric acid tacked on to the molecule. The appearance of phosphoric acid is not as surprising as it seems; in fact, quite the contrary, for phosphoric acid is constantly appearing in biological changes, whether they be digestion, fermentation, or the flexing of muscles.

A number of compounds like glycero-phosphoric acid, including glycero-phosphoric acid itself, are formed and decomposed again in the process of fermentation (see page 76). It looks rather as if the building up of the starch molecule in the leaves of the vine (and of all other plants) somewhat resembles the process of fermentation in reverse. As for the origin of the phosphorus, that is no mystery at all. All plants (as well as bacteria and animals) contain quite definite amounts of phosphorus, which come originally from the phosphates in the soil. Very little is necessary, for it is used over and over again by the plant.

The starch is formed in the leaf, then, by carbon dioxide changing to the three-carbon molecule of glycero-phosphoric acid, and this, in some way which is obscure, arranging to the recurring pattern of starch:

Carbon dioxide — Glycero-phosphoric acid — Starch

P = phosphoric acid

By mid-autumn, or earlier in the hotter parts of the wine-zone, the grapes are ripe and ready for picking. The usual time of vintage is mid-September to mid-October. It varies from year to year, of course, and is not, as it once was, a fixed date, but depends on the judgement of the *vigneron*. He looks at the colour of the grapes and notes how easily the berries part from the stalk, and the appearance of the fragment of pulp which adheres to the stalk, the colour and dryness of the stalk and the main stem, and, of course, he tastes the grapes. In modern vineyards, the chemists employed by the vine-growers take samples of the grapes, press out the juice in small laboratory presses and test it for sugar content. In former times, the lord of the manor decided the date of harvesting for the district, so that some *vignerons* watched their grapes rot while the lord's ripened, and others gathered theirs unripe and sour because the lord's had ripened first. This, the so-called *ban de vendange*, was abolished only in the nineteenth century in some parts of France and Germany.

In the cooler vineyards, those of the Mosel and the Rhine, the grapes are sometimes gathered as late as November, so as to take advantage of every hour of sunshine. In Algeria, although the general vintage is in September, as in Bordeaux and Burgundy, some places gather in mid-August because there, in the hot, dry coastal plains, the maximum sugar is reached earlier than in the cooler hillside vineyards inland. In these warm countries, like California and North Africa, a certain proportion of unripe grapes is included in the vintage, so that the acidity will be raised. Acid is a most essential constituent of wine (see page 85).

In some districts, for a special purpose, grapes are left on the vines after they are ripe (see page 62).

When grapes are just ripe, all the starch has migrated from the stalks into the fruit, where it has turned into sugar. This change is not difficult to visualize, for the starch molecule is a very long chain of rings of atoms, and each ring is to all intents and purposes a sugar molecule:

$$C \quad\quad C-O \quad\quad C \quad\quad C \quad\quad C-C$$

Once the oxygen bridges between these rings are broken, one is left with a pile of sugar molecules, each consisting of five carbon atoms and an oxygen atom, with another carbon sticking out as a sort of tail. (This is a very simple statement of the case.) The full formula for glucose, or grape sugar, is:

$$CH_2OH$$

In some vineyards, those of the Sauternes in the Bordeaux district, and in some of the vineyards of the Rhineland and elsewhere, the grapes are allowed to stay on the vines for a week or two after they are ripe. They are allowed to rot a little, in a judicious manner. The reason is a curious one.

Floating in the air of the vineyards is a host of yeast-cells, moulds, bacteria, all ready to live on suitable organic matter. Where they settle, they grow, if the right food is available. One of the moulds is known as *Botrytis cinerea*, and it is unique among moulds in at least two ways: its filaments can pierce the unbroken skin of the grapes, and it does not spoil the taste of the wine made from them. It forms as a greyish hoary coating on the fruit, which come to have a melancholy, half-rotten appearance, especially when the berries shrivel. *Botrytis* is a well-known mould: it occurs only too often on fruit in this country, on gooseberries in particular (see Raymond Bush's *Soft Fruit Growing*, p. 85. Penguin Handbook 1). In most countries it is ranked as an enemy of the horticulturalist, to be fought and extirpated. In the Sauternes and the Rhineland the vine-grower depends on it for his livelihood. The grapes lose water through the filaments of the mould, so that the pulp inside becomes stronger and stronger in sugar, which is the principal solid dissolved in the juice. It is true that the mould consumes sugar and acid from the juice, but this is a slow process, while the evaporation of the water is rapid. Juice from grapes ripened normally and picked when they are ripe contains about 15 to 25 per cent of sugar; the juice of grapes exposed to *Botrytis* sometimes has as much as 60 per cent of sugar: that is, more than three-quarters of the water has been lost. The wines from such grapes are much sweeter than usual, for only about 30 or 35 per cent of sugar can be fermented out of a juice; the ferments die when the alcohol reaches a certain figure.

Grapes which are grey with *Botrytis* are said in France to have *pourriture noble*, and in Germany, *Edelfäule*; both terms mean 'the noble rot'.

Some sweet white wines are made by picking the grapes and laying them out in the sun to dry on straw, or in warm rooms, when the water of the juice partly evaporates and leaves them in a condition half-way to raisins. In the Levant in particular, the stalks are twisted at a certain stage so that the sap can no longer flow, and the berries are left on the vine to dry. Wines from such grapes are, like those from fruit attacked by *pourriture noble*, sweet and luscious, rich in sugar and glycerine, but with as much alcohol as that from normally-ripened grapes.

These are special wines, and form only a very small proportion of those made.

THE HARVEST

The harvest, *la vendange*, has been traditionally a time of feasting at least since the time of Theocritus (Seventh Idyl: third century B.C.), and probably far earlier. The general air of joviality at vintage-time is perhaps best communicated in contemporary literature by Mr J. M. Scott's *Vineyards of France*.

The bunches of grapes are cut from the vines by curved knives or secateurs, usually by women, and taken in conveniently sized bins or baskets to the fermenting-vats. The particular conditions vary widely, but the picking is everywhere by hand still. Even California cannot yet (though they are trying) rival the mechanization of the hop-fields, where the hops are now gathered mechanically.

The conditions vary widely.

In America, the grapes are . . . 'brought to the winery in 20-ton side-dump trucks and trailers and lined up in lanes by variety. . . . Four samples are taken from each 20-ton load . . . the sugar test, made by means of a Brix or Balling hydrometer, gives the concentration of a sucrose solution of the same density as the juice being tested. . . . After acceptance, grapes are weighed on a 60 by 10 foot motor truck scale which handles a 20-ton truck and trailer simultaneously. The driver then waits his turn at the crusher, the crushing schedule being planned by the fermenting-room supervisor.'

That is Fresno, California.

In the Dordogne valley, 'the ox-carts take six of these *comportes*' (tubs containing 150 lb. grapes) 'but they have to be roped on, for the carts have sides, but no fixed front or back', says Mr Philip Oyler, describing a stay in the district. 'These carts are made, of course, by local wheelwrights, for they know what is needed and they alone can make them. . . . Foussac shouldered the long wand, still called an *aiguillon* or goad but not used as such, said "Ah" to his team and set out for home. . . . After the grapes are picked, they will be crushed at once to express the juice. They do this in a *comporte* (any wooden tubs would serve) with a wooden rammer with a round flat bottom and a horizontal crossbar at the top. Anyone can make such a thing for himself.'*

The method of the Dordogne peasants described by Mr Oyler is as representative as that used at Fresno. A large proportion of the world's wine is made by smallholders in much the same way as that described by Mr Oyler. Mechanization generally resembling the Californian procedure is practised in the large vineyards of Algeria, the Midi of France, and to some degree in Australia and South Africa. The fine classed wines of Bordeaux, Burgundy, and the Rhine are made with much less mechanization than the American, and very little more than in the Dordogne.

The grapes are sometimes freed of their stalks before fermentation and sometimes fermented stalks and all. This applies only to the making of red wines. The method of making white wines differs in a number of details and will be described a little later. The best opinion inclines to the practice of fermenting with the stalks, but in the Bordeaux district they are traditionally removed. In California they are removed, for they are said to give an unpleasant taste to the wine, and moreover without them the mixture of juice and skins can be handled by pumps for transfer to the fermentation vats. In at least one American firm, the stalks are treated separately to extract the 7 or 8 per cent of sugar which they contain. The object of leaving in the stalks, by those who do leave them in, is that the tannin in them, which is a valuable constituent of wine, shall be extracted. Further, the presence of the stalks prevents the mass of skins from compacting too solidly in the fermenting vat. Tannin is an essential part of wines, red or white: it adds what is described as zest, and also enhances the keeping qualities. It is commonly added to wine, especially white wine, which is naturally lacking in it.

If the stalks are to be removed, they are taken out either by hand or mechanically. In the first case, the bunches of grapes are thrown into a sieve with holes large enough to allow the individual grapes to pass through, and stirred around with a wooden stick, often with three legs on it; the grapes are by this means dragged off the stalks and fall through into a tub beneath. The mechanical appliances for separating the stalks, *égrappoirs*, are commonly of the form of

* *The Generous Earth.* Hodder and Stoughton 1950.

cylinders pierced with holes of a size to pass the grapes. Inside them the bunches are scraped against the cylinder by means of revolving arms furnished with brushes which push the grapes through the holes.

The grapes must in any event be crushed in order to free the juice, and it is usual to combine the crusher (*fouloir*) with the *égrappoir* and call the whole a '*foulo-grappe*'. Manual crushing is often carried out, commonly by means of a pole with a flat board fixed perpendicularly to it, just as described by Mr Oyler (page 63). Treading has by no means completely died out.

The mechanically driven *fouloir* is something like a domestic mincing-machine, but the cylinder is channelled parallel to its axis, and the clearance between it and the walls of the crushing chamber is great enough to avoid crushing the pips. It is important not to crack the pips, for they contain substances which impart an unpleasant taste to the wine.

The mush of skins, pips, and juice which comes out of the crusher is ready for fermenting. It will be already warm with incipient fermentation unless the weather is cold, and rapid transfer to the vat is essential. A delay of twenty-four or at most thirty-six hours is as long as can be allowed in Europe; in countries like Australia, two hours is quite long enough. If for any reason there is any delay beyond these times, the mush must be preserved with sulphur dioxide. Some degree of 'sulphuring' is all but universal, in any case.

Fermentation and Preservation of the Juice

Nowadays, fermentation is very rarely allowed to proceed without some modification of the natural course of events, and it is interesting to consider what would happen in the vat if there were no interference at all.

NATURAL FERMENTATION

The grapes as they grow collect in the waxy bloom on their skins numerous yeasts, moulds, and bacteria. These are floating in the air of the vineyards; they are part of the normal aerial flora and fauna of the district. In any case, *Drosophila*, the fruit-fly, as well as other insects, soon inoculates everything with yeasts. An actual count, made in

America, showed that on arrival at the fermenting vat, each grape harboured on its skin about 100,000 moulds, 100,000 wine-yeasts, and upwards of ten millions of other yeasts, the so-called 'wild yeasts'. This was in a wine-growing district. In newly planted vineyard areas, where no vines have grown before, wine-yeasts are absent.

Upon crushing the grapes and leaving them to ferment naturally, it is the wild yeasts which start the fermentation: they are greatly in the majority. The principal species is *apiculatus*, which forms lemon-shaped cells (see Figure 3*a*), and for about twenty-four hours the full burden lies on them. As it happens, they are feeble fermenters, and after about thirty-six hours they are finished. They have made about 4 per cent of alcohol, and at that concentration they die. There are

FIG. 3*a. Saccharomyces apiculatus*
(Wild yeast)

FIG. 3*b. Saccharomyces ellipsoideus*
(Wine yeast)

many species of wild yeasts, but at about 4 per cent alcohol they are all dead. They introduce a trace of off-flavour to the wine, and delay the action of the true wine-yeasts: they are a nuisance.

The true wine-yeasts, *Saccharomyces ellipsoideus* (Figure 3*b*), now take control. They are vigorous fermenters and raise the alcohol content of the vat to about 12 or 14 per cent, if there is enough sugar to give that amount. At this point they are very slow, and 16 per cent of alcohol is as much as they can tolerate. In the ordinary way, a grape juice will not contain more than enough sugar to give 11 or 12 per cent of alcohol; 10 is a good average in Europe, and much wine is sold at 7 per cent. In due course all the sugar will have disappeared, and the wine will be dry. But before this point has been attained, the next stage of natural fermentation will have started, unless something is done to stop further change. The fermenting vat will now contain a watery liquid with perhaps 7 to 12 per cent of alcohol, a little glycerine, acids, pectin, and albuminoid substances, while floating in the liquid will be the skins and pips, and of course all the dead yeast cells.

Suppose, instead of taking off the wine, the mass is left to its own devices. The next organism to take control will be the vinegar bacterium, *Acetobacter*. This attacks the alcohol in the wine and converts it to acetic acid. The liquid gradually turns to vinegar, and *Acetobacter* dies. The moulds and putrefactive bacteria now come into their own and finish off the affair: they break up the acetic acid, and almost everything else that is there, except the water, and reduce all to its lowest stage, that is, to water, carbon dioxide (which escapes, being a gas), and ammonium salts. All action ceases.

This is the natural course of events. The stages overlap, and before the wild yeasts have finished, *ellipsoideus* the wine-yeast is becoming busy; especially if the temperature rises too high in the vat, the acetic bacteria will have already started to destroy the wine as it forms, and the acetic acid will already be on its way to carbon dioxide and water before all the alcohol has disappeared.

One of the problems of the cellar-master is to have in his wine no more than the minimum of acetic acid, which will give it an acid, vinegary taste: it will be *piqué*. He must keep it below a certain amount by law (a quarter of one per cent in France, for instance). Further, he must bring his wine into such a condition that the putrefactive bacteria do not attack it, or else it will not keep.

Generally speaking, he must allow the minimum contact with air and he must get rid of the skins and other floating debris as soon as he reasonably can. These are the absolute minimum precautions, for there are a great many diseases which can attack wine (*tourne*, bitterness, *la graisse*, *la jaune*, *le bleu*, and the mildew). He is helped all along the line if he can kill, either before or after the fermentation, every organism except the wine-yeasts. This is conveniently, and very frequently, carried out nowadays by adding a certain amount of sulphur dioxide in some form. It happens, very fortunately, that the wild yeasts, which in spite of their wildness are really very sensitive little things, are killed off by far less sulphur dioxide than the wine-yeasts.

So it is very common nowadays to add a hundred parts of sulphur dioxide to each million of the grape-must to start with; that is, about three ounces to each ton. The wild yeasts are all killed, so that the off-taste which they introduce is avoided, as is also the delay in starting the full fermentation, although the trace of sulphur dioxide causes a slight delay on its own. Some cellar-masters believe that this treatment actually stimulates the wine-yeasts. Not only the piculate yeasts, but also most of the moulds and bacteria are also killed.

Sulphuring is a very sore point with wine-drinkers who have any palate, for far too many wines have a taste of sulphur dioxide left in them when they are sold. It is so easy for a maker of wine to put much more sulphur dioxide in after the fermentation is over and so save himself the trouble of making the wine sound in other ways. All the wine-making countries have their regulations for preventing over-sulphuring. France allows 450 parts per million, for instance; but less than 300 parts can be detected as an aftertaste quite easily in wine. Almost all cheap white wines taste of sulphur dioxide.

Sulphuring to some degree is almost essential, although at least one of the *grands crus* of Bordeaux is said never to employ it. Treatment with sulphur dioxide is used in many foodstuffs: jam, fruit, meat, and so on. It is quite normal. Camden tablets are recommended officially for preserving fruit, and Camden tablets consist of bisulphite, one of the most convenient ways in which sulphur can be used for this purpose.

FERMENTATION METHODS

The vats (or *cuves*) in which fermentation is carried out may be of any size, from a fifty-gallon cask to a 55,000-gallon tank. They may be made of oak, of cement, of stone (sometimes marble), masonry, or even metal. Metal is not used by respectable wine-makers, but it is used. Glass-lined tanks are scarcely employed at all, even in America, although it is generally recognized that they would be excellent for the purpose. It is their expense which limits their use.

Now one of the most important matters which must be attended to during fermentation is temperature. The process of fermentation itself gives out much heat, which is dispersed by radiation from the walls of the vat and the surface of the liquid, and carried away by the large volumes of carbon dioxide which are given off. The liquid is in turbulent motion and mixes itself. Nevertheless, in large vats there is always a tendency to overheat; in small ones, where the surface area of the walls is relatively greater, there is less trouble, except in hot climates. The climate is an important point. In Algeria and other warm climates, cooling is frequently necessary. On the other hand, in Burgundy, where the climate is much cooler, and can be quite cold in October, large copper kettles are kept at hand so that part of the juice can be heated up and poured back into the main mass to raise the temperature to starting-point.

If the temperature in the vat rises to 90°F., the yeasts weaken; a few degrees more and the process stops or 'sticks'. In this case it is sometimes very difficult to start again, and the wine will be prone to disease. On the other hand, for normal wine-yeasts, temperatures below about 40°F. are almost equally bad, for the fermentation may equally 'stick', and will certainly proceed very slowly. Between these extremes there is ample room for differences of opinion among the experts as to which is the ideal temperature. Putting the matter at its simplest, by keeping the temperature reasonably high, say 80° or 85°, the fermentation is soon over, with a consequently shortened time of exposure to air. Air encourages *Acetobacter* and its followers. On the other hand, a slow fermentation at low temperatures conserves the aroma in the wine and gives a wine which is in general superior to the usual run. In fact, American experiments are being directed towards the cultivation of yeasts which will remain still vigorous at low temperatures, so that a long cool fermentation using them will give finely-flavoured wines, it is hoped. This may be one of the important trends in the future of fermentation.

In fermentation for red wine, in which the skins and pips and sometimes also the stalks are left in, the solid mass is buoyed up by the rising carbon dioxide gas and forms a cap on the top of the liquid. It is important that this cap should be kept immersed, or at least constantly pressed under. It is in this cap that the acetic acid bacteria proliferate. The punching down of the cap is carried out by men with poles. This is exceedingly hard work and the old method is far from being obsolete: men stand on the cap and tread down the solid mass. The cap will very nearly support a man's weight in a vat of about 2,000 gallons, and a stay is fixed across the top of the vat for the man to hold on to. The liquid may also be pumped from beneath and back again over the cap, which is thereby kept wetted and for most of the time immersed. A simpler method, which is in fact not employed very widely, is to fit a perforated screen below the surface of the liquid and to keep the cap below this. The criticism of this expedient is that it is difficult to keep and maintain the screen clean, especially free from the moulds and bacteria.

This problem of cleanliness is a serious one. The vats are empty for all but a month or so in the year, and to keep them clean and free from putrefaction for eleven months is difficult, especially if they be of wood, as they most commonly are.

If the vats are kept covered during the fermentation, the atmosphere which builds up over the surface excludes the air (and the acetic acid bacteria), and this method is not uncommon. Instead of a bung, a valve which will allow the gas to escape but no air to enter must be fitted. Or in country parts, a vine-leaf held down by a stone. There are a number of special designs of vats, some of which cause a circulation of the must over the cap by the pressure of the gas given off. The difficulty is usually that they are troublesome to clean.

An ingenious method of *cuvage* which is due to the well-known French wine-expert, Semichon, is still used to some extent, especially in Italy. It is the *superquatre* or *superquattro* method. If a third of a tank of fully fermented wine, containing 12 per cent alcohol, is added to a tank which is two-thirds full of unfermented must (containing no alcohol, of course), the result is a full vat of must with 4 per cent alcohol in it. The wild yeasts are killed and only the true wine-yeasts are active. This deals neatly with the problem of the wild yeasts. The danger is that if one of the wine-diseases appears in the factory, it spreads rapidly to the whole winery. The Semichon method is for this reason not very popular.

In America it is (slowly) becoming standard practice to sulphur the grape-must straight from the crushers so as to kill the wild yeasts with three to five ounces of sulphur dioxide per ton, and then to add a pure culture of a selected wine-yeast, leaving nothing for the natural yeasts to do. By using carefully selected strains, control over the flavour of the finished wine is possible to a limited extent.

Making White Wine

In making white wine, the skins of the grapes are separated and the juice is fermented by itself. Either black or white grapes are used, for, except in one or two varieties, the juice of black grapes is not coloured. The colouring matter of the berries is contained in cells just under the skin, and unless these cells are ruptured, the colouring matter remains with the skins. The juice from some varieties of black grape gives a wine of more delicate and attractive flavour, and although some extra troubles are encountered in making white wine from black grapes – *blanc de rouges* – many wine-makers consider it worth while.

The juice must be expressed as soon as possible after the grapes are gathered, otherwise incipient fermentation will rupture the colour-cells and the wine will be tinted. Four pressings are given in most vineyards, and the *marc* of skins, pips, and stems is cut up with sharp-edged spades between each pressing. The earlier pressings alone are fermented to give the best wine – *vin de goutte*. The must from later pressings goes for lesser wines, *les suites*.

White musts, especially those from black grapes, are more sensitive to deterioration than red musts, for the tannin which is extracted in considerable quantities, from the skins of black grapes in particular, is a valuable preservative for wines. Wines which are low in tannin often suffer from the complaint known as 'the yellows', and their colour soon deteriorates, as well as their taste. White wines, even those from white grapes (*vins blancs de blancs*) with the skins included, are usually somewhat low in acid also, and this further reduces their resistance to disease.

It is the usual practice to add tannin and tartaric acid before the fermentation starts. Wines which lack sufficient tartaric acid have a flat and uninteresting taste, and this is perhaps the commonest fault of white wines (with the exception of over-sulphuring). Extra sweetness conceals this only from the inexperienced.

If it is a poor year, and the weather has not favoured full ripening, it is not unusual to add sugar also before fermentation, or even to put in a little alcohol (that is, brandy), although this is always delayed until fermentation is under way. These additions are regulated by law, and the amounts are restricted in most countries. Before *sucrage* (addition of sugar) is carried out in France, for instance, three days' notice must be given to the authorities, and sugar and tartaric acid may not both be added.

White wine fermentations are best carried out in small containers. About 400 gallons is a common size, and in making the finer wines, even smaller ones of about 55 gallons are often used. The reason is that already mentioned in connexion with red wine fermentation: the necessity of keeping the temperature down. Where internal refrigeration coils are fitted in the vats, size is of less importance, and in America and the more highly rationalized Continental vineyards, large tanks holding thousands of gallons are employed.

Before running the must from the presses into these containers, they are sulphured so as to make sure that there is no residual mouldiness lurking in any corner. (See the following section on sulphuring.) Generally the must has enough yeasts in it, picked up from the skins during pressing, to ferment as it is. The use of pure yeast cultures is spreading slowly, but is as yet far from universal.

In the making of cheap, sweet, white wines, fermentation is stopped ('muted') when the appropriate amount of sugar remains unfermented, by sulphuring further, or pasteurizing. White wines from white grapes made in presence of the skins have a yellowish or yellowish-green colour which is generally absent from those made by fermenting without the skins.

At this point it may be useful to consider the subject of 'sulphuring'.

Sulphuring

Sulphuring, that is the treatment of wines with sulphur dioxide in one form or another, is not at all new. It has been practised for a century or two.

Sulphur dioxide is a very powerful disinfectant. It is a gas with a characteristic odour and much pungency even in small quantities. It is easily compressed to a liquid, and this is supplied by manufacturers in siphons, steel cylinders, or tank wagons. Wine-makers use it either in this form, or dissolved in water, or combined as potassium bisulphite, which is a pale yellow powder, usually made into tablets. It is still not uncommon for wine-makers to make the gas as required by burning sulphur, especially when casks or vats have to be sulphured (*méchage*). 'Sulphur candles' are used for this purpose; these are lengths of cloth impregnated with sulphur. A suitably-sized piece is cut off, fitted into a sort of metal lantern, lit, and the lantern lowered into the cask. The lantern prevents drops of molten sulphur or scraps of burnt cloth dropping into the cask; the presence of these in the wine would have the most strikingly unfavourable effects on its taste.

Wine in bulk is sulphured by bubbling liquefied sulphur dioxide through it, or by adding the appropriate amount of the solution in water (which normally contains 6 per cent of the gas) or of a solution of bisulphite. Sulphuring is a more or less temporary measure. That is to say, the sulphur dioxide gradually disappears, by changing to sulphuric acid, and then ceases to have any perceptible antiseptic action. This is the reason that careless wine-makers tend to over-sulphur.

In France, wines may not contain more than 450 parts per million of total sulphur dioxide; this corresponds to about $6\frac{1}{4}$ ounces per hundred gallons. In Germany the limit is 250 parts (only 25 parts if the wine is to be sold bottled); Italy allows 165 parts, Spain, like France, 450 parts.

Rosé wines are made in various ways in different localities. Light pressing of red grapes and a quick removal of the juice is the basis of most methods. Fermentation is carried out quickly – forty-eight hours or less – by allowing the temperature to rise a little higher than usual. Since *rosé* wines are sometimes difficult to clear, in some parts the must is muted for a few days by sulphuring heavily, so that during this standstill period pectins and albumins will settle out.

THE YEASTS

In order to understand what is happening in the fermentation vat, it is first necessary to consider the yeasts, which are the agents by which the fermentation is carried out.

Yeasts are plants of a very lowly order indeed: a sort of fungus. They consist of single cells which commonly reproduce by the simple means of budding off another cell. In favourable surroundings they can reproduce at an enormous rate; in unsuitable conditions they remain quiescent and solitary for long periods. They are the agents responsible for the rising of bread and the fermentation of beers, ciders, and other alcoholic liquors, for some have the capacity of converting starch or sugar into alcohol. They are among the most important of the lower organisms, for it is to their efforts that we owe the fact that much of our food is palatable, and that we can absorb it into our bodies whether it is or not.

At one time it was thought that fermentation could take place only when living organisms (like yeasts) were present, but in 1897 it was found that it was not the yeasts in themselves which were the true agents, but substances in them. These substances are called ferments or enzymes: the words are derived from Latin and Greek roots respectively which signify 'to boil'. Hundreds of enzymes are known; all are proteins, that is, chemical compounds without life. A single yeast cell, which is about one five-thousandth of an inch across, may contain a thousand different enzymes.

Enzymes have the peculiar property of causing changes to take place without suffering any permanent change themselves. Only a minute amount of enzyme is necessary in order to carry out a change: a single drop of an extract of rennin, one of the enzymes of rennet, will curdle four tons of milk in ten minutes, it was found. All living cells contain enzymes; that is to say, all cells in all plants, animals, and bacteria. Many of the chemical changes associated with life are carried out by enzymes.

It is by means of enzymes that the starch of the plant is converted into the sugar of the ripe grape; it is they which break the oxygen bridges of the starch molecule (pages 59). In fact the very same enzymes occur in the human body, in the saliva and the intestines, and convert the starch in our food into sugar, which we absorb (with the help of other enzymes).

A vast amount of work has been done on finding out how the sugar of the grape becomes the alcohol of wine. These investigations started long ago, but it is only ten or fifteen years since they reached the point when the whole complicated process of fermentation could be visualized and broken down into its successive steps, which can all be reproduced in the laboratory. Pasteur did not start the inquiry, but it was he who did the lion's share of the early work, and put the problem into such a form that it could be attacked by the methods of modern science.

In 1861, he considered that the reason yeast grew so prolifically in grape-juice was that it needed oxygen and the grape-juice supplies it. 'Since yeast assimilates oxygen so actively in the free state, it proves that the cell needs it in order to live,' he said, 'and therefore, if this element cannot be obtained in the free state, it must be taken from the fermentable material. The cell then appears to use it for the breakdown of sugar.' This, though not quite correct, was a good theory to start from. It was not until 1942 that Meyerhof proved that what fermentation provides the yeast cell with is not oxygen, but energy.

The fact is that during the various steps in the transformation of sugar to alcohol, a considerable amount of energy is set free, and it is this which enables the yeast cell to carry on the family of *ellipsoideus* so prolifically.

What Happens in the Vat

The problem of what happens in the fermentation vat is simply, given the rules of chemistry, to find out how the sugar molecule changes into alcohol. It had been known for a long time that the sugar in grapes is converted into about half its weight of alcohol, and that the other half goes off as the gas, carbon dioxide.

The sugar in ripe grapes consists of about half glucose (or grape-sugar, or dextrose: same substance) and half fructose (or fruit-sugar, or levulose). Both of these have the formula $C_6H_{12}O_6$, and the arrangement of the atoms is as shown on page 61. The difference between the two, although of great interest to chemistry students, is of no moment to fermentation, for they behave identically in the vat. Alcohol has the formula C_2H_6O, and carbon dioxide, CO_2. One molecule of sugar gives two of alcohol and two of carbon dioxide:

$$C_6H_{12}O_6 \quad \rightarrow \quad 2C_2H_6O \quad + \quad 2CO_2$$

To give a detailed account of all that happens would be long, involved, and tedious, but it is not difficult to get an idea of the sort of thing that goes on, especially if we confine our attention to the skeleton formulae.

In the first part of the transformation, the six-membered ring of the glucose-fructose is converted to a five-membered ring, called, after its discoverers, 'Harden and Young ester';

There is still the same number of carbon atoms in this, that is, six, but another has slipped out of the ring, so that Harden and Young ester has two tails onto a five-membered ring. What is even more surprising is that each of these two side-arm carbon atoms has attached to it a tail of phosphoric acid (here again abbreviated to 'P').

It had been known even to Pasteur that phosphoric acid played some part in fermentation. He suggested adding some to the vat to see what happened. There is ample phosphoric acid in the grape-must and the yeasts to supply the normal needs of fermentation (although it is good practice to add some phosphate to a 'stuck' vat). Compounds of phosphoric acid are profoundly implicated in an enormous number of biological changes, as already mentioned.

For simplicity, three steps have been treated as one stage to arrive at the Harden and Young ester, and for these three steps, three separate enzymes are needed, one for each step. Enzymes are in their very essence specialists, and work to the strictest union rules: each enzyme can cause only one particular compound to be converted into another particular compound. Moreover, each enzyme needs its 'co-enzyme', and can do nothing without it. (It is interesting, though irrelevant to the subject of wine-making, that several of these essential co-enzymes are very similar indeed to some of the vitamins.)

In the next step, the Harden and Young ester breaks down into two identical halves, each containing three carbon atoms and a phosphoric acid tail. This change also needs an enzyme (zymohexase, found also in the cells of animal muscles). We are now down to a three-carbon chain, to a molecule of the glycero-phosphoric acid type in fact. It might seem that we have only a little way to go to reach alcohol, which has two carbon atoms. But glycero-phosphoric acid is not convertible into alcohol by the enzymes of wine-yeast so easily. There are six intervening steps. Five of the steps (each with its attendant enzyme and co-enzyme) are concerned with three-carbon compounds with phosphoric acid attached to them; then at last the phosphorus is thrown out and an acid without phosphorus is formed. This is called pyruvic acid.

Harden and Young ester   Glycero-   Pyruvic
                              phosphoric acid   acid

Pyruvic acid is of peculiar importance because when, in 1910, Neubauer discovered that this acid (made by chemical means, quite apart from fermentation or enzyme action) could be fermented, research workers realized that they were at last on the home-stretch of the prolonged investigation. In 1897, Éduard Buchner had succeeded in showing that the presence of living cells was not necessary for fermentation to take place, but that an extract of the yeast cells would do just as well. This was of great importance, for it killed the oldest fallacy in wine-making: that living organisms were necessary to make wine; the date is an important one in science: 9 January 1897. Later, in 1906, Harden and Young showed that the extract which Buchner had made was a mixture of two separate materials, both of which were necessary for fermentation: the enzyme and the co-enzyme. This was another landmark.

Pyruvic acid is a comparatively simple compound and we can now jettison the skeleton formula and write it out in full. It is $CH_3.CO.COOH$, that is, a carbon atom with three hydrogen atoms attached, joined to a carbon with a single oxygen, and this in turn linked to the carbon group, COOH, which is known as carboxyl, and is characteristic of an acid. It is this last part of the molecule which is attacked by the next enzyme, carboxylase; Von Karczag contributed this piece of information. The enzyme carboxylase is found in bacteria, most fungi, and plants. It is a protein which contains magnesium as well as the inevitable phosphorus, as Green proved in 1941. Its action on the pyruvic acid is to remove carbon dioxide, which escapes in bubbles from the vat and so provides the most obvious evidence that fermentation is going on. Acetaldehyde is left. This is, of course, $CH_3.CO$—H, usually written $CH_3.CHO$.

It is a rather sweetish-smelling liquid, of which traces always remain in wine and also in spirits. It is very easily turned into acetic acid, which as already mentioned (page 67) is one of the enemies of wine: it is what wine becomes if not well cared for. Fortunately another enzyme steps in and quickly converts the acetaldehyde into alcohol, our goal:

$$
\begin{array}{ccccc}
CH_3 & & CH_3 & & CH_3 \\
| & & | & & | \\
CO & \longrightarrow & CO & \longrightarrow & H_2C\text{—}OH \\
| & & | & & \\
COOH & & H & & \\
\text{Pyruvic} & & \text{Acetaldehyde} & & \text{Alcohol} \\
\text{acid} & & & &
\end{array}
$$

So, successive enzymes, each ready with its mate, its co-enzyme, to take over when the previous one has finished, break down the ring-molecules of glucose and fructose, first to Harden and Young ester, then to members of the glycero-phosphoric series of compounds, and so to pyruvic acid, then to acetaldehyde, and finally to alcohol.

When we drink alcohol, or leave it to the mercies of *Acetobacter* and the bacteria, in either case it turns back to carbon dioxide and water, which is how it started in the leaf of the plant.

It is easy to work out, from the equation on page 75, that 180 parts of glucose/fructose produces, or should produce, 88 parts of carbon dioxide and 92 parts of alcohol. (Just give each atom in each formula its relative mass: hydrogen, 1; carbon 12; oxygen, 16.) That is, the sugar gives almost exactly half its weight of alcohol (51.1 per cent to be more exact). If the grape-juice contained 20 per cent of sugar, the wine should have an alcohol content of about 10 per cent. This is in fact roughly the amount of alcohol in ordinary table-wine.

In point of fact, the enzymes are not so completely efficient as that, and there is some loss. One hundred parts of sugar give about $47\frac{1}{2}$ parts of alcohol in practice. The discrepancy should not be blamed on the twelve enzymes concerned in the alcoholic fermentation, however, for besides these there are hundreds of other enzymes in the yeast, and occasionally one of them will come across the compound which is its own particular food, perhaps among the glycero-phosphorus compounds. In that case it converts it into something not in the alcoholic series. So much is lost to the production of alcohol.

The Harden and Young ester is a weak point: a few molecules, instead of keeping to the normal path through the glycero-phosphoric acid compounds, are converted into glycerine itself. That is why there is always a little glycerine in wines; it adds slightly to their sweetness. This is particularly the case when *Botrytis cinerea* (see page 62) has attacked the grapes. Then, there may be three times as much glycerine as usual: 2 or 3 per cent instead of rather under 1 per cent.

Wine as it is run out of the fermentation vats contains a large number of substances besides alcohol and water, and this is lucky, for alcohol and water plain is not an interesting drink. Nevertheless, the wine is not drinkable as it stands. It is cloudy with live and dead yeast cells, bacteria, and moulds, with pectins and albumins, and mineral matter caught up with the grapes in the gathering. Dissolved in it are acids and glycerine, tannin, colouring matter (very little in white wines of course), a little unfermented sugar, phosphates, and other soluble salts. Some of these improve the wine by their presence, others must be removed. There may be too much or too little acid, or tannin, or pectin, or alcohol. Apart from these, it is very necessary to make sure that there is not within the wine the seeds of its own destruction, in the form of *Acetobacter* or moulds.

The wine must now be treated.

CHAPTER 5

FROM THE VAT TO THE BOTTLE

Of the processes of fermentation and treatment of wines, Robinet, a practical expert, says 'the question . . . is more complicated than one can well imagine'. Dr Jules Guyot, another expert, says, 'the great art of making good wine is of primitive simplicity'.

Bearing in mind both of these pronouncements simultaneously, we may now consider what must be done to the product of the fermentation vat to turn it into sound wine which will keep.

The fermentation is virtually over. If it is red wine the cap of skins is still and no wine oozes through, forced up by escaping gas; if the vat contains white wine, an occasional clump of yeast cells, or fragment of debris, rises slowly to the surface, floated up with a gas bubble. All the tumultuous stage of the process is finished. There is a little sugar left: perhaps 1 per cent, no more, unless the wine is to be a sweet one, when the fermentation will have been stopped some time before, so as to leave the desired amount of sugar.

The first thing to be done, fairly obviously, is to run off the wine, free from the cap and the lees, into another container. There it is left in great barrels ranged in long rows on their sides in a cool cellar. The small amount of yeast suspended in the slightly cloudy liquid will then ferment out the remaining sugar. A dry wine should contain no more than one part of sugar in five hundred of wine (0.2 per cent).

The murk of skins, stalks, and pips is pressed to obtain all the wine possible. It is shovelled into presses such as those shown in Plate 5, and the cover of the press forced down either by hand, through long arms which are turned around a central screw, or pressure exerted by means of hydraulic pumps. The final pressure is between 200 and 1,000 pounds per square inch of surface.

Especially during the first month or two, the wine shrinks, and it is necessary to make up the ullage. The shrinkage is partly due to the wine cooling (after the warmth of the fermentation), but the chief cause is absorption by the casks. New casks will absorb between 5 and

10 per cent of the wine in them in the first year, and even old ones take up 1 or 2 per cent. The wine passes through the pores of the wood and evaporates off into the air. Unfortunately, alcohol passes through more easily than water, and so there is a tendency for the wine to become weaker as well as less. Faulty cooperage can lead to much greater losses, of course, and casks are frequently inspected for weeping.

The filling-up of the casks (*ouillage*) must be carried out with a sound wine of the same year, or the year before, and is done every few days for the first month or two, then less frequently. If the casks are small, it is common practice merely to push an inverted bottle full of wine through a hole in the bung; then, as the wine-level sinks in the cask, more liquid flows in from the bottle. There are patent contrivances to do the same thing. In some places, a few handfuls of washed pebbles are thrown into the cask at intervals so as to bring the level up.

The remaining cloudiness in the wine is meanwhile settling down to a new sediment and the wine is racked from this at intervals, that is, it is drawn off through a pipe from above the sediment, which must not be disturbed. These intervals vary somewhat. In hot countries it is well to start early with the racking and to do it frequently. Fabre, the expert on Algerian wine-making, says roundly, 'premature racking carried out properly cannot harm a wine. Late racking, or one carried out badly, can spoil a good wine irreparably', and in North Africa racking is ordinarily carried out first in mid October after the August or September vintage, then again in November, January, March, and July. In Bordeaux, however, it is sufficient to rack first some time during the winter, for the second time in March, and again in June, with occasionally a fourth racking in August, or even late September, and this practice is fairly widespread in Europe.

Now the greater part of the wine of every country is drunk within the year after making, and it is clear that the long standing in the cellar with careful and frequent racking is unnecessary, and in fact impossible, for wine of this sort – the *vin ordinaire*, *Konsumwein*, and *consumo*. It is filtered through the conventional type of horizontal filter-presses, familiar in chemical works. Such wines sell for a few pence the litre, or are supplied free with *prix-fixe* restaurant meals.

To wines which are for export or to be kept to mature (*vins de garde*), special consideration must be given. This is the province of the cellar-master, the *maître de chai*, an all-powerful and experienced man, upon whom the responsibility for the health of the vintage depends: upon his palate and his knowledge. In many places, expert chemists and biologists are supplementing and even supplanting *monsieur le maître*, but the science of oenology has not yet arrived at the stage of completely correlating quality and composition. Moreover, it has been found that if a wine tastes earthy or musty, no chemical or biological report will placate the buyer. The *maître de chai* decides what treatment a wine must have to correct its deficiencies, if any. Most wines need no more than racking and fining and slight sulphuring.

Fining is necessary to remove the very small particles which do not settle out during cellaring. Yeast cells are so minute that unless they agglomerate into clumps they will never settle out, and there are other fragments of various descriptions which would float for ever unless forced to sink. Fining consists in adding some materials to the wine in which the minute particles will be entangled and so carried down. (What really happens is fairly certainly not as simple as this: the 'entanglement' is probably due to the attraction of the floating particles, which are usually charged negatively, to the positively-charged particles of the fining agent, but this is by the way.)

This operation of fining (or *collage*) is carried out with a wide variety of substances. Fish-glue, gelatine, the seaweed colloid agar-agar, white of egg, tannin, various clays, charcoal, milk, casein, and ox-blood are all used in one vineyard or another, and there are innumerable patent powders and liquid preparations on the market in addition. Egg-white beaten up with salt is frequently employed for the fine wines of Burgundy and the Bordelais. Generally speaking, for white wines purified fish-glue (isinglass) is used, never gelatine. In California, an absorptive clay, bentonite, is used for the cheaper wines. Clearing of the wine after fining takes between ten and twenty days (depending on the nature and the age of the wine, the temperature, the direction of the wind, and many other factors).

This, then, is the treatment which all good wines must have: a cool cellaring, with frequent *ouillages*, and periodical rackings, with fining before the last racking (or the last but one).

It sometimes happens that the weather during the growing and vintage periods has caused the wine to be low in alcohol, to be too acid or not acid enough, to be infected with disease, or to be almost impossible to clear satisfactorily. To treat one of these faulty wines so as to finish with a high-class wine for the cask and the bottle tests the experience and the knowledge of the cellar-master, often to their limits. Some of the great Bordeaux vineyards do not bottle under their own name if the wine is likely to harm their reputation, and in fact some proprietors own an inferior vineyard in the district, so that its yield in poor years can be swollen by the access of the shameful product of the great château. (Château Lafite bottled no wine at all at the château from 1885 to 1905.)

The average dry red or white wine contains 10 to 12 per cent alcohol, rather more for the 'standard' wines of the U.S.A. and Australia. Of the rest, nearly all is water, but apart from the contribution from the alcohol, the taste, aroma, and colour are due to the one or two per cent that is neither water nor alcohol: the scrap of un-fermented sugar and the half per cent of glycerol that is always formed (see page 78), and the miscellaneous lot of oddments which occur in only very small quantities indeed: colouring matter in red wine, a little tannin, esters, pectin (which occurs in all fruits and is only partly broken up by the enzymes), and, very important indeed, acids.

There are three matters to which the cellar-master pays particular attention. (There are others, but we must simplify a little: these are the chief.) The first is the amount of alcohol in the wine; the second is the amount of acid; and the third is any evidence of disease.

The Alcohol in Wine

Most of the wine-countries insist that there shall be a certain minimum amount of alcohol in wine offered for sale. The figure is usually 8 or 10 per cent. (*Appellation Contrôlée* wines each have their own minimum, see page 96.) In any case thin wines don't sell, although in Italy (and elsewhere) many ordinary local wines contain as little as 7 per cent, and a comprehensive series of tests of German wines produced between 1903 and 1911 showed that about one in three had less than 10 per cent of alcohol in them.

The cellar-master knows fairly certainly by vintage-time whether he will have trouble with the alcohol content of the wine he is going to make. In the fine sunny years, like 1945, 1947, and 1955, he is all smiles; otherwise he is not to be approached without trepidation, for he is anxiously balancing in his mind the various ways he can correct the wine. He can boldly add alcohol to it. This is *vinage*. But alcohol is expensive, especially if it is of such quality as not to impart the taste of its origin to the wine; also, there is an excise duty on it. *Vinage* is not popular for beverage wines; it is not allowed in France, and in Germany forbidden except for wines to be sold on draught.

Of course, the wine may be mixed off with another which has plenty of alcohol in it. Wines made in hot climates always have more than the 8 or 10 per cent minimum and they are often a little short in acid, while wines made from grapes which have scarcely ripened are high in acid. Nothing could be luckier: just send a telegram to one of the wholesalers of Algiers or Sète or Málaga and arrange for the delivery of a few hundred hectolitres of good twelve- or thirteen-degree wine, to mix in with your thin stuff. Millions of gallons of wine are made in this way every year – by *coupage*, as it is called. It is the recipe for making *vin ordinaire*. So long as the flavour does not matter and there is no worry about the bouquet, it is the simplest way there is of adjusting the alcohol in wine. Of course, you will not expect to sell the wine very advantageously, for having spoiled its aroma and dulled its flavour it will not fetch the price of a fine wine, and the competition to sell *ordinaire* is very fierce. Flavour is an elusive quality and its delicacy is easily destroyed.

The most favoured method of increasing the alcohol in a thin but delicately-flavoured wine is to sugar the must before, or during, fermentation. This is called *sucrage*, or *chaptalisation*. The *maître de chai* knows before he carries out the fermentation how much short of the desired alcohol the wine will be, and he can calculate the amount of sugar that the grapes lack. In Spain and Portugal sugaring as such is forbidden, but the addition of evaporated must is not merely allowed but very widely practised.

The addition of sugar to finished (beverage) wines is forbidden in most countries; in France and Algeria, it may be carried out if the wine is to be drunk 'by a member of the family or a domestic servant'.

The expedient has been adopted of refrigerating the wine so that some of the water freezes out and leaves a liquid richer in alcohol. This is a wasteful method, for it is impossible to free the ice-crystals from the liquid wine completely, and although there is a certain gain in alcoholic strength, some wine is lost. The practice was first suggested by Paracelsus, in the sixteenth century ('Congelation').

In very bad years, or when none of these methods of improvement is convenient, the wine is sold to manufacturers of spirits, who distil it. It goes to make not cognac or armagnac, but an inferior brandy.

The Acid in Wine

The commonest reproach levelled against a wine is that it is acid, or 'vinegary'. It is the easiest reproach to deserve, for acidity can very readily occur in wine. The way acetic acid is formed during – or after – fermentation has been noted on page 67. The cellar-master keeps the acetic acid out by taking care to keep the conditions in the vat and the cellar unfavourable to the growth of *Acetobacter*, which needs air to live as much as human beings do. Once acetic acid has got into a wine, there is no cure: it will taste vinegary.

Some wines have no taste of vinegar, yet are too acid. They have a tart, acid taste, like sour apples, and the reason is usually the same: it is due to incomplete ripening of the fruit. In the southern vineyards, of the Rhône and the Mediterranean, wines that are tart or *vert* are rare. Not so in Alsace and on the Mosel; even on the Loire and in Burgundy they are not very uncommon. It is largely a matter of latitude, although it depends to some extent on the variety of grape.

There are several acids which contribute to the tart taste of wine in sunless years. The principal is tartaric. If a wine has less than about two parts per thousand of tartaric acid, it will not keep well, and will tend to taste insipid. On the other hand it will be hard to the palate if there is more than about ten or fifteen parts. Malic acid, which is so called because it occurs in apples, is always present in grapes, and some carries through to the wine. As grapes ripen, the malic acid diminishes, for in fact it is a primary food of the cells in the fruit, and as the cells mature, the malic acid is burnt up to sustain them. The higher the temperature, the more rapidly it diminishes. In the wine there may be as much or even more malic acid than there is tartaric; on the other hand, there may be a mere trace.

The other acids in wine are of comparatively minor importance;

they are citric acid, succinic acid, and lactic acid. Lactic acid (the acid of sour milk) has a certain interest. Normally there is only perhaps a quarter as much lactic as tartaric acid, but occasionally quite a considerable amount is present, for some enzymes convert sugar into it in the fermentation vat, and also, wines may be attacked by a bacterium which produces lactic acid.

In all fresh wines there is a bacterium which destroys malic acid, *Bacterium gracile*. There are several, but this is the most important. It sets to work on the malic acid and converts it into lactic. One might conclude that this is nothing gained, but lactic acid is a much less 'acid' acid than malic. This is not really very abstruse. The mark of acids of this sort is the presence in the molecule of the COOH group (see page 77), and the molecule of malic acid has two of these groups while that of lactic acid has one. So after *B. gracile* has carried out its fermentation (for its action is classed as a fermentation) the wine is less acid. The process largely takes place in the wine after it has been bottled. It is of little interest to the wine-makers of the South, for the sun has already burnt up most of the malic acid in their grapes. But in the wines of Germany, Austria, and Switzerland it is an important aid in improving acid wines. In the course of the 'malolactic' fermentation some carbon dioxide is given off (by the splitting of the COOH group, as in normal alcoholic fermentation, see page 77), and this is sufficient to impart a very pleasant freshness to the wine. The loss of acidity resulting from this fermentation was one of the unsolved puzzles of vinification until Seifert and a number of other biologists discovered the bacteria responsible, in 1900 and the following year or two.

However, the malolactic fermentation cannot always be relied upon to reduce the acidity; the bacteria will not do their work if there is more than a trace of sulphur dioxide present, for instance. If the extra acidity is due to tartaric acid, it will not be susceptible to the action of bacteria of this sort, and it must be removed in some other way. There is a very simple method, of the most venerable antiquity. Most of the tartaric acid in wine is half-combined with potassium. This is not a very scientific way of putting it, but it may serve to explain the position. Like malic acid, tartaric acid has two COOH groups in the molecule, and one of these is combined with potassium while the other is free. This half-combined tartaric acid, popularly known as potassium bitartrate or 'cream of tartar', does not dissolve at all easily in wine, especially when the temperature is low. One of the principal reasons for keeping the wine cool during cellaring is to encourage the tartar to come out of solution. It falls to the bottom of the cask in crystals which, if they were not discoloured by the lees, would be white. In warm countries – Algeria, the U.S.A., Australia – it is usual to put the wine through a refrigeration process in order to bring out the tartar.

The southern wine-maker is more likely to want to increase the acidity of his wine, and this problem is rather more difficult to solve than the converse. In ancient times, the wine-maker would cheerfully throw in a few handfuls of plaster – plaster of paris. Plaster of paris is calcium sulphate, and when it is added to must or wine, there is, in effect, an exchange with potassium bitartrate which is present, so that calcium tartrate forms and settles as a sludge at the bottom of the barrel, while free tartaric acid and potassium sulphate form in the wine. The tartaric acid makes the wine taste more acid and the colour is also improved. The presence of sulphate in wine is not a good thing, at any rate if carried out in excess. Pliny complained of the practice about two thousand years ago, and the modern French, German, Italian, and Spanish wine-laws are as one in forbidding more than two parts per thousand of sulphate to be present in wine.

However, one can avoid introducing sulphate into wine by using calcium phosphate instead of plaster. In this case the tartaric acid is replaced by phosphoric acid instead of sulphuric. Phosphoric is not such a strong acid as sulphuric, but the acidity of the wine is quite considerably increased. In Germany and Switzerland this practice also is forbidden by law, but in Algeria and the Midi of France it is common. Mixed solutions, containing sulphur dioxide as well, are sold under fancy names to small wine-makers. The use of these is not recommended by everyone; one expert says that some give the wine a 'taste of soda and a smell of damp dogs'.

Of course, one can buy tartaric acid or citric acid and put it into the wine. Not in Germany, however; in fact, one may not even import into Germany wines which have had acid added to them. The best way to avoid being saddled with a low-acid wine in the South is to pick early and to include in the vintage a proportion of unripe grapes. This means sacrificing sugar, that is, alcohol, of course.

Apart from the amount of alcohol and the acidity, a wine may need some attention in one or two other respects. The sweet white wines made with the help of *Botrytis* are particularly liable to give difficulties in filtering (as well as in fermentation). They are tender things, these fine white wines, and too severe a treatment will destroy their delicacy. Otherwise they would be dealt with by heating in closed containers: a sort of pasteurization. The best thing to do with Sauternes or Barsac which filters badly is to add a rather larger amount of tannin than usual and then to fine once more, perhaps with gelatin this time, although as gelatin is rather fierce in its action, there is some danger of the wine turning yellow. Sometimes the trouble is more difficult to deal with. A certain number of the Sauternes and Barsacs of 1917, after the usual long cellaring and very careful fining, were bottled in 1921 in apparently perfect condition. Very soon after in some cases, but not for a year or two in others, the wine turned cloudy; it was presumed that some bacterial companion of *Botrytis* had taken four or five years to declare itself.

If a red wine is simply rather pale, it is possible to mix it with one of the dark wines from Spain, which are especially made to help *Kellermeisters* in distress. These are known in Germany, where pale wines are not uncommon, as *Deckweine*, and quite a brisk little trade is done from Alicante and Valencia in these 'cover-wines'. Alicante Romana, Alicante Monovar, Priorato, Benicarlo, and Liria travel around Cape Finisterre to unload at Rotterdam for the Rhine towns.

Long fermentation extracts more colour from the skins, and so does a hot fermentation (short of sticking-point – see page 69) or heating part of the must with the skins and adding it to the fermentation vat. One can include more of the *vin de presse*, obtained by later pressings of the fermented murk. Salt can be added if one holds the old and now discredited belief that *salage* improves the colour. There is an even simpler way: in Italy, at least, one can buy 'oenocyanine' in tablets, and these, when dissolved in the wine, deepen its colour marvellously.

It is becoming increasingly common to give wines which are not quite first class a final filtration: in California it is called a 'polishing filtration'. Pasteurization is also frequently carried out, by pumping the wine through heated pipes so that it spends several minutes at a temperature of about 140°.

After considering this outlisne of a few of the adventures which may befall a wine before it passes out of the cellars into the hands of the merchants, the force of M. Robinet's statement, quoted at the beginning of this chapter, will be appreciated. Nevertheless, the best way to make wine is to avoid trouble beforehand, even as long before as the choosing of the vinestocks and the scions and the clearing of the ground in which they are to be planted. The wine from the really great vineyards rarely needs much treatment at all; in one or two of the Bordeaux châteaux even sulphuring is avoided, and in some of the vineyards of the Rheingau, the precautions taken against the danger of accidental contamination seem almost grotesque (see page 158), but their wines are prized by many above all others. Dr Guyot's dictum applies to the making of the best wines: avoid complications.

The description given in this and the previous chapter of the making and treatment of wine applies to wines which comply with the requirements of the laws of the country and are offered for sale in the usual way. In all the vine-growing areas of the world, 'little' wines are made for local consumption from the pressed *marc* of skins and pips. In France the resultant drink is called *piquette*, *vinade*, or *pique*; in Germany, *Tresterwein*, *Nachwein*, or *Haustrunk*; in Italy, *vinelli* or *vini piccoli*. They are made by putting the *marc* into barrels and pressing down, then adding water and a little potassium bisulphite as preservative. After a few days, during which it has been stirred occasionally, the liquid has a pale red tint (if the grapes were black) and contains 5 or 6 per cent of alcohol. It is hard and rough, but sound, unless the skins were left too long. Acid grapes give a better *piquette* than those grown in the South, which of course tend to be short of acid. In South Germany, citric acid is often added to the *Haustrunk*, which is frequently mixed with fruit wines. Such wines as these are not bottled, or sold outside the localities in which they are made. Of French *piquette*, Robinet says 'it is a sound and innocent drink in which the crudity of water is suitably corrected'.

In the early 1930s, the so-called *vins de café* (café wines) became popular in the South of France. They were generally drunk between meals, and tended to be bright in colour rather than deep; they had more colour than *rosé* wines but less than red. They were made by fermenting only overnight, or at most for twenty-four hours, but had a fairly high alcohol content with little body.

Since, as is well known, the difficulty of making enough money honestly considerably irks some people, there have been a number, a large number, of occasions during the past centuries when wine-makers and wine-merchants have increased the volume or improved the apparent quality of their products by some sort of sophistication, such as the addition of sulphuric or nitric acid, or of pigeon-dung (see page 41). Apart from these, many much more easily defensible expedients have been adopted for much the same purposes. When Phylloxera reached the Midi, in 1863, the production of wine dropped rapidly to rather over half normal. For a long time before, the wine-producers in this area had been importing a certain amount of raisins which they added to the fermentation vats so as to raise the amount of alcohol in the wine. Now that they were faced with a serious shortage of grapes, they increased the size of their orders on Valencia, Genoa, and the Piraeus. The grape-growers were up in arms at once, for, apart from losing half their crop, they were not even getting scarcity-prices for the harvest they could gather. When the vineyards re-covered, the traffic was much reduced, and it eventually fell to very small proportions. But the detection of the presence of raisin wine in ordinary wine is still not possible with certainty.

Although, as already mentioned, it is illegal to add sugar to wines in many countries, there are other methods which are quite legal of making a wine sweet. The use of grapes which have been subject to the attentions of *Botrytis* is the commonest of these. Wines from such grapes are made in the Sauternes district of Bordeaux, on the Rhine, in the Tokaj-Hegzalja district of Hungary, and in Anjou. In other places – Alsace, Baden, the Tyrol, and the Jura – the so-called *vins de paille*, or straw wines, are made. Only sound sweetish grapes are used; they are laid out in an airy room on straw or reeds and there they slowly dry. The sugar is slowly concentrated in the juice, and by fermentation to about the normal 10 to 12 per cent of alcohol, a wine with residual, unfermented sugar is obtained.

Most fortified wines have concentrated must added to them to increase the sugar content. The concentration of must has been practised from the earliest antiquity and a good deal of confusion has arisen because the ancients often used the same word for wine and for must, either evaporated or not. It may be mentioned that must does not remain long unfermented in hot countries, and in order to preserve it, boiling and, better still, evaporation is necessary. Aristotle mentions some wines of Arcadia which were quite solid, and it is clear that in this and many other cases referred to in classical times, evaporated must is meant.

In ancient Greece and Rome the must was often boiled down sufficiently to prevent fermentation until it was syrupy. It was then known to the Greeks as *hepsema* or *siraion*, and to the Romans as *carenum*, *defrutum*, or *sapa*. For travellers, must was also dried and made into cakes with flour and other materials. Evaporated must is still made and sold nowadays. It is used as it stands as a sweetmeat, for making confectionery or in cooking, all over Southern Europe and in both South and North America. Around the Mediterranean it is known as *moût cuit* or *mosto cotto*. When more highly concentrated to a honey-like consistency, it is sold as *miel de raisin* or *mosto agustin*. Vacuum evaporators of modern design give a pale product, but *mosto agustin* is more frequently dark brown. In Asia Minor, *pekmez*, the local variety of *miel de raisin*, is made from a mixture of grape and other fruit juices and honey, and is so widely made and used by the peasants that sugar is rarely seen, or needed.

Apart from the coarsening of the taste of the wine to which evaporated must has been added, there is also introduced the characteristic taste of 'burnt sugar' or caramel.

The By-products

Wine-makers are economical men. They waste as little as the porkpackers of Chicago. The grape-husks, after refermenting to make piquettes or *marc* brandy (see chapter 11), are treated to obtain the tartar which is mixed with them, and this is purified by crystallization and sold for use in dye-works or for making baking-powder. The grape-pips are separated and ground up, then extracted with a solvent to obtain the oil which is present to the extent of about 10 per cent of their weight. This has a pleasant taste and can be used, after hydrogenation, to make cooking-fat or margarine. Poorer qualities go to soaperies or to make oil-colours. The exhausted *marc* may be used as cattle-food so long as there is not too much tartaric acid left in it. (If there is, the cattle tend to drop their calves prematurely. It is not considered as very high-class feeding-stuff in any case.) In many places it is used as manure; there is an old belief in Burgundy that the best grapes should be manured with nothing else. In fact, it has a higher mineral content than stable manure, but no bacteria, and is rated very low by experts. The lees can be treated to give 'yeast wine' (*Hefewein*), which on distillation yields 'yeast brandy'. At Roma, in California, the grape-stems are treated to obtain the sugar in them.

The Maturing of Wine

The fact that some wines improve on storage has been known for three or four thousand years; it is mentioned by ancient Hebrew writers, and in the days of Solomon, wines were either drunk soon after making, or, if they were suitable, stored away in great jars underground to mature.

Few white wines improve much on keeping, and many deteriorate. Red wines of mediocre quality scarcely change over the years, and very rarely for the better. A great or fine red wine, on the other hand, improves for a time, which may be many years, and then slowly its quality fades. Burgundies generally mature more rapidly than clarets and deteriorate sooner, but the wines of each year and each *vignoble* and even each vineyard vary in their longevity. Claret of 1825 matured after twenty years, but the 1828 wine was at its best in seven years, and somewhere between these two periods is the average maturing time of a fine claret. A red burgundy would be at its best in half the time, but would be fading before the claret was fully mature. Some clarets have almost incredible lasting powers. Château Latour of 1874 and 1875 are said to be still perfect; at a reception held in 1926, a bottle of Château Lafite of the 1811 vintage was opened and, to the amazement of everyone, it was found to be in perfect condition. Generally, it is only such fortified wines as Madeira which can live so long without falling into senility.

The basically important factors in the improving of a wine by its maturing seem to be the tannin and the acid content. These must be present in fairly large quantities. A hard, somewhat acid claret will take longer to mature than a softer one, but will at last be the superior. Given enough tannin and acid, which are insurances against deterioration, the gradual improvement in quality appears to be due to, first, the slow continuation of the reactions between the substances present in the new wine, which leads to a loss of all harshness, and to a slow, a very slow, oxidation by means of the oxygen of the air present in the bottle-space and dissolved in the wine. The effect of the oxidation is to convert a trace of the alcohol into acetaldehyde; this is equivalent to the retracing of the last step of the fermentation series of reactions (see page 77). Acetaldehyde is a pleasant-smelling liquid (in small quantities) and contributes directly to the aroma. It also enters into the reactions which go on with the other substances present: the 'marrying' process.

The marrying consists of a number of reactions which go on, some consecutively, some simultaneously. Traces of the acids present combine with the alcohol; that is perhaps the main effect. The result of this is to form esters, which have a sweetish, fruity smell, some of well-known fruits, some of fruits which never were. The acetaldehyde also combines with some alcohol to give yet another sweetish-smelling liquid, called acetal. Other changes which take place are connected with the higher alcohols of the wine, which together make up fusel-oil and are formed from the proteins of the grape in the course of the original fermentation. These are turned into acids by oxidation (just as acetic acid results from the oxidation of ordinary alcohol), and then these new acids combine with the alcohols present. Too much air will destroy a wine, by taking these reactions further to form unpleasant products. The whole marrying process involves only traces of the various substances present, but it is upon these traces that the original taste and aroma, and their improvement upon maturing, depend.

The malolactic fermentation (page 86) has some slight effect upon the changes of maturation, for it takes place even in wines which have only moderate amounts of acid in them, red as well as white.

All sorts of processes have been suggested, and patented, for the rapid ageing of wines. They can almost all be classed under one of two heads: they either involve some sort of electrical treatment, which may possibly accelerate some of the chemical reactions, or they aim at hastening the oxidation. It is very doubtful indeed if any of these artificial methods is actually used.

The Wine Industry

One of the most striking aspects of the wine industry is the degree to which it is organized in co-operative societies of grape-growers and wine-makers. The members of these societies are generally small-holders who find it convenient to combine into associations for the purchase of agricultural machinery, fertilizers, and insecticides and for sharing labour, and often to hold cellars jointly so that the fermentation and subsequent operations can be carried out on the large scale. In many cases the selling of the wine is carried out by a co-operative also. None of the great wines and only a small proportion of the fine wines is made by these co-operative associations, but co-operatives do make much of the common wines of Languedoc and Algeria, Germany, and Italy, not to mention those of Turkey, Luxembourg, and parts of Burgundy.

There is no place for the co-operative system in Bordeaux, where the average holding is fifty-seven acres. This is traditionally the home of the large estate, where the wine is made in the château itself, or in buildings attached. Many of the fine wines are handled by large firms, such as Calvet's, which is the largest, and perhaps the largest in France, for it has branches at Beaune and Cognac. Calvet's have cellars which hold bottles by the million and casks by the scores of thousands. They buy fine, and nearly-fine and not-perhaps-quite-so-fine wines from all over the Bordelais, finish and age them, blend them if they are to be blended, bottle or cask them, ship them, sell them. They store and sell even château-bottled wine. Ginestet, another large firm, deals with Châteaux Margaux, Cos d'Estournel, and Durfort among the Médocs, and others in Saint-Émilion and elsewhere. Eschenauer's, another Bordeaux firm, handles much of the middle-class wine.

Wine Auctions and Wine Fairs

All wine is not sold prosaically by means of letters starting 'yours to hand of the 15th inst.' In many places auctions are held annually, although only a fraction of the wine produced passes through them. The most well known of these auctions is the Sale of the Wine of the Hospices de Beaune. The Hospices de Beaune is a charitable foundation which originated in 1443 with a gift of Nicholas Rollin to found an almshouse. Legacies over the centuries have made of the foundation a very valuable property, for in all they comprise some 130 acres of fine vineyards in Burgundy, in the district of Beaune itself, Meursault, Savigny, Corton, and elsewhere. All are first-class wines and sell at high prices. The actual price they fetch is a fairly close indication, the expertness of the buyers being what it is, of the quality of all Burgundy wines of that particular year. The auction takes place each year on the second Sunday in November, and before and after are feasts and the tasting of wines in a manner which is truly Burgundian. At Dijon, and at Mâcon, as well as in many other parts of France, and in Germany and Austria and Switzerland are held wine fairs in either the spring or the autumn.

Wine Regulations

The earliest laws and regulations concerning wine were concerned with preserving and extending the prerogatives of the ruler and the perquisites of his friends, and it is only during the last century and a half that ordinances regulating the quality and conditions of sale of wine have been passed.

The Phylloxera plague of the 1870s had a very considerable effect in pointing out the necessity for stringent laws to protect the producers and consumers, not only in France but in the other wine-producing countries also. Nevertheless, laws take long in gestation, and it was not until the turn of the century that any move was made. France had passed her first wine law in 1350; in 1905 wine was legally defined and it was admitted that some treatments might be necessary. A decree of 1907 summarized the position, and a succession of edicts passed at intervals since have shown successive approximations to the ideal. (In 1907 also, the General Confederation of Vignerons was formed to represent the wine trade; it has about 100,000 members.) The most important and comprehensive simplification of the law of 1905 is that passed as a decree on 10 August 1921, where wine is once more defined carefully (as quoted on page 16), with careful exclusion of diseased wines and a detailing of allowable treatments of wines and musts, with further regulations as to labelling.

The other wine-countries followed suit. The comprehensive German Wine Law is dated 1930, with another on vermouth, herb wines, sparkling wines, and so on, in 1936 and an extension to fruit wines in 1952. Spanish wine-making is covered by the Estatuto del Vino of September 1932. Italy defined wine in 1925, amplified the definition in a regulation of 1926, and in laws passed between 1931 and 1936 made orders concerning grape cultivation. The law of 1953 covered the export of wines, and the making of vermouth and aperitifs.

In France, apart from the regulations as to the making and treatment of wines, there is a series of decrees dealing with the denomination and labelling of wines, and these are of great importance to all those interested in consuming fine wines. Following the war of 1914–18, there was a sudden large increase in the demand for wine; it would be interesting to inquire into the reason, but this is not the place to do so. Faced with mounting sales and neglected vineyards, the moral fibre of the *vignerons* weakened, and wines appeared whose origin by no means corresponded with the labels on the bottles. In May 1919, with commendable despatch, a law was passed defining the *appellations d'origine*, so as to bring into correspondence the origin and the name of the wine. It was, in effect, a refinement of the original ordinance on this subject of 1851. It did not in fact have the desired effect: it was too easily evaded. In 1935 a further decree was passed to 'control' the *appellation d'origine*. Within a few months a series of specifications, not unlike the B.S.I. specifications issued currently in Britain to cover a wide variety of articles, began to appear.

Each applied to a particular wine and consisted of seven or eight clauses, all quite short and lucid. Generally, the first article of an *Appellation d'Origine Contrôlée* defines the area in which the grapes must be grown. Next, the varieties of vine which must be employed to make the wine are enumerated. Beaune wine, for instance, one of the first batch to have an *Appellation Contrôlée*, is to be made only from grapes of the defined varieties grown in sixty-three named vineyards, which vary in area from five and a half to over fifty acres and total 11,800 acres in all. (This is a district wine and comes from a comparatively wide area.) White wines and red are covered by the same *appellation*, and it is stated that up to 15 per cent of white grapes may be used in the making of the red wine. The third article defines the minimum amount of sugar in the must and of alcohol in the wine. If the must is to be sugared, its original sugar content must exceed the minimum (17·8 per cent) before this is carried out. If a Beaune wine is to be sold under the name of a particular vineyard, the sugar must be rather higher (over 19·6 per cent): wines coming from a single vineyard command higher prices than district wines. The next article limits the yield of wine, averaged over the previous five years: 311 gallons per acre in the case of Beaune. This provision is to prevent overcropping to produce more, but inferior, wine; in fact these yields are seldom reached in good vineyards. The fifth article forbids the artificial drying of the grapes on the vines (to increase the proportion of sugar) by twisting the stems. Lastly the grapes may be gathered only at full maturity and fermented 'according to local usage'. There is also the necessary note on labelling of the bottles.

This is the general form which an *Appellation d'Origine Contrôlée* takes. Certain wines require special provisions: the straw wines, for instance, and the fortified wines of Banyuls and the V.D.N. (page 134). Moreover, cognac and armagnac are also covered by A.O.C.'s.

Just after the Second World War, there was some tendency to evade the regulations, and the French Minister of Agriculture actually passed a law in 1946 to improve further on the previous ordinances by issuing a 'certificate of quality' for the wines of *Appellation Contrôlée*. However, the industry itself took steps to put its house in order and the law has never been applied. Wines covered by A.O.C. comprise about one-tenth of the wine-production of France.

Wine-testing and Investigations on Wine-making

Each wine-producing state has regional testing stations where wine is examined by chemical and biological methods to make sure that it complies with the current regulations. In France, inspectors are empowered to stop and sample consignments of wine travelling by road or rail, for this purpose.

A certain amount of investigation into methods of vinification is also carried out at some of these stations, which are situated in the vineyard areas themselves: Bordeaux, Montpellier, Blois; Trier and Oppenheim; Kishinev (Moldavia) and Krasnodar (Ciscaucasus); Valdepeñas, Haro (Logroño), and Benicarlo. The researches of J. Ribereau-Gayon, Director of the Bordeaux Oenological Station, mostly carried out in collaboration with Professor L. Genevois of Bordeaux University, are among the most important of recent years.

In addition, the large wine-companies carry out research and there are Government-sponsored institutes in most countries, such as that at Narbonne under M. Flanzy and at Freiburg-im-Breisgau under Professor Vogt. In Australia, research on the horticultural side is carried out by the state of New South Wales under H. L. Manuel, and by Victoria under A. G. Strickland, while some of the most interesting work being done anywhere on fermentation methods, and especially the use of various strains of yeast, is that of J. C. M. Fornachon and Bryce Rankine at the Waite Institute, Adelaide, which is sponsored jointly by the Commonwealth Treasury and the wine trade. Fornachon's work on the *flor* process is a classic. In the U.S.A., Professor W. V. Cruess, with M. A. Amerine and M. A. Joslyn, has for many years investigated every conceivable aspect of viniculture. Research in South Africa is concentrated under Professor C. J. Theron of the University of Stellenbosch and Dr C. J. G. Niehaus at the K.W.V. Russian research appears to be carried out through the regional 'Magarach' institutes in each *vignoble*; the principal workers seem to be Durmishidze, Gerasimov, Burkvits, Beridze, and (especially on quick-ageing processes) Manskaya.

The results of these laboratory investigations find their way into large-scale working, where they may be adopted and so influence the current vinification procedures. A process of this sort, that of Semichon, has already been mentioned on page 70. In the last ten or fifteen years methods have been investigated in which grapes have been held before fermentation in an atmosphere of carbon dioxide, or the fermentation carried out in sealed, glass-lined tanks in an atmosphere of carbon dioxide. The former of these seems to have been a French innovation and the latter German. The results have apparently not come up to expectations in either case, but it may be a little early to draw final conclusions. A process may be very successful technically yet be uneconomical for large-scale adoption. On the other hand, the scale may be tipped in favour of a process because plant suitable for carrying it into production has become redundant elsewhere in a winery.

Other changes in the age-old methods of wine-making have been mentioned already in this and the previous chapter. Sulphuring is now all but universal practice; the use of selected yeast cultures is being gradually adopted.

CHAPTER 6

CHAMPAGNE AND SPARKLING WINES

Champagne

CHAMPAGNE, the best known of the sparkling wines, has a curious reputation. It has an air of high society and dissipation about it; it is drunk to toast actresses and newly-christened babies; some connoisseurs despise it and some adore it; it is the traditional favourite of Slavs and Englishmen; it is expensive.

Champagne is one of the sparkling wines which are made in minor amounts in almost every vineyard area in the world. The champagne district near Rheims, some eighty miles east-north-east of Paris, is the only area of importance in which sparkling wines preponderate over still wines, and are the generally acknowledged peer of the best of them.

Effervescing wine is quite easy to make. It is merely necessary to bottle wine firmly before the fermentation has quite finished. If the bottle does not burst, you then have an effervescing wine. It will not sparkle, for it will be cloudy with the impurities listed in the previous chapter. It will be the 'new wine' of the ninth chapter of Matthew (verse 17), which bursts old wine-skins. True sparkling wine was invented in the champagne district and all other modern wines of this sort are imitations of it. Nevertheless, a century or two before champagne was born, effervescent wines were sold in Italy as *Refosco* and *Moscato spumante*. They were cloudy and were not especially prized or even popular.

Some time at the end of the seventeenth century it was realized that a very attractive drink could be made by clearing wine of cloudiness and at the same time retaining some of the carbon dioxide in it. The credit for this invention is by common consent given to Dom Pérignon, the cellar-master of the Benedictine Abbey of Hautvillers, near Rheims, from 1668 to his death in 1715. In order to make a sparkling wine and keep it, good bottles and efficient corks are necessary. Before this time wine bottles were loosely stoppered with tow or hemp and a little olive oil dropped on to the surface of the wine to prevent the access of the vinegar bacteria. Improvements in the strength of bottles and the quality of corks made Dom Pérignon's invention possible. It was not until 1718 that the sparkling wines of Hautvillers were called 'champagne', but since that time they have become world-famous, and about forty million bottles have been made each year for the last half century.

Methods of Making Sparkling Wine

There are three ways of making sparkling wine, but only one of making champagne. The champagne method is used for some other sparkling wines, but not for all.

The three methods are:

(a) The Bottle Method: the champagne method.
(b) The Tank or Chamat Method.
(c) The Impregnation Method.

(a) THE CHAMPAGNE METHOD

Champagne is, with the rarest exception, a white wine, but part of the grapes used in making it are black grapes. In some vineyards the proportion is as high as four black to one white. The fine Burgundy grapes are used: the *pinot noir* and the *pinot blanc*.

In growing the grapes and making the wine which is to become champagne, even greater care is necessary than usual. The very fact that the wine is a sparkling one means that its taste will be appraised more critically and its appearance noticed with much more particularity. The pinots are tender grapes and need more care than the gamay and the meunier, the inferior grapes of this region of France. If the black pinot is allowed to become too ripe, it will be almost impossible to prevent a little colour getting into the wine. In the gathering unusual care is taken to prevent bruising, for bruising leads to premature fermentation, and if fermentation starts in the panniers used for gathering, viscous materials and colour are extracted and the fermentation is abnormal, the wine is difficult to clear and may even become diseased. If rain falls on the grapes during vintage-time, mildew may appear and putrefaction set in. Frost, much more common at this latitude of 48° than in the South, may be disastrous, for then the grapes are soft and flabby.

Pinot blanc is no less susceptible than black. Any trace of mildew results in the wine contracting the disease known as 'the yellows', and the delicate taste of champagne makes it dangerous to adopt the more drastic curative methods which may be used for a still white wine.

The pressing of the grapes is carried out with equal care. Only the first part of the expressed must (the *cuvée*) is used for champagne. This amounts to a little over half the juice which could be extracted. The rest of the juice goes for inferior wines: the second and third pressings are the *tailles* and the rest *rebèche*. The *tailles* are made into lesser but sparkling wines, the *rebèche* into *vin ordinaire*.

It is more necessary than ever to keep the fermentation going, and to take the wine off the lees as soon as possible. There is nothing which more feeds the natural feeling of superiority of the champagne-vignerons over those who make sparkling wines in Touraine, the Bordeaux, and the Rhône districts than the custom in those places of leaving the wine on the lees a little longer than in the Champagne. In cask the secondary fermentation continues until spring. A small addition of alcohol and of tartaric acid is sometimes made and tannin is frequently added, as in the case of other white wines.

Fining is a delicate operation, and isinglass, which has a mild action, is much the commonest agent used. It is best added in the first cold weather: that is, about five months after the wine was made. Some wines refuse to clear, but remain bluish and opalescent. In that case one takes a deep breath and adds alcohol, citric acid and then tannin, and, after waiting anxiously for twenty-four hours, fines with gelatine and offers up prayers, for '*le bleu*' is serious. Robinet calls this (all but the last stage of the treatment) 'a brutal proceeding', but an opalescent champagne is unthinkable, and, of course, unsaleable.

The wine is now clear: a clear, still, white wine, slightly more acid than some white wines, for that is a characteristic of sparkling wines. It now needs the sparkle. For champagne this is produced by bottling and then carrying out a supplementary fermentation *in the bottle*. Especially thick strong bottles are used, free from flaws, and the wine is filled into them together with some sugar – for the wine is dry – and a pure yeast culture. Rather under an ounce of sugar is added, as a strong syrup, and beet-sugar syrup will not do: it taints the champagne with its own faintly earthy taste, imperceptible in any other medium but champagne. The yeast is a specially cultured yeast which acts vigorously, but is not sensitive to high concentrations of carbon dioxide. A little tannin is usually added at the same time.

The bottles are stored at 60 to 65°F. and inside them the yeasts display their normal activity on the pure sugar. All the enzymes sidle forward in turn, each taking the compound produced by the previous enzyme in the series, exactly as in the vat, until the relay race is run and the sugar all turned to alcohol, the yeasts exhausted, the enzymes without further work to do. The bottles contain a dry wine once more, but also a pressure of carbon dioxide of up to 90 pounds per square inch. The corks have been wired on and nowadays very few of the bottles burst. At one time, before the bottle manufacturers became so expert, a considerable proportion of breakages took place and to work in a champagne cellar was a dangerous occupation. When the fermentation is almost complete the temperature of the cellar is lowered to about 40°F.

Now the bottles contain good champagne, but also dead yeast cells – nothing else, for all the original debris was removed before bottling. The difficulty is to get these yeast cells out without releasing the pressure. It is a difficult and tedious process only to be carried out successfully by very patient and very expert men. The bottles are stood, neck downwards, on a rack: tens of thousands of them: millions. The sediment floating idly about the liquid begins to fall into the neck: very slowly, for it is very fine. If the original clearing has been inadequate, it will be very very slow and particles will stick to the sides of the bottle.

Every day a man goes along the almost endless rows of up-ended bottles and helps on the settling process: he is the *remueur*, a highly-skilled man. (Plate 25.) He takes each bottle by its base and gives it a slight twist to the left and a slight twist to the right. It is done in a flash, but each bottle when he leaves it is an eighth of a turn round from where it was before – thirty thousand bottles a day if he is an expert. In the first place they were by no means quite vertical, but in the course of six or eight weeks of daily visits by the *remueur* they have slowly taken up a more nearly vertical position, so slowly that only another *remueur* could detect the daily change. At the end of the two months the bottles are *sur les pointes*, like a gigantic chorus from *Swan Lake*. All the sediment rests on the cork, if the *remueur* has done well, and the really difficult operation follows.

This is *dégorgement*, or disgorging, which sounds a little crude in English. The expert *dégorgeur* takes each bottle and removes the cork with one hand and allows the sediment on the cork to fly out; after the correct period of a fraction of a second, he puts his thumb over the mouth of the bottle, so that a negligible amount of liquid is lost, and deftly inserts a new cork. It takes five years to train a man to do the job properly. If he is too slow, liquid and pressure will be lost; if he is too impatient the sediment floats back into the wine.

The task of the *dégorgeur* is eased slightly by the modern method, due to Walfard, of freezing the neck of the bottle for about an inch above the cork so as to enclose the sediment in a plug of ice. Upon removing the cork the ice-pellet is ejected, but the *dégorgeur* has still to recork the bottle before the rest of the contents escape.

The champagne which results at this stage is dry, and it does not quite fill the bottle. It is described as *brut*, and needs some sweetening to be saleable, although *brut* champagne can be purchased and some connoisseurs prefer it to any other. In the ordinary way, *brut* champagne is given a *dosage* of sweetening to suit whichever market it is to be sold in. This tailoring to suit the market has already started before the fining operation, for champagne is a mixed wine. For good-class still wines, *coupage*, the mixing of the products of different vineyards, is deprecated; in the Champagne it is the rule, and highly skilled tasters decide the circumstances of the mixing.

Generally, the English buyer prefers a drier champagne which has more taste and is slightly more alcoholic than others; the Germans want a light wine, rather sweeter but with greater delicacy of taste; the Mediterranean prefers it a little sweeter still than Germany; champagne for the Slavs is very sweet and rather high in alcohol.

Formerly, *dosage* was carried out with a mixture of cognac, fortified wine, flavouring, and bouquet material, but nowadays pure cane-sugar syrup alone is used. For the driest champagnes about 1 per cent sugar is added, for the sweetest 5 per cent. The taste for sickly-sweet sparkling wines is dying out: at one time some 12 per cent sugar was used for *dosage*.

The *dosage* over, there only remains for the bottles of champagne to be corked finally, capped, wired, and covered with metal-foil, labelled and slipped into their straw *capotes*.

Some champagne is not mixed, but sold as 'vintage champagne' by the year; it sells at a rather higher price than non-vintage.

It will be appreciated that champagne is an expensive wine to produce. The business is in the hands of about 200 firms, of which a dozen or so have a universal reputation: Bollinger, Veuve Clicquot, Heidsieck, Irroy, Krug, Lanson, Moët et Chandon, Mumm, Perrier-Jouet, Pommery et Greno, Louis Roederer, Pol-Roger, Ruinart. These firms are all at least a century old, and Ruinart, the oldest, was founded in 1729.

During the nineteenth century the consumption of champagne increased greatly. In 1835, five million bottles were exported; in 1866, twenty-two million. The United Kingdom bought most, but Belgium, Russia, and Germany were not far behind. The area in which grapes for champagne were grown gradually extended and grapes were imported from other parts of France. There was a considerable danger that the quality and reputation of champagne would suffer. The growers were split into two organizations, the General Confederation of Vignerons of the Aube, the southern part of the area, and the General Confederation of Vignerons of the Marne, the northern. By 1907 the bitter rivalry between these two prompted the Government to intervene in order to prevent the industry damaging itself. In 1908, a law was passed limiting the area within which grapes for champagne might be grown. The limits were set too narrowly and in 1911 a second law was made. There was still disagreement, and after the First World War a third law was passed in 1919 and revised in 1927. This is now in force and controls the champagne areas.

The production of champagne commonly varies between six and seven million gallons a year, but in 1934, for instance, it was as high as thirteen million, and in 1910 less than a quarter of a million. Champagne is classified according to the pressure within the bottle. *Grand Mousseux* has a pressure of 67 to 75 pounds per square inch, *Mousseux* between 60 and 67, and *Crémant* below 60.

Still champagne, champagne without the sparkle, is made in minor quantities. A little pink champagne is also sold. Its chief interest is as a novelty and, to some minor degree, as a selling point. The law forbids the addition of artificial colouring matter, but considering the care necessary to prevent normal champagne from becoming tinted, it will be understood that to make pink champagne presents no difficulty.

(b) THE TANK METHOD

Early in the nineteenth century, the French chemist Maumené, and others, suggested that it should be possible to avoid the expensive and complicated procedures of *remuage* and *dégorgement* by carrying out the secondary fermentation in a closed tank. This method is quite widely used nowadays, and a considerable proportion of sparkling wine is made in this way, though Maumené gets no credit, for it is called the *Charmat*, or sometimes the *Chaussepied* Method, or of course simply the Tank Method. In Germany the product is popularly described as *Grossraumgärwervahren Schaumwein*.

Enamelled steel tanks are used, and after the first vigour of the secondary fermentation is exhausted, the temperature is lowered and the yeast cells allowed to settle; then the wine is filtered (under pressure) into another tank from which it is bottled. The dosage of sugar is usually mixed with brandy and is placed either in the empty bottles or in the tank.

It is a good deal cheaper to make sparkling wine by the Tank Method than by the lengthy process of Champagne, but the product is of lower quality: the sparkle is that of Strauss rather than Mozart.

France bottles something like a million gallons of sparkling wines each year from tanks.

(c) THE IMPREGNATION METHOD

With the further advance of modern civilization it became clear that the tank method was too expensive and complicated, especially for the production of sparkling wines for those who had never tasted champagne.

Cheap sparkling wines are made by cooling a suitable wine and forcing carbon dioxide into it under a fairly low pressure. Upon allowing the wine to warm to room temperature the pressure increases. A fairly high alcohol wine is used, for alcohol dissolves carbon dioxide more readily than water does. The sparkle of these wines rapidly disappears in a glass: it is the sparkle of Litolff rather than Strauss. Sparkling wine does not foam in the way beer does, and there is no incentive to add saponin, which is such a valuable aid to the effervescence of some other beverages.

Some years ago the difference between true champagne, in which the bubbles continue to rise steadily for a considerable time, and sparkling wines made by the impregnation method was explained. A year or two ago the Russian chemists Parfentov and Kovalenko confirmed the truth of the explanation. It appears that when the carbon dioxide is made by a second fermentation in the wine it is combined chemically with the alcohol (in the form of the substance ethyl pyrocarbonate), whereas in sparkling wine made by impregnation, the gas is simply dissolved. In the first case the chemical forces tend to retain the gas, and although these forces are weak they do act as a sort of brake on the effervescence. In the second case the chemical forces do not exist, for no ethyl pyrocarbonate is formed when the gas is simply dissolved in the wine.

Statistics of the production of sparkling wine made by the impregnation method are not easy to come by; it is not a product of which its manufacturers are proud, presumably.

The Sparkling Wines of France

Besides Champagne, sparkling wines are made especially on the Loire, in Burgundy, and in Bordeaux.

THE LOIRE

It is in Touraine that some of the best moderately priced and very pleasant sparkling wines are made. They are usually rather lighter than the still wines of the region and when drunk young are unsurpassed of their kind. The districts around Vouvray and Saumur produce the most well-known sparkling wines, which are imported into Britain and sold at very reasonable prices.

SPARKLING BURGUNDY (BOURGOGNE MOUSSEUX)

Sparkling burgundy, red, white, and *rosé*, is made in considerable quantities and has a considerable reputation. The industry started at

Nuits-Saint-Georges, but is now chiefly centred at Rully, Beaune, and Savigny. The white wines of Rully are especially suitable for making into *mousseux* and it was the Rully wines which first gained sparkling burgundy a reputation outside France.

The regulations for making wine to be sold as *Bourgogne Mousseux* direct that the champagne method shall be used and that at least one-third of the grapes must be pinot (in the Côte d'Or). Not less than one year may elapse before *dégorgement*. Red sparkling burgundy is said to be 'a particular favourite' with Anglo-Saxons and in the Scandinavian countries.

SPARKLING BORDEAUX

Sparkling Bordeaux has never quite 'caught on'. It was the idea of a M. Nathaniel Johnston, a wine merchant of Paris and Bordeaux, who in the course of time acquired a number of Médoc vineyards, one a very fine one, Château Ducru-Beaucaillou, and also the castle of Bourg-en-Gironde. Here, in the extensive cellars, he began to make sparkling wine, which he sold as *Royal Médoc Mousseux*. Part of the production of Ducru-Beaucaillou, which is still owned by M. Johnston's successors, commonly goes for *mousseux* as well as much of the claret from the *palus* vineyards.

The Sparkling Wines of Germany (Sekt, Schaumwein)

The sparkling-wine industry of Germany started in Württemberg and Silesia in 1826. Nowadays about 200 concerns make *Schaumwein*, mostly on the banks of the Rhine, the Mosel, and the Main.

The same grapes as for making champagne are used, although rieslings and other *cépages* are employed for special varieties of sparkling wine. A golden wine is made from the riesling in the Rheingau. Champagne yeasts or, for sparkling red wine, the Ass-mannshausen cultures, are used. The champagne method is usually employed, but most *Sektkellerei* bottle at least part of their sparkling wine from the tank.

In Germany, sparkling wines, known as *Süsskratzer, Sauser*, and *Federweiser* are very popular. Fruit wines, that is wines not made from grape-juice but from other fruit-juices, are also frequently made into sparkling wines, usually by the tank method. Including these, approaching twenty million bottles of sparkling wine are made in Germany each year. *Perlwein* is a sparkling wine bottled at a pressure of only 20 pounds a square inch.

Other Sparkling Wines

Spain seems not to be interested in sparkling wines, but Italy produces one of the most well-known ones at Asti, in Piedmont. *Asti spumante* is a light sparkling wine, usually rather over-sweet to English tastes, which is not fermented to dryness in the primary fermentation.

In Eastern Europe, sparkling wines have always been popular and, especially in Russia, are now made in considerable amounts. Thirty-six times as much 'Soviet Champagne' was produced in 1940 as in 1936, most of it in the Krasnodar region and near Rostov ('Zimlianskaia Sparkling Wine'). However, the largest 'champagne' factory in Russia is near Tiflis, in Georgia. Georgia makes more than one-quarter of all Russian sparkling wines, that is, about four million bottles annually. But sparkling wines are produced all over the vineyard areas of Russia: the Ukraine, the Crimea, Moldavia, Uzbekistan, at Alma-Ata in the Cossack country, and even in the Kirghiz. Russian experts say that 'Soviet Champagne' is not matured long enough, and much is certainly made by the impregnation method; it is described by a percipient Englishman as sweet and nasty.

Romania was once well known for her sparkling wines, mostly made by the firms of Mott et fils, and Rhein et cie. She still makes a certain amount, not especially notable for high quality. Hungary also produces a little, which is rather sweet even by Eastern European standards.

AMERICAN SPARKLING WINES

Sparkling wines are made in Canada, in the U.S.A., and in Argentina and Chile.

Canadian 'champagne' is made in the Niagara peninsula from American white grapes. The history of sparkling wine in this region goes back almost a century, for Henry Parker, in 1858, made 'champagne' here, both red and white. Nowadays, it is an established industry, although sparkling wine in Canada takes a very subordinate place, as do the still table-wines, to fortified wines. Like U.S. 'champagne', Canadian is slightly more alcoholic than European sparkling wines, which rarely exceed 12 per cent alcohol and are often as low as 7 per cent, while Canadian 'champagne' contains between 12 and 13 per cent.

In the U.S.A. sparkling wines are all called 'champagne', but are not all made by the true '*méthode champénoise*'. The tank method, which is referred to as 'the modern process', is that most commonly employed in California, although more than half of the sparkling wine is in fact made east of the Rocky Mountains, where the champagne method is used.

Typical of Californian practice is that of the Roma Wine Company. Here tanks of 500 to 1,000 gallons are used and the process is controlled scientifically from beginning to end, in the usual American manner. The tank fermentation lasts for about a month and then the *dosage* is added. This is a mixture of sugar and brandy. The wine is cooled and filtered without releasing the pressure, and after resting for a month, bottled, and aged.

The Fingers Lakes region of New York State, on the shores of Lake Erie, is the centre of the main manufacture of sparkling wine in the Eastern United States, though some is made in nearby Ohio: the vineyard area extends over the state boundary. Two native wines are used: Catawba and Delaware. These are both crosses of *Vitis labrusca* and, especially Catawba, have a somewhat foxy odour and taste. Wines are usually blended in any case, for they tend to be rather too acid and with not enough sugar. For blending, other Labruscas, whose taste is less distinctive, are used. Ageing of the primary wine, that is, of the wine before bottling, is carried out in small oak casks, and after two years, sugar and yeast are added, and the wine bottled. The bottle fermentation takes place at about 50°F., and when this is over, the cellars are cooled to 41° for a month to allow the sediment to settle. The necks are surrounded by refrigerating brine-coils and *dégorgement* and *dosage* carried out in the usual *méthode champénoise*.

In round figures the U.S.A. makes annually rather less than half a million gallons of sparkling wine in California, rather more than half a million gallons east of the Rockies, and imports about 600,000 gallons. But these figures vary from year to year.

Buying Sparkling Wines

As in buying all wines, the important thing is to try everything and decide for yourself. However, there is the important question of snobbery, which can never be ignored for long in dealing with a subject like wine. If you have to impress anyone, choose a good vintage champagne if you can afford it: 1947, 1945, 1942. Nevertheless, there is nothing absolutely contemptible in choosing a non-vintage wine, with the name of a reputable shipper on the label. Half-bottles are sufficient for two people, unless the meal is to be romantic; and even so . . .

On the other hand, if it is very inconvenient, or impossible, to find over 30 shillings for a vintage champagne, or over 25 shillings for a non-vintage one, then the best one can do is to order an Asti Spumante if your companion has a sweet tooth, or a sparkling Saumur or Hock or Mosel if not, and laugh the matter off by saying, 'Champagne's too serious for an occasion like this', or 'Hope you don't mind, but champagne always tastes like soapy water to me' (this requires fortitude).

Returning to the happy contingency, for a moment, of cost not being a confining factor, if there are four or more in the party, and champagne is to be the drink, it establishes a definite ascendancy to decide on a magnum, which costs no more than two bottles; this may impress even the wine-waiter, who will expect a proportionate tip.

It is impossible in a book of this length to cover other contingencies connected with ordering champagne and the sparkling wines.

CHAPTER 7

THE FORTIFIED WINES

THE 'fortified wines' are those which have been strengthened, during or after fermentation, by the addition of spirits, so that their alcohol content is about 20 per cent – almost double that of the beverage wines. In France, fortified wines are called *vins de liqueur*, and wines with naturally enhanced alcohol content (the *pourriture noble* and straw wines) *vins liquoreux*. Germans use the term *Likörwein* for a fortified wine, the Spanish *vino generoso*, the Italians *vino di lusso*. Vermouth, which is a fortified wine, is treated separately in Chapter 16.

The fortified wines are sherry, port, Madeira, Marsala, Malaga, angelica, Californian 'tokay', and a number of wines of more or less local interest, such as the French V.D.N., the wines of the Greek islands, and so on. Wines with more than about 18 per cent of alcohol are not subject to many of the ills which may attack the lighter beverage wines, for although the bactericidal properties of alcohol are often exaggerated, the organisms which attack wine either die or are very poorly themselves in liquids containing as much alcohol as the fortified wines. It was doubtless in order to preserve them that wines were fortified in the first place, whenever that was.

Fortification is practised, as *vinage* (see page 84), on light wines when, because of bad weather, they are a little too light, and although the practice is nowadays severely limited by law, it has in the past led to the downfall of wines of repute. Constantia of the Cape, once a very popular wine, owes its eclipse until recently, in part at least, to the habit of improving it until its quality foundered under the brandy added. In 1872 that shrewd oenologist Dr J. L. W. Thudicum wrote: 'Constantia begins to share the fate of all sweet liqueur wines; they are so easily falsified or imitated that the genuine products themselves can no longer be distinguished with certainty and are constantly distrusted and neglected.'

Sherry

Sherry is the most popular of the fortified wines. A first-class dry sherry is a unique, inimitable drink. (Sweet sherries are not quite so difficult to simulate, and are in fact simulated.) Dry sherry is a blended wine by its very nature, so that vintage sherries do not exist. Part of the fermentation is carried out by a yeast which differs considerably from the ordinary wine (or beer) yeast.

Sherry, true sherry, is made only in a restricted area in the Spanish province of Cadiz, in Andalusia. The vineyards lie in a triangle, about twenty miles or less each way, bounded by Cadiz, Sanlucar de Barrameda, and just north of Jerez. (See map 8.) Some, but only a small proportion, of the grapes come from the province of Estremadura, a hundred miles north of Jerez.

Although Andalusia was famed in Roman times for its fine wines, they were not fortified. In the sixteenth century some 'improvement' may have been made, for Falstaff soliloquized on his favourite wine, 'sherris-sack': 'If I had a thousand sons, the first human principle I would teach them should be, to forswear thin potations and to addict themselves to sack' (*Henry IV, Part II*, iv. 2).

The name 'sherry' undoubtedly comes from the town, Jerez, in which the trade is centred. Jerez is pronounced *hereth* by Spaniards, with the initial *h* guttural. It was once called *Xeres*, and by the Moors *Sherisch* or *Saris*. Before them, the Visigoths named it *Serit* and the Romans *Ceret*. It is very probably the town which the Phoenicians named *Xera*. A venerable antiquity: twenty-five or more centuries.

It was the Moors who encouraged viniculture so greatly in Andalusia, which was, in the eighth to the eleventh centuries, the greatest centre of civilization in the world. Córdoba, their capital, had half a million inhabitants; now it has less than 100,000. The *Calendar of Córdoba*, promulgated in 961, embodied their directions to winemakers as well as to other agriculturalists. It was their advice which guided the viniculture of the Americas, which was everywhere founded by the Spanish Jesuit missionaries.

Sherry is an Anglo-Saxon drink, and exports average over three million gallons in cask and a quarter or a fifth as much in bottle, a total of over twenty million bottles. Much more sherry is bottled in London, Liverpool, and Bristol than in Spain.

Andalusia is a triangle of land thrusting up from the coast north-eastwards into the *meseta*, the tableland which forms the heart of the Iberian peninsula. It is roughly equivalent to the basin of the Guadalquivir, which flows down to Sanlucar from mountain heights of over 11,000 feet. The vineyards of Andalusia depend for their moisture on the melting of the snows of the Sierra Nevada ('the snowy mountains'). This is one of the most fertile regions of Spain, and, besides the vine, the olive, the chestnut, and the oak, maize, rye, and wheat, oranges and lemons all flourish. In the flat *vergas* near the coast are fields of cotton and sugar-cane.

Although there are about twenty inches of rain in the year, less than 10 per cent of this falls in the four summer months, June to September, and the vineyards must be irrigated from the Guadalquivir and its tributaries. It was irrigation that the Arabs were so expert in, resting on their experience in the Yemen and the oases of their homelands. Summer in Andalusia is hot. Its maximum is 116°, which is the maximum also of the Sahara, and the highest in Europe. For the rainless months the temperature averages over 78° and the grapes are plump and sweet. The table-grapes of Almería are well known. When the wind blows, it comes from the south-east, the *solano*, and brings scorching dust from the Sahara. The grapes and the wines suit themselves to these hot, arid conditions, and if the rain comes early, before the harvest is gathered, as it did in 1923, the must is thin and the wine poor.

In the best vineyards the soil is the calciferous *albariza* (see Plate 27), dazzlingly white in the summer sun. The small, sweet *palomino* grape is the characteristic sherry grape, although some *Pedro Ximenes* is used for blending. Much of the soil hereabouts is *barros*, a mixture of clay and limestone, and when the palomino is grown on this, the wine is not so good but there is more of it. Near Sanlucar, where the dry *manzanilla* wines are made, the soil is sandy (*arenas*).

As the grapes ripen they are gathered, and a vineyard is worked over several times as more and more bunches ripen. The basketfuls are brought in by mule-carts to the crushing sheds, where they are laid on esparto mats to dry out under the fierce sun, like the grapes for straw wine in France and elsewhere. If they are intended for dry sherries (*finos*), they are dried for twenty-four hours, but if for the fuller, sweeter *olorosos*, they are left for longer. The Andalusian temperament being what it is, vintage-time in the sherry vineyards is a period of singing, hard work, and dancing, in roughly equal proportions. The age-old vintage fête, *La Fiesta de la Vendimia*, which had not been celebrated for some years, was revived again in 1948 to canalize the general exuberance.

The grapes are next trodden out to express the juice, for sherry is essentially a *vin blanc à blancs* – with variations, as will be seen. Treading takes place in shallow wooden trays (*lagars*) which have a run-off for the juice on one side (Plate 26). All sherry musts are 'plastered', that is, treated with gypsum to increase the acidity (see page 87). This is another peculiarity of sherry: a practice which is much frowned upon in other wine-districts is here an essential part of the process. Spain happens to be one of the half-dozen largest producers of gypsum in the world and exports it by the million tons, so there is no shortage. Left with its natural acidity the must would be subject to bacterial attack. After the treading, for which the men wear special boots (*zapatos de pisar*), the murk must be pressed to obtain more juice, and this is carried out by a method which is typically Spanish in its uniqueness. The mush is piled up around a vertical screw erected in the centre of the lagar. A shovelful of gypsum is added now and again and the whole is bound in position with a long strip of esparto matting. A plate is slid down the screw to rest on the top of the *pie* of skins, etc., and a two-handled lever above that. The lever engages in the threads of the vertical screw so that when the lever is turned the juice exudes through the grass binding and goes to augment the juice expressed by treading. In some crushing-houses (*casas de la gares*) crushing-machines and modern filters are being introduced, but even so, the traditional methods are still used in combination with them.

The must is fermented in 100-gallon casks, after being lightly sulphured, and then left outside until it is first racked in December. The mean November temperature is 60°; for December it is 53°. After racking, the wine begins to turn itself into sherry: a long and curious process. First, a film of yeast forms on the top of the wine as white isolated patches which coalesce to a continuous layer over the whole surface. This is known as *flor* (flower); it has puzzled wine experts more than any other phenomenon in wine-making (except the great enzyme-problem). The *flor* yeast is a variety of *Saccharomyces ellipsoideus* which takes the film-form, can live in higher amounts of alcohol than the ordinary *ellipsoideus*, and introduces a peculiar flavour into the wine by fermenting sugar and alcohol to aldehydes and other, probably more complex, substances. Pasteur found it growing on the vines of his native Arbois. The reason for much confusion was that it resembles the ordinary *ellipsoideus* under the microscope, while other film-forming yeasts (*Pichia* and *Hansenula*), which are characteristic of pickle-spoilage, are also found amongst the Jerez film-yeasts. The main problem now seems to have been solved in the sense described, by the efforts of Cruess of California, Fornachon of Australia, and the Spanish oenologists Bobadilla, Marcilla, and others.

Only some sherries develop the characteristic taste of a *fino*. Tasting, nowadays supplemented by chemical analysis, makes the decision, and the casks of wine are classified into *palmas*, *cortados*, and *rayas*. *Palmas*, the finest and most delicate, are earmarked to make the best dry sherries, the *finos* and the *amontillados*. *Palmas* are lower in alcohol than the other two classes and are brought up to 15 per cent alcohol by adding brandy. The *cortados* are fuller and rather more alcoholic; they are the embryo-*olorosos*, and are made up to 18 per cent alcohol. *Rayas* wines of slower maturing, or of coarser type, are possible candidates for *finos* and *olorosos*, and are left to see how they will turn out. Some will obviously do no good and so they are distilled to make brandy.

Next comes the complicated blending process, which again is peculiar to sherry. The process, which includes ageing in wood, is carried out by the *solera* system. Imagine a row of perhaps ten casks, each holding 115 gallons, and above them another identical row, with a third row on top, and so on: five or six lines of casks one above the other. The lowest row is full of wine which has passed through the system; the uppermost contains new wines, callow young things which have only just decided whether to become *finos* or *olorosos*: they have just matriculated. When wine is wanted, it is run off from the casks of the bottom line, which has spent five or six years in the *solera* and has graduated. The ullage is made up equally from all the casks in the second rank up, and the ullage in them from the third row; all casks in the system contribute directly or indirectly, although the transfer is made from underneath the *flor* yeast, which is not disturbed. *Soleras* of *oloroso* and *amontillado* wines are too alcoholic to support *flor*, but they are otherwise identical with soleras of *fino*.

Of course, the wine from the lowest casks of a *solera* is not yet a finished sherry. It must first be fined and probably filtered. The fining at Jerez and the other sherry towns is carried out with egg-albumin. No one who has eaten a Spanish meal will need to be told that eggs are plentiful in Spain. Somewhere between half a dozen and a score of egg-whites are beaten into a gallon of wine, and this is then added to a full, hundred-gallon cask, and followed with a slurry of two pounds of 'Spanish Earth' in two gallons of wine. Spanish Earth is a clay of high absorptive capacity from Lebrija, a small town about fifty miles north of Jerez. After settling, the wine is racked off and, especially if it is to go for export, filtered.

Except for the facts that it is too dry, not alcoholic enough, and too pale, the sherry is now all but ready for shipment. As to the dryness (and even dry sherries contain a little sugar), that is corrected by adding a little sweet wine from Pedro Ximenes grapes, which have been sun-dried. The must is only partially fermented, then muted so as to leave much sugar in the wine. For colour, *arrope*, which is thick, evaporated grape-juice, or *vino de color* is added. *Vino de color* is made by adding *arrope* to must or new wine and fermenting almost to dryness. If too much *arrope* is added the taste of caramel is detectable in the sherry, as it often is in *olorosos*. The alcohol content is adjusted by addition of brandy, distilled from rejected *rayas* with a high degree of rectification (see pages 208 and following) so as not to impart any particular flavour of its own. Most sherries are sold under a name like *Tio Pepe*, *Bristol Cream*, *Dry Sack*, *Dry Fly*, and so on, and as it is necessary that there shall be no variation from year to year in branded goods, a final blending is made to ensure uniformity before shipment from Jerez.

The sherry-types as sold are as follows:

Finos are pale and dry, drunk as aperitifs before meals.

Olorosos are sweet and rather dark dessert wines.

Amontillados are *finos* with a little more alcohol than usual and are not quite as dry as ordinary *finos*.

Amorosos are a little paler and a little sweeter than *olorosos*.

Brown Sherry or *East Indian Sherry* is rather darker and sweeter than the usual *oloroso*.

Manzanilla and *Montilla*, from Sanlucar and near Córdoba respectively, are dry sherries with a sort of bitter taste.

The alcohol content of sherries lies between 16 and 20 per cent; on the whole *finos* are less alcoholic than *olorosos*.

It may be mentioned that the district around Jerez is an admirable place for holidays, with unlimited sunshine and a bathing beach at Sanlucar which is not overcrowded. At Jerez, Puerto Maria, and Sanlucar, the *bodegas*, which are mostly in old convents, may be visited without difficulty.

From this description of how sherry is made it will be appreciated that a cheap sherry is unlikely to be made properly. Sherry is one of the most often imitated wines. In 1873, ten million gallons were consumed in Britain; in the same year, Spain produced 3·6 million gallons. A good part of the wine used to make up the ullage in the exports of Spain came from South Africa, where overproduction and a decline in quality were freeing much wine for use in sophistication. Nowadays, South Africa makes one of the best sherry-type wines there are.

SOUTH AFRICA

When the wine-industry of Cape Province revived in the 1920s, especial attention was paid to sherry. For one thing, the climate of the vineyard area behind Cape Town somewhat resembles that of Andalusia. It is not as hot as in Spain; the rainfall, which shows a maximum in June, corresponding to November and December in the northern hemisphere, when Andalusia has most rain, is about the same. The soils of the Cape are shales and sandstones, with none of the calcareous admixture which makes *albariza*, except in small diffused patches. But what is most important, on keeping Cape wines, they were found to develop something of the *rancio* taste of the *fino* sherries. Dr Niehaus, the chief wine expert of the Co-operative Wine-Growers' Association, and the University of Stellenbosch commenced investigations and it was found that *flor* yeasts were indigenous to the area. (They are not easy to re-acclimatize.) Dr Niehaus brought *palomino* vinestocks from Andalusia; at the Cape the *palomino* is called the *fransdruif*. Another import, the *steindruif*, is also employed. The sherry process was imitated carefully; until local deposits were found, gypsum was imported for plastering.

In fact, South Africa now produces passable imitations of sherry. Dr Niehaus says boldly, 'judge them on their merits as sherries, not as "South African sherries".'

AUSTRALIA

Australia exports little of her sherry-type wine, but domestic wine-lists show over ninety brands. It is a reasonable presumption that few of these have been through a full *solera* system. *Flor* yeast is not indigenous to Australia and strains were therefore imported from Jerez. Young wines are sterilized and filtered before inoculating them with *flor*, which takes two or three weeks to spread its film over the surface. This process is carried out in casks, as in Jerez, or latterly in concrete tanks. Australian taste is rather for the sweeter sherries, and in making these, *flor* plays no part. Mr Fornachon, the head of the Oenological Department of the Commonwealth Scientific and Industrial Research Organization, is an acknowledged expert on the sherry process, and there is no lack of expert knowledge in Australia of how to make sherry properly.

RUSSIA

Flor yeast is indigenous to Armenia, now the Armenian S.S.R., and it is very probable that sherry-type wine is made there, for Russia is showing much interest in the sherry-type wines. Only vineyard areas such as those of the Turkestan oases in the Uzbek and Tadzhik regions have summers hot enough for making sherry-type wines, but these are well known. They contain about 20 per cent alcohol, which is at least as high as an average Spanish sherry. The *flor* yeast is apparently used, but there is no information as to the employment of the *solera* system.

CALIFORNIA

The wine described as Californian sherry is not even sherry-type. For reasons which it seems idle to pursue, in California they imitate

Madeira and call it sherry. (The wine sold as Madeira is usually a baked angelica – see page 132.) Professor Cruess of the University of California, the doyen of American oenologists, has for some years waged a campaign on behalf of *flor* sherry in the U.S.A. He and Drs Amerine and Joslyn have studied the process in Spain and in California, in laboratory and field. One vineyard, the Almadén, now makes *flor* sherry by the *solera* process.

Palomino grapes are used for Californian sherry. The fermentation is made after separating the skins, and when all the sugar has gone, neutral brandy is added at once to the dry wine (called sherry material, or *shermat*) to bring the alcohol content to 20 or 21 per cent. This fortified material is then 'baked' either by circulating hot water through copper coils immersed in the wine, or by storing the casks in a room at about 120°F. In the hot San Joaquin valley insolation may be sufficient. After fining and ageing in oak, perhaps after a light sulphuring, it is ready to sell, at one-third to one-sixth the price of Spanish sherry. It is said to resemble real sherry somewhat in odour but not at all in flavour. It is somewhat confusing that the flavour it *has* got (that is, the taste of burnt sugar or caramel) is described as *rancio*, which is the word used by Spaniards for the very different flavour of *fino* sherry.

Californian sherries are sweetened with angelica.

CANADA

Of all Canada's range of wines, 'sherry' is the most popular. It is made in the Niagara peninsula district of the Province of Ontario by much the same methods as those used for Californian sherry. The *flor* yeast is not employed. In Canada 'sherry' is frequently drunk mixed with soda or ginger-ale, as a long drink.

Port

In a French wine-merchant's list you will see, on the last page, as an afterthought as it were, 'Porto'. Just that: no description, no vintage year, no shipper's name. The catalogues of German wine-merchants are works of art, with gold and silver decorations everywhere; little gnomes and wood-sprites, *Kobolds*, dryads and satyrs clamber all over the headings and playfully poke their heads through the lines of print. Hundreds of wines are listed; dazzled and exhausted, you reach at last the final page. The last item, just a single item, is 'Portwein; original Douro'. In English wine-lists, port wine usually comes first, and two or three pages are devoted to it. Each item is carefully denominated by shipper, quality, body, and, if it is a vintage wine, by year. In the U.S.A., port is the most popular wine, leading sherry by a short head; in Canada, it is second only to sherry in popularity. In Australia it sells better than hot cakes (the climate being what it is) and is imitated in eighty or more varieties. Port is, in short, an Anglo-Saxon drink.

It is illegal in England to sell wine as 'port' unless it comes from Portugal. Not so in other countries; that is why the German wine-lists add the qualification, 'original Douro'. Port-type wines are made in large quantities in Australia, the U.S.A., Canada, and South Africa. Port wine is made only in a closely specified area of the Upper Douro valley in Northern Portugal by a method which is specified by Portuguese law.

The soil in the Upper Douro is in part granite and in part a schistose rock which is soft where it has been weathered by the rains and winds of past millennia but underneath the surface very hard. (A schistose rock is one which has been subjected to great pressure by movements of the earth's crust and so has a finely-layered structure, like slate.) The best wines come from the schistose soils which contain traces of manganese and titanium, although it is not known whether these influence the quality of the wines. The Douro slopes are steep and must be terraced to hold the vines; it is hard labouring on the Douro. The climate runs to extremes: summer shade temperatures may top 100°F., but in winter deep snow is not unknown. Wet winds from the Atlantic bring the rainfall up to between thirty and fifty inches, almost all of which falls in the winter months: the maximum is in November. If the rain comes early and there is a sudden deluge just before the vintage, which takes place in September or early October, the grapes become swollen with water which rises up the stems and dilutes the juice in the grapes; moreover, wet grapes quickly develop mildew which taints the wine.

Since Phylloxera, which came to Portugal in 1868, scions of the native Touriga, Tinta Francisca, Tinta Carvalha, and other varieties have been grafted on American root-stocks. The grapes are trodden in *lagars* somewhat like those of Jerez, but without the central screw. Ox-carts are still widely used for transport, although lorries are slowly ousting them. Fermentation is continued for two or three days, but long before all the sugar has gone, brandy is added and the yeasts die. The sweet, evaporated *jeropiga* is also added at the same time.

Silent spirit (see page 209) is used only for cheap ports; for the better qualities, the brandy is distilled at comparatively low proof (about 78 per cent alcohol) so as to conserve the congenerics. The sweet, brandied wine remains in the fortifying vats for several months. Then, when spring comes, all is activity again in the *quintas* in the mountains. The boats from Oporto (Plate 28) arrive with their cargoes of empty barrels, which are of a slightly unusual shape, with narrow ends. *Pipes* they are called, and hold 115 gallons, about half a ton of wine. Pinhão (Plate 29), Torre, Tua, and Regoa are the principal river ports on the Alto Douro, and from there the empty pipes are taken up to the *quintas* by ox-cart, filled, and brought back to the boats. The picturesque river-boats, now being replaced by lorries and the railway, return to Vila Nova, across the river from Oporto. At Vila Nova are all the great wine-lodges, and it is here that the wine lies maturing and where it is blended and despatched to its Anglo-Saxon destinations. Almost all (98 per cent) port wine leaves Vila Nova in pipes, to be bottled in the country of its consumption.

Port, the deep purple-red wine with some 20 per cent alcohol and 6, 7, 8 per cent or more sugar, is a modern invention, only some five human generations old. But before 1820, there were incipient ports: the idea was there. Portuguese wines were red beverage wines imported into England for drinking with meals, like claret and burgundy, the cheaper varieties of which they resembled very closely, for the very good reason that they were much used for the *coupage* of cheap claret and burgundy. No one knows exactly when the wines of Portugal became well known in England, but it was a very long time ago. The general belief is that some of the Crusaders, stopping off on the way to the Holy Land for water and fresh food, were impressed by the opportunity of fighting the infidel comparatively near home and stayed in Portugal. Ferdinand I of Castile was at this time (the tenth century) waging a private war against the Saracens who occupied most of Lusitania. The Crusaders liked the wine of the country, and in due course a colony of English merchants settled in Vianna do Castella, rather over fifty miles north of Oporto, at the mouth of the river Lima. Vianna later lost its wine trade to Oporto, but it is still a flourishing and picturesque little port, with some 13,000 inhabitants and a fair trade in cod-fish.

In the early part of the seventeenth century, heavy duties were placed on French imports to Britain, and at the same time Florence wines, which had formed a considerable proportion of the wine drunk in England, deteriorated so greatly that they lost their popularity. Portuguese wine exports to Britain increased considerably and the merchants of Vianna and Oporto became wealthier than ever.

In 1703 a treaty, the Methuen Treaty, named after the diplomat who signed it, was negotiated between Britain and Portugal. It gave a heavy preference to Portuguese wines and severely damaged the wine trade of France and Germany. British ships which returned with Portuguese wine, cork, and fruit took out from England woollen cloth and cotton goods. English wine merchants established their headquarters in Oporto, and many of them still flourish there.

Portuguese wines were not really very good at this time, and, cosily sheltering under the shelter of the Methuen Treaty, they became worse. The English merchants, who held practically all the trade, tried to improve affairs by personal visits to the vineyards to overlook the methods of viniculture and vinification. They were very prosperous indeed, and were doubtless inclined to hector and domineer. Few today are really poor. The Portuguese, after an abortive attempt in 1755, brought out a scheme, sponsored by the powerful Marquis de Pombal, to limit the rights of the English merchants and at the same time to meet some of their criticisms by specifying conditions up-country. Before this, £2 a pipe had been paid to the Portuguese wine-producers; afterwards, £6.

The provisions of the scheme were evaded; bribery ensured this. Nevertheless, the trade was established on a more formal and stable basis, and everyone, merchants and consumers alike, benefited. The English merchants built the magnificent 'Factory House' in 1786, club and business premises combined, which still stands in Oporto. During all this time the wine was a beverage wine, sophisticated a little in bad years so that the colour and the alcohol content and the flavour remained uniform. A little spirit brought up the alcohol, elderberries improved the taste and certainly gave the wine a fuller colour. In 1811, Sabine, in his handbook, *The Complete Cellarman*, described port as 'a wine more in use and indeed, I may almost say, generally speaking, more in estimation than any other', and gives hints as to how the smart cellarman could imitate it. The vintage of 1820 was a magnificent one and sophistication was unnecessary. Nevertheless, it was practised, for it was the custom.

In 1844, J. J. Forester, an Oporto merchant, campaigned with vigour against additions to port. He would have returned to the simple beverage wine: to do so would in fact have killed the trade. His fight probably did much good although he was defeated. The port trade gave up the use of elderberries but kept the brandy. It was a reformation slowly carried out, for twenty years after Forester, Cyrus Redding says, 'since 1820, the wine of Oporto has been more doctored than ever – twenty-five or twenty-six gallons of brandy to the pipe, elderberries for colour, treacle for sweetness, and imperfect fermentation'. Redding was fighting the cause of French wines. The later history of port wine is uneventful. Besides the Anglo-Saxon countries, Belgium, Norway, Holland, Ireland, and Switzerland take the bulk of the exports.

Basically, there are two sorts of port wine: vintage port, and blended port, or 'port from the wood'. Vintage port is the product of a single year. Only in fine years is vintage port made: 1950, 1948, 1947, 1945, 1943, 1942, 1935, 1934, 1927, 1924, 1922, 1920, 1917, 1912. The year 1926 was a record bad year: not only was no vintage wine made, but the yield of wine for blending was poor in quality and low in quantity. Port destined to escape blending is kept in cask in Oporto for two years, then at once shipped to its destination, where it is promptly bottled and laid away in utter peace and quietness. A splash of whitewash is put on the uppermost side so that, when it is at last disturbed, it can be laid down properly in the purchaser's cellar, with the splash uppermost. Vintage port matures in bottle for seven to ten years, and rather more slowly beyond this period to perhaps as long as forty years. After that, it deteriorates, and some last not quite so long. The late Mr Maurice Healy said, 'nobody drinks a vintage port until it is at least twenty years old'. At least it may be said that a vintage port should never be drunk until it is eight or ten years old. The decanting of an old port requires a steady hand and much experience. Without these the last part of the bottle will be muddy and must be filtered through fine muslin or a filter-paper.

BLENDED PORT: 'PORT FROM THE WOOD'

Most port wine is blended after lying in casks for some years beyond the two of the vintage ports. Port for blending is called 'Red Port', although it is purplish. It gradually turns ruby-coloured and is bottled as 'ruby port': thereafter it does not change much in colour. If it is left longer in wood it becomes somewhat brownish and is then sold as 'tawny port'. Before bottling, ruby and tawny ports are blended with similar wines to ensure uniformity. Vats holding up to 10,000 gallons are often used. A vintage port is a much fuller wine than a wood port, and costs a good deal more. Tawny ports do not improve on keeping, but a full-bodied ruby port may be laid down for a few years. Old port often deposits a transparent flaky material: it escapes the decanting process and comes down in the glass. From its appearance it is called 'beeswing', and consists of cellular tissue from the grapes.

White ports made from white grapes are of little importance except as a curiosity.

PORT-TYPE WINES: AUSTRALIA

Since 1925, when preferential duties on Empire-produced wines came into force, port-style wines have outweighed in value and importance the other wines exported by Australia. They must be described as 'port-style' in Britain and Eire. In fact, they are made in the same way as the Douro wines, and with a more modern attention to methods of production. They lack nothing but the precise taste of port. In Australia, white port, as well as ruby and tawny types, is quite popular, and sometimes vintage ports are made. Maturing periods for Australian port-style wines are less than for true port, presumably because the annual variation in temperature is not so great.

PORT-TYPE WINES: SOUTH AFRICA

The first port-type wine was probably *Constantia*, a sweet red dessert wine made a few miles south of Cape Town. In the first half of the nineteenth century it was for the ladies what port was for the men. It was not so heavy as port and had a marked muscat flavour. The grapes were of old *cépages*, pontac and red muscadel, brought from no-one-knows-where early in the seventeenth century, and the Frontignan muscat (see page 135). The South African *vignerons* later replaced the frontignacs and pontacs by hermitage, but this unwise move resulted in the deterioration of Constantia, and their efforts to improve their wines by brandying made matters worse. After a period of decline, fortified (and unfortified) wine from Constantia is once more on the market.

Various unsuccessful attempts were made to produce port-type wines at the Cape from a series of combinations of grapes, but it was not until the *cépages* of the Douro were used that any success was attained, and even yet the experiments continue. Cape soils are perhaps too light and too various. Professor Theron's dictum on the subject is perhaps the last word, and is applicable with equal force to other Empire wines. 'South Africa', he said, 'can never produce Douro wines, but she certainly can produce very interesting ones in that class.'

PORT-TYPE WINES: U.S.A.

In the United States, quite a range of port-style wines is made: there are 'California Port' and 'California White Port', 'Muscadel' and 'Red Muscadel'. Before Prohibition set in, 'California Tawny Port' and 'Trousseau Port', both tawny in colour, were made. Angelica (see page 132) is of the same general type. California White Port is made from port by decolorizing with charcoal; this also takes out some of the flavour and occasionally introduces a curious taste of its own. White port in California really is white, unlike Portuguese white port, which is merely very pale. All these American wines are made in much the same way: that of the Douro. The Muscadels are made from the muscat grape, which imparts its own peculiar flavour. Normally none of these wines is aged much, but the pre-Prohibition Tawny Port was aged long enough to attain to a tawny colour. Trousseau Port was made from the French grape of that name and was not, more than any other wine, commonly packed in the bridal outfit. It also had a tawny colour. The usual large-scale, efficient, scientifically-controlled Californian methods of vinification are not so widely applied to the making of dessert wines. Pure yeast strains are not commonly used, for instance. Fortification is carried out gradually in the best wineries, so that fermentation is slowed down, not abruptly halted. The wine which results is mellower and softer than that from dead-stop fortification. The brandy for the fortification is partly obtained from the *marc*.

PORT-TYPE WINES: CANADA

Canada makes her own port-type wines in two varieties. 'Canadian Port' is a deep ruby and on the heavy side. 'Concord Sweet Red Wine' is very sweet and less deeply-coloured than Canadian Port. It has the peculiar flavour of the Labrusca grape. Both are made in the Niagara peninsula, between Niagara and Hamilton, Ontario. Although the Canadian taste runs to sweet dessert wines, port-types take second place to sherry-style wines.

Madeira

Madeira lies some 500 miles out in the Atlantic off the coast of Morocco, south of Casablanca and north of Mogador. Rumours of its existence may possibly have given the ancients their myth of Atlantis. It was not officially discovered until A.D. 1419, however, and without delay the vine was introduced (from Crete) by the Portuguese seamen. Within a few years Madeira wine established itself as a favourite in all Western Europe. Until about 1700, Madeira was an unfortified wine, but since then about 10 per cent of spirits has been added.

The great days of Madeira were before the coming of *oïdeum* (see page 53). Already in 1856, C. W. March writes, 'the old days of unbridled luxury and lavish hospitality are now gone'. After *oïdeum* had been conquered, the sugar-cane and pumpkins which succeeded the ravaged vines were only slowly replaced by the grape, and

Phylloxera dealt the reviving industry another blow before it had fully re-established itself. American stocks are largely used, with the old scions of *Sercial, Bual, Verdeilho,* and *Malvasia.* The interior of the island is rocky and mountainous, and in fact rises to over 6,000 feet, but in every valley running down to the sea are vineyards, although these are much more extensive in the south than on the north side of the island. The largest area – four or five miles by about three – is around Funchal, the capital.

Since the soil of Madeira, a decomposed volcanic tufa, is exceptionally fertile and its climate is described by everyone as idyllic, viniculture is not so difficult as in many parts of the world. The rainfall is quite sufficient (27 inches in Funchal, more on the north coast) and comes between October and March. Irrigation is carried out through *levadas* (ditches) and *furos* (tunnels). Even the easterly wind from the Sahara (the *Leste*) has become humid and not unpleasant in its long passage over the sea.

The vines are grown on pergolas (see Plate 22) which vary in height but are most commonly five or six feet from the ground, so that the grapes can be gathered from the inside. They are trodden in shallow *lagars* like those of Jerez de la Frontera, and gypsum is usually added. The wine is fortified in stages: some spirit is added during the treading, and more when the fermentation is about finished, and then again in cask after the lees have been removed. Sugar-cane spirit, a highly rectified rum, not unlike the spirit of Puerto Rico, is used. Clarification with egg-whites or ox-blood is carried out before the last fortification, or just after it.

The peculiarities of sherry-making are the use of the *flor* yeast and the protracted blending in the *solera*; Malaga is unique in being synthesized from *pantomima, tierno, arrope,* and *maestro*; Madeira owes its characteristic caramel-like flavour to the *estufado* system of ageing. The wine is casked in pipes which are rather smaller than those of port (93 against 115 gallons) and stored in hot rooms for several months. The better-quality wines stay for longer periods (six months or more) in the cooler *estufados*, the common wines for a shorter time at higher temperatures, even as high as 140°F. This 'baking' darkens the wine a little and imparts the flavour of slightly-decomposed sugar. In the smaller wineries in the country districts the *estufados* are of glass and the sun provides the heat. The wine loses 10 or 15 per cent of its volume in the *estufado*, oozing imperceptibly through the wooden casks and evaporating in the warm atmosphere.

At one time, a century ago or so, Madeira wine was made from a mixture of grapes: *verdelho*, *tinto*, and *bual* chiefly. Nowadays, at least in the larger vineyards, each variety of grape is fermented separately. The *bual* gives a delicate medium-sweet wine, the *sercial* a paler and drier, almost an aperitif, while *malmseys* (*malvasias*) are dark, sweet, heady Madeiras. *Verdelho*, from white grapes, is dark and full-bodied.

No wine lasts longer than a Madeira; a good Madeira never reaches senility. The trade is largely in the hands of British firms – Cossart, Gordon; Blandy; Leacock; Rutherford and Miles; Shortridge Lawton; and Welsh Brothers – who are members of the Madeira Wine Association, which is registered in Portugal but largely financed with British capital. By far the largest buyers of Madeira are the Scandinavian countries. Sweden has a positive passion for it and takes 40 per cent of the exports, Denmark another 20 per cent. In 1943, the U.S.A. imported nearly half a million gallons, but neither before nor since has taken any notable quantity.

Marsala

Marsala, the principal *vino di lusso* of Italy, is made on the hills behind Lilybaeum, where wine has been made for some twenty-five centuries, at a moderate estimate. Lilybaeum, now called Marsala, was a Phoenician port six or seven centuries B.C., and a wine-centre perhaps before that, for the indigenous Elymians may, for all we know, have been *vignerons*. The Greeks turned the Tyrians out of Lilybaeum, but the vineyards continued to flourish, and Drepanum (the modern Trapani, where Samuel Butler's girl-Homer came from) was built in the third century B.C. to defend the wine- and grain-port. When, a little later, the Romans ejected the Greeks, the vineyards may have suffered a partial neglect, but Augustus Caesar in the first century A.D. restored some of its old fame to the 'fiery wines' of Lilybaeum. In the following few centuries history dozed, and not only in Sicily.

When the Saracens came, in the ninth century, they brought their knowledge of agriculture to the aid of the vineyards, and Marsa-Ali (the port of Ali), as they renamed Lilybaeum, became one of the most important wine-ports of the Mediterranean area. Palermo, only forty-four miles to the north-east, was one of the greatest Arab cities.

The conquest of Sicily by the Normans at the end of the eleventh century left the island's prosperity scarcely impaired at first, although the rapacity of the Normans, and to a greater degree that of the Spaniards who followed them, gradually impoverished the *vignerons*. The population in Arab times was approaching three millions; by 1570 it was under one million, and not until the latter part of the nineteenth century did it again rise above two millions. Roads became mule-tracks, the vineyards were neglected.

Towards the end of the eighteenth century an enterprising Englishman, John Woodhouse, decided that the wine of Marsala was worth consideration. The house of Woodhouse was founded in 1773. In 1813, the reputation of the wine was made and another English firm, that of Benjamin Ingram, was started. The two firms survived independently until 1929 when they were both absorbed by Florio, an Italian firm founded a century before.

The grapes of the Marsala vineyards are of *cépages* peculiar to Italy, the Cattarato and Insolia, and small proprietors own the land and carry out the cultivation and vinification. Much of Sicily is volcanic soil, for the vast expanse of Etna occupies the centre and encroaches upon the eastern part of the island. The north is occupied by a range of mountains, essentially part of the Apennine range, and this falls away in the north-west, around Marsala, to hills of comparatively recent rocks. These are the products of wind, water, and weather on the mountains and consist of sandstones and the mass of cemented pebbles known as conglomerates. The top soil is made of detritus from these and from the limestones of the interior. The plains around the coast, still not quite free from marshlands and malarial swamps, are not much cultivated, but only a little inland the soil is fertile and the country healthy. The northern part of this area, around Palermo, has long been famed, as the 'golden shell' (*conca d'oro*), for its fertility. There is no volcanic rock hereabouts, and those who detect the volcanic taste in Marsala wine are mistaken: it is burnt sugar.

The climate is full Mediterranean, tempered by sea-breezes in these hilly slopes which are rarely more than twenty-five miles from the sea. The grapes are roasted by the intense insolation, and the must has a high sugar content, and correspondingly low acidity. The average August temperature, just before the vintage, is just under 77°, and even in January, the coldest month, ranges around 50°. The wettest month is December, with four and a half inches, and altogether the westerly sea-breezes prevent this district from being as arid as the eastern coast; it has an annual rainfall of thirty inches.

The must is plastered before fermentation to bring up the acid, and when the wine is made, it is mixed with *vino cotto*, which is evaporated must: a dark-coloured, thick, sweet liquid, and fortified – usually by adding a must to which alcohol has been added. In exceptional years, vintage Marsala is made, unblended and even not sweetened with *vino cotto* or fortified. This is very unusual, however. *Vino cotto* is made nowadays by mixing must evaporated over an open fire and fresh must with alcohol added. Tannin is added to tone up the whole.

Good Marsala is matured in casks for between two and five years. It is a dark, almost treacle-sweet wine, not to everyone's taste. There is a dry variety, sold in England as Virgen, but Marsala unqualified has commonly 5 or 6 per cent of sugar and 20 per cent, or a little more, of alcohol. The taste of burnt sugar is of course derived from the *vino cotto*.

Marsala for consumption in Italy is not so alcoholic as that for export – only 15 or 16 per cent alcohol. It is usually sweeter, however.

Marsala is sold quite widely in Germany and other North European countries, as well as in America. The total production is about four million gallons a year.

In the United States, Marsala-type wine is made in almost exactly the same way as the sweet sherry-type wines, that is by baking *shermat*. Mission grapes or Carignanes (otherwise used for port-type) are commonly employed.

Malaga

Anyone entering Málaga by car or train will see how packed the hills are with vineyards. Even so, there are insufficient grapes from them to make enough Malaga wine, and imports from the neighbouring provinces of Almería and Granada help to make the favourite *vino generoso* of the Western Mediterranean.

Málaga is a sizeable port on the south coast of Spain which has been well known for 2,500 years. Before Buddha or Plato was born, at about the time of Daniel, the Hebrew prophet, the Phoenicians here founded a port and traded Eastern luxuries for salted fish, whence they named the place Malaca, from *malac*, to salt. They established vineyards, and they are there still, on the terraced hills of Axarquia a few miles out of the town. Málaga now has almost a quarter of a million inhabitants, and has added sugar and cotton to its old exports of wine and fish, besides Picasso, who left at the turn of the century.

The modern Málagueño is apt to boast that Malaga wine is still much the same as the old Phoenician wines.

The components of Malaga are *arrope*, *color* (sometimes known as *pantomima*), *vino tierno*, and *vino maestro*, besides ordinary wine from grapes, to which 5 per cent of spirit has been added. *Arrope* is an unfermented grape must, evaporated over an open fire until it has the consistency of syrup and a clear brown colour. By itself it has a sweet, bitterish acid taste.

Color is very similar to *arrope* but is evaporated almost to a paste, so that it is very dark indeed, even when diluted with must to its original volume.

Vino tierno (*tierno* means 'tender' or 'delicate') is a wine made from grapes which have been dried off in the sun to half their weight. About 6 per cent of spirit is added. It is rather thick, although not like *arrope*, of course. *Vino tierno* is kept to 'improve' wines (this is the wine-makers' international term for putting up the alcohol).

Vino maestro ('master wine') is also called *calebre*. It is made by fermenting must long enough to replace much of the grape-odour with a winy smell, and then muting the fermentation by adding enough spirit to bring the alcohol content up to 17 per cent. It is a rather syrupy liquid with a penetrating fragrance.

The basic wine is made in the usual Andalusian manner: the grapes are destemmed, and then trodden in the tray-like *lagars*, the skins separated by the screw (page 114 and Plate 26). Muscatel grapes are used with P X for the *vino maestro*, *vino tierne*, *arrope*, and *color*. Fermentation of the clear must lasts for six weeks or so. Then 5 per cent of spirit is added, next either *vino tierno* or *vino maestro* to put up the alcohol or improve the bouquet, and about 8 per cent of *arrope* to enhance the body of the wine, and then enough *pantomima* to enrich the colour.

After this, there is really very little more to do to the wine, except the usual racking and fining. Malaga wine is much about the colour of a strong infusion of coffee and naturally has all the properties in the way of body, alcohol, colour, and bouquet which have been donated to it. For *vino de postre* (dessert wine) Malaga is unsurpassed, in the Spanish view. (Anglo-Saxons are apt to find that, except in limited amounts, it has somewhat dramatic effects on their metabolism.) Malaga wine is sometimes blended by a modified *solera* system and, like sherry, has a very long life. It contains between 17 and 19 per cent alcohol and up to 15 per cent sugar.

Special types of Malaga are made based essentially on *vino tierno*, that is, produced to a great extent from sun-dried grapes: a sort of fortified *vin de paille* known as *Lagrima* (i.e. tears). This is paler: a beautiful bright golden colour. Little is exported.

The Málagueño *vigneron* has his troubles, but the weather is not often among them. The *terral* wind from the north-west is the only one which can discompose him, for in the summer it is hot from the baked *meseta* and in winter cold from the icy peaks of the Sierra Nevada. The east wind, the *levante*, brings moisture which is generally welcome. The *leveche*, which comes in from the south-west in summer, is cool and invigorating.

Other Fortified Wines

Port and sherry, Madeira, Marsala, and Malaga are the only fortified wines readily obtainable in Britain, with the exception of sacramental wine. There are several hundred others made all over the wine-growing parts of the world, and it would be impossible to list them all.

Let us consider first the fortified wines made in California: angelica and 'Californian Tokay'.

ANGELICA

Angelica seems to be the only contribution of North America to the world's battery of drinks, with the exception of the cocktail. No one knows where the name came from, but the wine was being made over a century ago, by mixing three parts of must with one part of brandy, and some similar method was still being used up to Prohibition.

Californian angelica is a sweet, white, fortified wine, differing little from Californian white port wine. In fact the difference seems to be solely in the labelling, in some wineries at least.

The best angelica is made from the black Mission grape, fermented off the skins. The must from these grapes is practically colourless, but in the Californian climate it is necessary to separate the skins very quickly, and to avoid with care the use of bruised or infected grapes. Only a short fermentation is given before fortification, and an almost neutral spirit is used so that the colour will not be spoiled. The first racking is carried out after about a week. Angelica is usually aged for three or four years; if shorter periods are used the flavour will not be smooth.

Angelica contains about 19 per cent alcohol and perhaps up to 15 per cent sugar. It has no burnt-sugar taste.

CALIFORNIAN TOKAY

Californian Tokay has never had anything in common with real Tokay. It is made by adding to angelica some port to give it a reddish tinge and enough sherry to make it taste of burnt sugar. It has about 19 per cent alcohol, and perhaps 10 per cent sugar. It is in fact tinted angelica with a caramel flavour.

MUSCATEL WINES

Many, probably most, of the fortified wines which proliferate in France, Italy, Spain, and other Mediterranean countries are made from one of the many varieties of muscatel grapes. Many are the local variations in making these wines. Some have *vino cotto*, *vin cuit*, or *arrope* added to them, when they have the caramel-taste of burnt sugar, some have spices added, some are fortified with all-but-neutral spirit, some with a brandy with plenty of congenerics, some with cane-spirit. The grapes are sometimes passulated by twisting the stems and letting them dry on the vine.

'NATURAL SWEET WINES' (*Vins doux naturels*: V.D.N.)

In the old French province of Roussillon, now the *département* of the Pyrénées-Orientales, and also a little further north, in Aude and Hérault, there has been a tradition of making fortified wines for many years. When, in the latter part of the nineteenth century, Hérault and Aude became part of the vast prairie of vineyards pledged to make more wine per square centimetre than anywhere else in Europe, the *vignerons* of these villages kept their independence and continued to make the sweet red and white wines of their fathers. In 1872 they found it expedient to obtain some measure of legal recognition, and when the *Appellations Contrôlées* were issued in 1936 (see page 96) they were among the first to have schedules issued for their wines.

The principal districts making these 'natural sweet wines' (*vins doux naturels*, usually abbreviated to V.D.N.) are Rivesaltes, Banyuls, Maury, Frontignan, Lunel, Rasteau, and Côtes d'Agly and Côtes de Haut-Roussillon. This little archipelago of fine wines in the great sea of wines of the Midi amounts to some four million gallons a year; in 1952, a record season, it was over six million gallons: more than the total annual production of wine by Cyprus or Turkey.

These wines are made by fermenting about half the sugar in the must and then adding brandy bit by bit to bring the alcohol up to between 16 and 22 per cent. The grapes used, mostly muscatels, ripen in this corner, sheltered by the peaks of the Pyrenean Canigou, to a high sugar content and a good part of this goes into the wine. The acid is quite healthily high. There are just over 9,000 producers, and the total area of their vineyards is about 32,000 acres: very small holdings.

The *Appellation* schedules are very similar for all these districts: the grapes to be used differ a little from place to place, the maximum amount of must allowable per acre varies a little: 220 gallons per acre at Maury to 310 at Rivesaltes and the Côtes. Upon ageing in casks these wines take a peculiar faintly bitter taste and are then labelled as 'Banyuls-Rancio', 'Maury-Rancio', and so on.

The proportion of red to white wines varies from place to place; some *rosé* is made too. They may be *sec*, when the sugar is between 3½ and 7 per cent, *semi-doux*, with sugar from 7 to 9 per cent, and *doux* (*doux vin doux naturel*), with more than 9 per cent.

Banyuls is the most southerly of these little towns, scarcely more than villages. It has a population of just over 3,000 and lies right under the Pyrenean heights: if 'Africa begins at the Pyrenees', it is the last village in Europe. (See Plate 15).

Maury has only about 1,300 inhabitants. It lies inland, beyond

Perpignan, and, like Banyuls, specializes in red and *rosé* wines. Rivesaltes, a few miles from Perpignan, is on the river Agly, which enters the Mediterranean not far from the salt lagoon of Leucate; all the coast along here is fringed with extensive lagoons. The Agly, a little river only fifty miles long, comes down from the Corbières, a range of hills which rise to over 3,500 feet and form the boundary between Aude and the Pyrénées-Orientales. It is on their lower slopes that the Côte d'Agly wines are grown. These are just about equally white and red and have not quite the reputation of Banyuls and Maury.

Frontignan and Lunel are further north, both a little larger than the other V.D.N. villages. Lunel, in fact, with its 7,000 inhabitants, is able to do a certain amount of shipbuilding, and also distils some of the heathen *vins ordinaires* which grow all around. Although it has its *Appellation*, Lunel makes only a mere 8,000 gallons of V.D.N., all of which is white. Frontignan wine has a very high reputation. It too is all white. It has received the compliment of being imitated: Australia makes 'Royal Reserve Frontignac', 'Gold Crown Frontignac', 'Blue Stripe Frontignac', and even, what Hérault knows nothing of, 'Red Frontignac': five or six shillings a quart. South Africa, too, sells a red and a white 'Frontignac'. 'Muscat de Frontignan', the only grape allowed in the *Appellation Contrôlée* of Frontignan, is much used in California for making muscatel wines; it is named there Muscat Canelli. It is a well-known grape elsewhere, especially of course for fortified wines, where the delicate muscatel flavour is often desirable. Australia finds it useful on Rupestris and hybrid stocks; it was one of the *cépages* used for the original Constantia at the Cape.

Only 180,000 gallons of Frontignan are made and the regulations are a little stricter than for the other V.D.N. The yield may not exceed 220 gallons to the acre; no sugar may be added, and congelation (see page 85) is specifically forbidden. It is sold in a special bottle with a moulded pattern.

These V.D.N. wines are not easily obtained in England, and if you are motoring through to Barcelona, the Costa Brava, or Seville, it is worth taking the opportunity of sampling them, not least because, as a wine-merchant of Collioure who specializes in these wines says in his wine-list, they 'dispense a large optimism' when taken as aperitifs and 'cradle one in a sweet beatitude' if drunk as dessert wines.

PINEAU DES CHARENTES

To be logical some mention should be made here of the curious drink known as *pineau des Charentes*, or simply as *pineau*. In the region of the Charentes (where cognac comes from), the brandy-producers sometimes find themselves with an overproduction of brandy. More than a century ago, an ingenious manufacturer mixed his surplus with fresh grape must and so made a sweet strong drink which sold well, although at first only locally. In the 1930s it had quite a vogue and is still made in very considerable quantities. The French government issued a circular on the subject in February 1935, regularizing the drink. It contains between 18 and 22 per cent of alcohol, and of course a considerable amount of sugar. It is rather like a fortified wine.

It is possible that a nineteenth-century visitor from Charente to North America suggested the invention of angelica (see page 132).

CHAPTER 8

VINEYARDS OF THE WORLD

France

THE variety of French wines is such that if all the other countries of the world ceased making wine, well. . . the world could carry on. We should certainly miss the hocks and Mosels, and there is nothing like Spanish sherry or Portuguese port. Nevertheless. . . . If all French wines were erased from the lists, on the other hand, the winescape would be quite unrecognizable: no clarets – only Spanish *rioja* and Yugoslav *cabernet*; no burgundies but the imitations from Australia; no Sauternes, no Chablis, no Saint-Émilion, no Beaujolais; neither the cheerful light wines from the Loire nor the fuller Rhônes; no champagne. Thousands of the most civilized folk on earth would die of thirst.

There are almost four million acres of vineyards in France, and of the eighty-nine *départements*, only a few near the English Channel make no wine at all. Even Brittany produces a few muscadets. As recently as the end of the nineteenth century, wine was made from vineyards at Versailles: the second worst in France, the nadir being that from Suresnes, across the Seine from the Bois de Boulogne. Only a small proportion of French wine is of any repute and many *départements* make large quantities which is either drunk locally or passes anonymously down the throats of the lower classes of Paris, Marseilles, Clermont-Ferrand, and Lille. Much of the production of the Charente and Gers is distilled for brandy. On the other hand, there are many places where good and even fine wine is made which is unknown abroad for one reason or another. Many of the little wines of the Loire, the Savoy, and the Jura are unobtainable in this country. Neither can the V.D.N. (page 134) be purchased easily here. In the great vineyard areas of France, such as Languedoc, the dangers of monoculture have become increasingly obvious in recent years and in some districts the land is going over to the cultivation of other fruits, or to those sorts of grapes, such as chasselas and muscat de Hombourg (i.e. trollinger), which sell well for eating or as grape-juice. (France bottled ten times as much grape-juice in 1945 as in 1939.) Meanwhile, the laws passed against alcoholism in France have the effect of increasing the amount of surplus wine, which was said to amount to about 17 per cent of the total production in 1950–3.

The *département* making most wine is Hérault in Languedoc, but after the three wine-gushers of the Midi, Hérault, Aude, and Gard, comes the Gironde, and among its seventy-odd million gallons are the select few tuns from the Château d'Yquem, and the great clarets, and no one would barter a bottle of Château Margaux for all the million bottles from Hérault, unless of course he were really desperately thirsty.

BORDEAUX (Map 3. Plates 1, 2, 3, 4, 6, 9, 11, 13, and 23).

For the variety of its wines, no vineyard area in the world can rival that of Bordeaux. If one wants a light red wine, there is nothing anywhere to approach even the quite ordinary fine clarets in flavour, bouquet, colour, or staying-power. The only red wines of the heavier type which surpass the Saint-Émilions are the burgundies. There is no better sweet white wine than Château d'Yquem from the Sauternes district of Bordeaux, although a few great hocks rank as its peers. Half a dozen of the best white wines from the Graves are outclassed only by Chablis and the white burgundies: there are good dry wines on the Rhine and the Mosel, in Touraine, the Vosges, and in Switzerland, Franconia, and Austria, but none surpasses the best Graves.

Altogether, from the 320,000 acres of vineyards, Bordeaux produces nearly eighty million gallons of wine, and no less than three-quarters of this is of *Appellation Contrôlée* quality (see page 96). To the north of the city of Bordeaux, on the left bank of the Gironde, is the district of the Médoc, an area some fifty miles long, in which the vineyard region is the strip six or seven miles wide bordering the estuary. (See map 3.) The northern part of the Médoc (the Bas-Médoc) gives clarets of somewhat inferior quality, inclined to have an earthy *goût du terroir*. It is from the southern part, the Haut-Médoc, that the great clarets come. The soil which produces these incomparable wines varies in different parts: somewhat sandy marls or even river alluvium (this not the the best soil for vines), in many places pebbly, and below, a sub-soil, in part the hardened iron-bearing sand called *alios*, in part the compacted and pebbly *arène*. Even more than in the southern and eastern regions of the Bordelais, the warmth natural to a latitude of 45° is tempered by cool westerlies from the Atlantic, which bring some thirty inches of rain every year. The warmest month, July, has an average temperature of 70°. Instead of the anticyclones from the region of Iceland, which control the climate of Northern France, it is the depressions coming north-east from the Azores which dominate the Bordeaux.

The best Médoc clarets – there are no *bad* Médocs – were classified in 1855 by a committee of Bordeaux experts. It was not the first time the clarets had been graded, but this time the task was carried out with such efficiency that it is still valid and is criticized only in minor details. The wines from the sixty-two best claret vineyards were graded into five classes : 4 *premiers crus* ('first growths'), 15 second, 14 third, 11 fourth, and 18 fifth *crus*. One of the first growths (Château Haut-Brion) comes from the Graves district, just south of Bordeaux, but all the rest are from the Haut-Médoc. This list, the claret-drinker's breviary, is given on page 144, together with the commune (parish) in which the vineyard is situated. The wines are named from the château of the estate. These châteaux are quite unlike the great châteaux of the Loire. Some of the Bordeaux châteaux are in fact modest country houses, some are very ancient; in many the grapes are pressed and the wine is made, in others the proprietor lives: in some he cannot live, for he is often a limited company nowadays. The château system of naming vineyards is peculiar to the Bordeaux district. There is one, and only one, alteration in the 1855 classification which is universally accepted: the promotion of Ch. Mouton-Rothschild from second class to first class. The classification is largely based on price (which is controlled by average quality). Sometimes a vineyard falls on bad days, perhaps because the *maître de chai* is too old, or ill, or too young, or ill-chosen, but the quality of the wine which can be produced in the best circumstances depends on the soil and the exposure of the vineyard. This is why the general placing of such wine has remained unchallenged for just over a century. Nevertheless, to despise a wine because it is only a fourth or fifth growth is quite wrong. To everyone but the experts, the differences between the wines in the different classes are all but imperceptible, and there are few experts who are not professionals. The relative prices paid (wholesale) for the wines are: 1st *cru* – 100; 2nd – 45; 3rd – 35; 4th – 32; 5th – 30. Mouton-Rothschild often fetches a premium even over that being paid for first growths. Some years there is a brisk market in futures. 1955 was one of these: spring was so dry and sunny in the Médoc that by the first days of June many gallons of non-existent wine were sold from grapes which had not yet appeared: 300,000 francs the *tonneau* (252 gallons) for first *crus*.

If you leave Bordeaux going north by the rue Fondaudège and the Avenue de la Libération, then fork right at km 7·50, you will be on the D2 road going through the heart of the Médoc. At km 27·50 is the village of Margaux; you will have passed Cantenac rather earlier: the parish of Cantenac contains Ch. Brane-Cantenac, named after the Baron de Brane, the eminent viticulturalist, who made Mouton-Rothschild great. Margaux commune is the home of the great Ch. Margaux itself (Plate 13), which is half a mile east of the village. All clarets from this commune have a splendid bouquet and an extreme delicacy of flavour, even the cheaper ones, such as Ch. Desmirail and Ch. Ferrière, which are both a few hundred yards to the north-west of the village. The two adjoining vineyards of Ch. Rausan-Ségla and Ch. Rauzan-Gassies, once under the same owner (1661–1860), are on the southern outskirts of the village. These are two very fine growths which lead the second class if Mouton is promoted. The village of Saint-Julien, at km 43·50, is just past the six second-growths of its commune: the three Léovilles, the two Gruaud-Laroses, and Ducru-Beaucaillou. Ducru wine has a dry, almost hard taste, unusual in a claret, which is very attractive. These are all towards the river, but Ch. Talbot is on the left of the road: it was named after John Talbot, Earl of Shrewsbury, and produces a fine claret, much of which comes to Britain. This wine, according to the poet P. Béarnez, is a 'nectar dear to lovers and beauties'.

Pauillac, which produces more fine claret than any other commune, is at km 48, on the river-bank. Château Lafite is just under two miles to the north-west of the village, on the right of the road, which here climbs up and away from the river. It was bought in 1868 by the Baron James de Rothschild (for 4½ million francs); Ch. Mouton-Rothschild, which the Baron Nathaniel de Rothschild had brought into the family fifteen years before, is just south of Lafite. Château Latour, with its ugly little tower, is near the river, on eastward-facing slopes. The wine of Latour is said by experts to have more body than Ch. Margaux or Ch. Lafite, but less bouquet and delicacy.

There are several hundred unclassified vineyards in the Médoc, graded roughly as Bourgeois growths (about 250), Artisan growths, and Paysan growths. Most of these wines are mixed off and sold as Margaux (not Château Margaux), Pauillac, La Rose-Pauillac, Haut-Médoc, Moulis, Médoc, etc. Some of the bourgeois growths sell under their own name and are often very good. Châteaux Angludet, La Gurgue, Citran, Parempuyre, Pomys, Lalande, and others are worth trying. A bourgeois growth fetches 20 to 25 per cent of the price (wholesale) of a first growth. Many are vinified by co-operatives.

Books have been written about claret, for it is a wine which inspires a peculiar affection. There are clarets which do not come from the Médoc, in particular the red Graves, which have an excellence all their own, and which have been somewhat neglected. They are on the whole rather more full-bodied than the Médoc and last for a very long time, though they mature more quickly. The outstanding red Graves is Château Haut-Brion, which ranks with the great, and whose vineyard is at the very gates of Bordeaux city. The château here is very ancient and the wine itself was well known in Britain in the seventeenth century. Graves soil is a sandy gravel (as the name implies) and underneath is either limestone or *alios*. Other fine red Graves are Chx La-Mission-Haut-Brion (across the road from Haut-Brion itself), Haut-Bailly, Chevalier, Carbonnieux, Malartic-Lagravière, Latour (there are about eighty La Tours in the Bordeaux), Laville-Haut-Brion, Smith-Haut-Lafitte, Olivier, and Bouscaut.

But this is not all. There are some 280 vineyards of merit in the Saint-Émilion district producing red wines which are rather more full-bodied than the Médoc clarets or red Graves. They are, in this respect, nearer to burgundies than are the western clarets. To reach Saint-Émilion, one turns left on to the N670 at Saint-André de Cubzac when coming into Bordeaux from the north by the N10 road. (Cubzac is just short of the bridge over the Dordogne.) The town of Libourne is some twelve or thirteen miles along the N670. Its 20,000 inhabitants, like the quarter of a million of Bordeaux, live on wine, although it is true that its half mile of quays handle petroleum also. The road to Saint-Émilion starts close by Libourne railway station and runs along the chalk hillside bordering the Dordogne valley for five miles to the small and ancient town, which is quite hemmed in by its vineyards (Plate 11). It is so picturesque and contains so much of historical and artistic interest that it is much visited even by teetotallers.

The Saint-Émilionnais contains one great vineyard, the Château Ausone, which is on the west of the hill upon which the town itself is built. Château Ausone, named after the Roman poet Ausonius whose vineyards were on the same spot sixteen centuries ago, was excluded from the 1855 classification of clarets only because its production was very small: it makes only 3,000 gallons a year. Château Ausone and Château Cheval-Blanc are the outstanding wines of Saint-Émilion. Cheval-Blanc is away to the north-west of Saint-Émilion, close to Pomerol, on the belt of gravel known as Graves de Saint-Émilion. Many experts rank Ch. Cheval-Blanc wine with the *premiers crus* of the Médoc. The best of the Saint-Émilion wines, apart from these two, are Chx Belair, Magdelaine, Canon, and Fourtet in the Saint-Émilionnais proper, and Figeac, Croque-Michotte, Corbin-Despagne, and Ripeau in the Graves de Saint-Émilion. Pomerol, to the north-west of the Saint-Émilionnais, was separated as a vineyard region from Saint-Émilion in 1928. Its full-bodied wines, which resemble those of the Graves de Saint-Émilion, come from a plateau of 1,500 acres in extent covered with a gravelly sand or a gravelly clay above *alios*. The finest vineyard is the Château Pétrus, and the best of the other sixty-one classified ones, Châteaux Certan, Vieux-Certan, La Conseillante, Petit-Village, and Trotanoy.

An official classification of the Saint-Émilion wines was made in 1955. Those of Pomerol are to be dealt with next. It is very unlikely that any of those mentioned above will be dethroned. Other parts of the Bordelais make red wines which are sold under regional *appellations* and not by vineyard, such as Côtes de Fronsac, Bourg, Blaye, etc., not to mention 'Bordeaux' and 'Bordeaux Supérieur'.

For the fine white wines of the Bordelais, one must take the N10 road south towards Toulouse. The first thirty kilometres skirt the extensive district of the Graves on the east. For some odd reason, Graves in Britain is a white wine, in fact the most well known of white wines, but there is more than twice as much red Graves made (880,000 gallons) as white (330,000 gallons), and the red is much the better of the two. The best white Graves come from the Châteaux Carbonnieux, Chevalier, Olivier, Laville-Haut-Brion, and Bouscaut. The Graves vineyards were not officially classified until 1953. There is much mixing of white Graves with inferior wine and it is best to drink only wine from one of those mentioned or labelled with *Appellation Contrôlée* (from a reliable merchant), or else to refrain from passing judgement on Graves, for you may be drinking very inferior stuff. After thirty-six kilometres on the Toulouse road one reaches Cérons, the centre of a district making sweet white wines of quality, though not up to the standard of the best Sauternes. Cérons has only been officially recognized as deserving of an 'appellation' separate from 'Graves' since the war. It makes about 400,000 gallons of white wine, including a little dry.

Beyond Cérons is the district of the really first-class sweet white wines, the Sauternes. Barsac, three kilometres beyond Cérons, is the largest town, with just over a thousand inhabitants, some of whom make barrels to put the wine into. The communes making Sauternes are Bommes, Preignac, Fargues, Barsac, and Sauternes itself. This is the region of *pourriture noble* (page 62), and the wines have over 14 per cent of alcohol (sometimes up to 17), as much as 20 per cent of sugar, and 2 or 3 per cent of glycerine. They are so full and rich that they are best not drunk with the fish course, like other white wines, but with the sweet, or even sipped after the meal, like a port or an *oloroso* sherry. The French, who have not heard, at least officially, of the German *Edelfäule* wines, admit no competitors to the Sauternes. To step in where the French refuse to tread, it may be said that a Sauternes has not the somewhat overwhelming bouquet of a Johannisberger Kabinett wine (which is found by some almost to approach the vulgar) but has its own more delicate aroma. (After saying this, it is wise to step smartly out of the ring.) *The* great Sauternes is the incomparable Château d'Yquem, '*Grand* Premier Cru'. The *premiers crus* are Chx La Tour-Blanche, Lafaurie-Peyraguey and Clos Haut-Peyraguey, Rayne-Vigneau, Suduiraut, Coutet, Climens, Guiraud, Rieussec, Rabaud-Sigalas, and Rabaud-Promis.

THE GREAT AND THE FINE WINES OF BORDEAUX

MÉDOC

CH.   *First Growths*

Lafite	Pauillac
Margaux	Margaux
Latour	Pauillac
Haut-Brion	Pessac (GRAVES)

CH.   *Second Growths*

Mouton-Rothschild	Pauillac
Rausan-Ségla	Margaux
Rauzan-Gassies	Margaux
Léoville-Las-Cases	St-Julien
Léoville-Poyferré	St-Julien
Léoville-Barton	St-Julien
Durfort-Vivens	Margaux
Gruaud-Larose	St-Julien
Lascombes	Margaux
Brane-Cantenac	Cantenac
Pichon-Longueville-Baron	St-Julien
Pichon-Longueville-Lalande	St-Julien
Ducru-Beaucaillou	St-Julien
Cos-d'Estournel	St-Estèphe
Montrose	St-Estèphe

CH.   *Third Growths*

Kirwan	Cantenac
Issan	Cantenac
Lagrange	St-Julien
Langoa	St-Julien
Giscours	Labarde
Malescot-St-Exupéry	Margaux
Cantenac-Brown	Cantenac
Boyd-Cantenac	Margaux

MÉDOC

CH.   *Third Growths*

Palmer	Cantenac
La Lagune	Ludon
Desmirail	Margaux
Calon-Ségur	St-Estèphe
Ferrière	Margaux
Marquis d'Alesme-Becker	Margaux

CH.   *Fourth Growths*

St Pierre-Sevaistre	St-Julien
St Pierre-Bontemps	St-Julien
Talbot	St-Julien
Branaire-Ducru	St-Julien
Duhart-Milon	Pauillac
Pouget	Cantenac
La Tour-Carnet	St-Laurent
Rochet	St-Estèphe
Beychevelle	St-Julien
Le Prieuré	Cantenac
Marquis-de-Terme	Margaux

CH.   *Fifth Growths*

Pontet-Canet	Pauillac
Batailley	Pauillac
Haut-Batailley	Pauillac
Grand-Puy-Lacoste	Pauillac
Grand-Puy-Ducasse	Pauillac
Lynch-Bages	Pauillac
Lynch-Moussas	Pauillac
Dauzac	Labarde
Mouton-d'Armailhac	Pauillac
Le Tertre	Arsac
Haut-Bages-Libéral	Pauillac

MÉDOC

CH.   *Fifth Growths*

Pédesclaux	Pauillac
Belgrave	St-Laurent
Camensac	St-Laurent
Cos-Labory	St-Estèphe
Clerc-Milon	Pauillac
Croizet-Bages	Pauillac
Cantemerle	Macau

SAUTERNES

CH.   *Grand First Growth*

d'Yquem	Sauternes

CH.   *First Growths*

La Tour-Blanche	Bommes
Peyraguey	Bommes
Rayne-Vigneau	Bommes
Suduiraut	Preignac
Coutet	Barsac
Climens	Barsac
Guiraud	Sauternes
Rieussec	Fargues

SAUTERNES

CH.   *First Growths*

Rabaud-Sigalas	Bommes
Rabaud-Promis	Bommes

CH.   GRAVES: RED

La Mission-Haut-Brion	Pessac
Haut-Bailly	Léognan
Chevalier	Léognan
Carbonnieux	Léognan
Malartic-Lagravière	Léognan
Latour	Martillac
Laville-Haut-Brion	Talence
Smith-Haut-Lafitte	Martillac
Olivier	Léognan
Bouscaut	Cadaujac

CH.   GRAVES: WHITE

Carbonnieux	Léognan
Chevalier	Léognan
Olivier	Léognan
Laville-Haut-Brion	Talence
Bouscaut	Cadaujac

Other sweet white wines, before which it is not necessary to bate one's breath, are made in the regions of Sainte-Croix-du-Mont and Loupiac, both just across the River Garonne from Sauternes, and, of course, in Cérons. Drier white wines are produced in Entre-deux-Mers (that is, between Dordogne and Garonne) to the volume of no less than ten million gallons annually, and in the Blaye and Bourg districts (across the Gironde from the Médoc) and on the *palus*, the alluvium of the river-valleys. Finally, besides the sparkling Bordeaux mentioned on page 107, about fifty thousand gallons a year of 'Bordeaux Clairet' are made: it is a more deeply coloured wine than *rosé* but less so than red.

BURGUNDY (Map 4, Plate 12)

The old Duchy of Burgundy, famed in history, fiction, and even musical comedy, is almost, but not quite, conterminous with the present-day *vignoble* of Burgundy. The modern *départements* of Yonne, Côte-d'Or, and Saône-et-Loire are common to both, but the extensive vineyards of the northern part of the *département* of Rhône produce much burgundy wine, but were not part of the ancient Duchy, while the wines of the Ain *département*, quite insignificant though they are, do not count as burgundies, although Ain was in the Duchy. The wines of Burgundy were well known before Burgundy became a duchy, and by the thirteenth century Chablis and Beaune provided some of the finest wines in Europe.

Apart from the small, select vineyards of Chablis, eighty miles away to the north-west, the vineyards of Burgundy stretch intermittently from Dijon south almost to Lyons: 120 miles. Of this strip, the northernmost thirty-five miles is by far the most important, for it produces Le Montrachet and Meursault, Richebourg, Chambertin, and Clos de Vougeot – all great wines, or very fine, as well as a host of fine red and white wines. This northern part is the Côte d'Or. It is shielded on the east by the Alps and the Jura mountains and on the west by the lower chain of the Hautes Côtes de Nuits and the Hautes Côtes de Beaune.

The road, from Dijon south, the N74, borders the Côte d'Or to the east for the whole distance from Dijon to Chagny, where it divides into the N6 and the N481. Beyond Chagny, the vineyards away on the hillsides to the west are those of Mercurey, where nearly 200,000 gallons of fine (but not great) wines are produced each year. These vineyards lie just to the west of the N481 road (fork right at Chagny) and finish just south of Montagny, where an unhappy stretch, which grows no vines, intervenes. However, at Tournus, the vineyards of the Mâconnais start. These give fine white wines, and include Pouilly-Fuissé, which misses greatness in good years only by a hair's breadth. If you rejoin the N6 at Mâcon itself, you will pass right through the vineyards, and by avoiding Châlon-sur-Saône will miss the steelworks. A few miles beyond Mâcon you come into the Beaujolais where the fine vineyards of Juliénas, Chénas, Moulin-à-Vent, and so on, are ranged along the hillsides to the west. The Beaujolais *vignoble* stretches for about thirty miles, finishing only a few miles north of Lyons.

The red burgundies are fine full-bodied wines, without quite the delicacy of the clarets, but making up for that by being more mouth-filling. Burgundy, according to Mr Maurice Healy, is 'one of the noblest and greatest of red wines'. He also says: 'you will only drink four or five bottles of truly first-class burgundy in your whole life . . . but you can drink claret of the highest class several times in the year: claret that should be drunk kneeling.'

About 60,000 gallons are made of the great red burgundies. Romanée-Conti, once one of the greatest, and nearly the smallest, with only four acres, succumbed to Phylloxera. It had never been replanted on American stocks, but the ground was treated with carbon disulphide (see page 56), which kept the pest at bay. During the Second World War this chemical was unobtainable and the vines succumbed. A sad story. It is now producing again, however, on ungrafted vines. Clos de Vougeot and Chambertin are the only great red burgundies made in any quantity (40,000 gallons between them).

The great white burgundies are few and by no means as reliable as the great hocks and Sauternes. They are dry, and at their best they are magnificent. There is Chablis, from a little limestone plateau in Yonne. Anything but *Chablis Grand Cru* is merely a fine white wine, and even so, one can be deceived. An elusive wine, Chablis. Le Montrachet, the great white wine from three or four miles south of Beaune, *is* a great wine as unique as real Chablis. The wines of Chevalier-Montrachet and Bâtard-Montrachet are not quite so good but are not to be sniffed at, all the same. Meursault is plentiful, but varies, too. Of the great white wines of Burgundy, only 35,000 gallons are made each year, and that does not go very far.

BURGUNDIES: GREAT AND FINE (Map 4)

Colour	Great	Fine
White		Chablis
Red	Chambertin (and Clos de Bèze)	Gevrey-Chambertin
Red	Clos de Tart	Morey-Saint-Denis
Red	Musigny	Chambolle-Musigny
Red	Clos de Vougeot	Vougeot
Red	Richebourg	Romanée-Conti
Red	La Tâche	Vosne-Romanée
Red	Grands-Echezeaux	
Red		Nuits-Saint-Georges

BURGUNDIES: GREAT AND FINE—*contd*.

Colour	Great	Fine
Red		Aloxe-Corton, Corton, Pommard, Volnay, Santenay
White		Meursault
White	Le Montrachet	Chevalier-Montrachet, Bâtard-Montrachet, Chassagne-Montrachet
Red		Chassagne-Montrachet
Red		Mercurey
White		Pouilly-Fuissé
Red		Beaujolais, viz.
		Brouilly, Chénas, Chiroubles, Fleurie, Juliénas, Morgon, Moulin-à-Vent, Saint-Amour

THE LOIRE (ANJOU AND TOURAINE) (Map 6, Plate 14)

The wines of the Loire basin are a study in themselves, and they must be sampled on the spot, for few come to Britain. Considerable numbers of English and other foreign visitors tour the Loire valley each year, attracted by the picturesqueness of the countryside and the beauty and historical interest of the great châteaux, but few know of the wealth of fine wines which the region produces. This is a district where local wines proliferate; there are scores of them. Most are white, and many sparkling wines are made; in fact the sparkling wines of Vouvray in Touraine and Saumur in Anjou are second only to champagne, and with this reputation are exported to Britain in considerable quantity.

Anjou, whose wines are generally superior to those of Touraine, is roughly equivalent to the *département* of Maine-et-Loire, for oenological purposes. Much of the vineyard soil is a shelly sand known as *faluns*, left by the great Miocene sea. Like all of the Loire basin, which is known as the 'Garden of France', it is very fertile. Anjou wine comes from the broad Loire valley itself for some thirty miles east and west of Angers, and especially from Saumur and the district south of it, and along the river Layon which joins the Loire at Chalonnes. There are smaller patches of vine along the Sarthe and the Loire, to the north of Angers, but Saumur and the Côteaux du Layon are the principal vineyard areas. *Rosé* wines are rather a speciality along the Layon; they are made from cabernet, transplanted here from the Bordeaux. A little further east on the banks of the little stream, the Aubance, are the pleasant wines of Brissac, Saint-Saturnin, and Vauchrétien, white and *rosé*, made since 1462 or earlier. Around Saumur, apart from its well-known *mousseux*, which may be dry or sweet, red and *rosé* wines are made. At Chaumes (as elsewhere on the Loire) there are sweet wines benefiting from *pourriture noble*.

In Touraine, further up-river, the well-known white wines are those of Vouvray, Montlouis, and Rochecorbon from the banks of the Loire. At Vouvray the vineyards are almost all about 400 feet high up on the hillsides. Montlouis wines are heady and those of Rochecorbon delicate in flavour. The red wines of Bourgeuil, between Saumur and Tours, are reputed the best of their colour on the Loire. Those of Chinon, which should be bottled for a few years before drinking, are for ever connected with the name of François Rabelais. These red wines are exceptions to the rule in being served stone-cold.

Far up the Loire, in the *département* of Cher, is the little vineyard of Sancerre, and facing it on the east bank of the river, that of Pouilly (no connexion with the Pouilly in Burgundy). Sancerre, where about 100,000 gallons of a greenish-white wine is made, is a district which prizes its independence from the rest of the Loire vineyards. Pouilly makes an interesting dry white wine: Pouilly-fumé.

RHÔNE (Map 6, Plates 5 and 10)

The valley of the Rhône is long and extends from a Swiss glacier to the Camargue west of Marseilles. The vines of the Valais and of Savoy overlook its waters. The vineyards of the Côtes du Rhône, so-called, extend only from just south of Vienne to Avignon, however, a stretch of about forty-five miles, broken into a northern and a southern part by a barren patch around Montélimar. Here we are on the edge of the Mediterranean climatic region, with its baked hillsides and its blazing sun, and the wines are full: 'big' is the word.

The weather is reliable here and harvests do not vary much. The *mistral* blows down from the north, bringing a cold flood of air from the Central Plateau of France and from the Alps, for the Rhône valley acts as a wind-siphon, just as the Adriatic Sea does for the *bora*.

In the northern stretch of vineyards the wines are mostly red: Côte-Rotie, Château-Grillet, and the Hermitage wines. Côte-Rotie, a fine-coloured wine with a characteristic bouquet, comes from near the little town of Ampuis, seven miles south of Vienne. Unfortunately little is now made, and it is not easily obtained. Château-Grillet, whose vineyards are only a mile or two further south, near Condrieu, on the N86 road, gives a white wine which reminds some of a hock. Hermitage (or Ermitage) wine has never recovered from the attack of Phylloxera. It is nowadays a fine full wine but not a great one. In the early part of the nineteenth century it was acknowledged to rank with, or above, the great clarets and burgundies, but its delicacy has gone. The vineyards lie on the river slopes behind the little town of Tain (or Tain-l'Hermitage) and facing Tournon across the river. The two towns, with a population together of no more than 7,500, handle all the wines from the Hermitage vineyards: Crozes-Hermitage, l'Hermitage itself, and Tain l'Hermitage. Some white Hermitage is made.

In the southern part of the Côtes du Rhône *vignoble* are just two wines of note: the well-known Châteauneuf-du-Pape, and Tavel. The vineyards of Châteauneuf-du-Pape make almost wholly red wine, although a little white, which does not come into commerce, is produced. Across the valley from the village and vineyards of Châteauneuf-du-Pape are the vines which give Tavel, the best *rosé* wine of France, and therefore of the world. Tavel is made by a co-operative society of *vignerons*.

ALSACE (Map 7)

The vineyards of Alsace are on the left bank of the Rhine in the French *départements* of Bas-Rhin and Haut-Rhin. The Rhine occupies a rift-valley, and the very fertile soil known as *loess* was deposited by the wind in the hollow during the glacial periods. Alsatian wines, which are not greatly different from the other Rhine wines, the hocks, and the Mosels, are predominantly white. A century ago Alsace was famed for its straw-wines, but these are no longer made, and now wines are specified by the grape they were made from – Sylvaner, Traminer,

Riesling, with the name of the village rarely added. The best-known white wines are those of Ribeauvillé, Gubwiller, Riquewihr, Kaysersburg, and Ammerschwihr in the Haut-Rhin, and of Wolsheim, Molsheim, and Gertwiller in the Bas-Rhin. The Molsheim Riesling wine is called *Finkenwein*. The red wines of Ottrot and Marlenheim have some reputation.

JURA (Map 7)

The *vignoble* of the Jura, sometimes known as that of Arbois, or of the Franche-Comté, lies to the east of the Côte d'Or, and in fact is shared between three of the French *départements*: Haute-Saône, Doubs, and Jura. In this small region, where vineyards occupy the inhabitants for half the year, and the making of clocks and watches the rest of the time, there is a surprising variety of wines made. There are red and *rosé* wines, which are somewhat hard until they are a few years old: the most well known are referred to as Arbois wine (or, after the names of the grapes, Poulsard or Trousseau. In any case they come equally from Conliège, Menetrux, Poligny, and other villages.) There are the straw-wines (*vins de paille* – see pages 62, 90). During the drying the malic acid content decreases considerably and this contributes to the peculiar bouquet and flavour as much as the vinification, which is very slow, and takes place in small casks, in which the wine is aged for five years before bottling. It is a dessert wine which has been compared to a Sercial Madeira (by Mr Morton Shand). The most well-known wine of the Jura is known as Château-Chalon, or *Vin Jaune*, for it is yellowish-amber coloured. It keeps almost for ever and resembles a dry sherry in bouquet and flavour. This is understandable, for *flor* yeasts are present during the ageing, which takes place in part-filled casks for at least six years. It is bottled in dumpy bottles (*clavelins*), which hold only four-fifths of an ordinary wine-bottle (620 millilitres). Finally, white and *rosé* sparkling wines (L'Étoile and Vassange) have been made (by the true champagne process) since 1671.

SAVOY (Map 7)

The alps of the Savoy are of limestone and on the slopes of the deep valleys cut out by the Upper Rhône and the Isère are red and white vineyards. The white wines come from around Lake Annecy (whose vineyards can be seen in some of Cézanne's well-known landscapes of the district), and the valleys of the Rhône and Arve as they enter Lake Geneva. The well-known vineyards are those of Crépy (a dry wine), Roussette, Chignin, Lucey, Frangy, and l'Aïse. The red wines, which are rather like Beaujolais, come from Montmélian (there is a little too much *goût du terroir* in this wine), Conflans, Brison, Touvière, and La Côte des Cent Marches (Sain-Jean-de-la-Porte). But the most well-known drink of Savoy is cows'-milk, of the famed *crus* of Abondance and Tarentaise.

PROVENCE

Provençal wines may be all that John Keats hints at in his ode, but connoisseurs rarely show very much enthusiasm. There are some quarter of a million acres of vines in Provence, and the wines of Bandol and Bellet and Cargueiranne and Fréjus have some reputation, which is scarcely more than local. Cassis makes a greenish wine which can be obtained in nearby Marseilles and has a reputation based probably on the fact that it is highly recommended as an accompaniment to *bouillabaisse*.

LANGUEDOC (Map 8 and Plate 7)

Some parts of Languedoc such as Lozère and Haute-Loire make practically no wines; the wines of Ardèche belong to the Côtes du Rhône (page 149); the Haute-Garonne, chiefly a cereal-producing area, makes a few wines of rather trivial interest at Villaudric, Capens, and Fronton; in Tarn white wine is made in some quantity, but that which is not used as *vin de coupage* has no more than local interest. The three *départements* of Hérault, Aude, and Gard make altogether 330 million gallons a year, more than ten times as much as Australia, seven times as much as Germany. Nearly half of it comes from the vine-prairies of Hérault. There is no nonsense of delicacy and bouquet about it; it quenches thirst and that is enough. The wine of Hérault, Aude, and Gard is not *vin de garde*; it is drunk within a year, or else thrown away to make room for the next year's vintage. At Marsillargues, twelve miles north-east of Montpellier, the co-operative claims to have the largest wine-store in the world: it holds rather more than three and a half million gallons (but see p. 186). Highly efficient co-operative societies of wine-growers deal with the greater part of the wine.

Nevertheless, there is a certain amount of wine with individuality and quality made in Languedoc. Tavel, the *rosé* wine of the Rhône (page 150), belongs to another *vignoble*, but apart from this, Lirac and the Clairettes de Bellegarde and the Costières from the borders of the Camargue are drinkable wines, covered by their own *Appellations d'Origine*. These are from Gard. Besides the V.D.N. (page 134), Aude has the sparkling wine of Limoux (the 'Blanquette') and the wines of Fitou, both of some quality, and, in addition, the region to the south, on the slopes of the Corbières, produces more than twenty million gallons of wine which is at least not ashamed of its name (although it goes under the A.O.C. of Fitou). Similarly, the north of Aude and the south of Hérault share the Minervois wines, which are mostly red and have some reputation.

CORSICA

Corsica has little space on its rocky hide for vines, but there are a few small plains around the coasts which are easy to irrigate, and interspersed between the groves of oranges and mandarins are the vineyards of Cap Corse and Bonifacio, Ajaccio, Bastia, Calvi, and Sari. Except for the full red Cap Corse, the most well-known wines of the island are the luscious Moscatello and Patrimonio.

Luxembourg and Belgium

Luxembourg, so near the northern limit of viticulture, naturally makes wines with high acidity: wines which are inclined to be rather hard but which at their best are crisp and refreshing. The vineyard area is all in the south, by the Mosel, and the wines are named by village and *cépage:* Ahner Riesling, Machtumer Sylvaner, Wiltringer Riesling. Bottling and labelling is supervised by State officials.

The very limited vineyards of Belgium are in the Meuse valley. Both red and white wine is made, but the quantity nowadays is less than 50,000 gallons annually and dwindles year by year.

Spain
(Map 8)

The Spanish grape-grower, unlike the French and the German, does not suffer from unpredictable weather conditions, which make every year's vintage a gamble in Burgundy, Bordeaux, and the Rhineland. Consequently, in Spain the quantity of wine produced is steady at rather under 500 million gallons: about seventeen gallons per head of population. Spanish table-wines, for the same reason, are good and dependable. Schoonmaker, the eminent American expert, considered that the finer ones were (in 1935) 'about the best wines for the money in the world', and this statement is probably still true. Nevertheless, Spain, with all her large production, claims only one great wine, and that the fortified sherry.

Although the largely coastal area of Catalonia produces more wine than any other of the main divisions of the country, it is surprising how much is made in the high arid tableland (the *meseta*) which forms Central Spain. In New Castile, all of which is over 2,000 feet in altitude, the temperature drops thirty degrees during the night in July. It says much for the hardiness of the vine that it can flourish in these conditions. The annual rainfall is only 15 inches; fortunately spring is the wettest season. In summer the land is a semi-desert, the air hazy with dust: the well-known *calina*. Here is Don Quixote's home, La Mancha, and vinification methods have not changed greatly since the days of Cervantes. This region was badly hit by Phylloxera, and American stocks do not take well in the soil. The red wines of Val de Peñas (the Valley of Stones) in La Mancha are in general better than the white. All the same, the white are better than the district wines of many places in Europe, but they tend to be cloudy. They are dry and may contain as much as 15 per cent alcohol.

The most frequently exported of Spanish table-wines are those from the *Rioja* district in Aragon, near Logroño. Both red and white Riojas compare on at least equal terms with the general run of claret, burgundy, and Sauternes wines: not, of course, with the château products. They have been famous since the sixteenth century, and have more than recovered their ancient renown: this is due principally to the vigorous efforts of José Elvira, a pharmacist of Fuenmayor.

Catalan wines are predominantly red, although grey wines, made by fermenting white grapes on the skins, are very common in the country inns. Innumerable local wines, all worth drinking, are made, both on the mainland and in the Balearic Isles, chiefly from malvasia or garnache (grenache) grapes. Spanish local wines are sometimes very interesting and are always good.

Portugal

(Map 8)

The part of the valley of the Douro where port wine is made forms a very small fraction of the area of Portugal, but table-wines are made throughout the length and breadth of the country. The areas of most intensive cultivation are in the province of Minho, which lies north of Oporto and borders the Spanish province of Pontevedra; in the northern part of Estremadura, that is, to the north of Lisbon; and inland from Setubal, in the Sadao valley, which is just south of the Tagus. There are altogether nearly a million acres of wine vineyards in Portugal. A generation ago most of the ordinary wines of the country were exported to Brazil and France, but since then Brazil has greatly increased her own production and France can no longer dispose of all the wine she makes herself. It was the American Eighteenth Amendment which caused the almost catastrophic reduction in French imports from Portugal, for when she found the North American market closed, the French government put a very heavy duty on imports of wine to protect her *vignerons*.

In the beginning of the nineteenth century the wines from Colare, a few miles north of Lisbon, were popular in Britain, and are still among the best in Portugal. The Minho wines made around Monção are much drunk in the northern part of the country. Portugal makes very good *rosé* wines, especially at Mateus in Tras-os-Montes, and even pink champagne near Setubal. The best wines of the Sadao valley are the red, which are somewhat heavy. In the north of Portugal the vines are trellised, for here the cool westerly breezes from the Atlantic keep the temperature down. In the south, where the summers are very hot, the vines are kept pruned down to bushes.

Italy
(Map 2)

Italy has a vast area of vineyards (some nine million acres) spread all over the country. Three-quarters of this area is shared with other crops, however, but even taking this into consideration, Italy has a slightly greater net area devoted to vines than France, and some 20 per cent more than Spain. Unlike Spain, only about 3 per cent of the grapes are grown for the table. Italian vineyards suffered much during the war, for not only were fifty-six million vines destroyed, but several of the war years were very dry and there was much loss because the ground was neither cultivated nor fertilized, and the plants went unprotected against mildews and blights.

It is impossible to do more here than summarily list a few of the more well-known Italian wines, many of which may be bought of any wine-merchant in Britain. The most well known of Italian wines is the Tuscan, Chianti. Red Chianti can be a very fine wine, although it sometimes is not; white Chianti is never very interesting. The Chianti Hills, on the slopes of which the vineyards lie, form a range of some fifteen miles long which rise to almost 3,000 feet. Tuscany produces other interesting wines than Chianti: the Vin nobile of Montepulciano to the south and the Vernaccia of San Gimignano to the east, in particular. Montepulciano is a red which is apt to be a little rough until it has aged for a year or two; San Gimignano is pale yellow and not too heady. One of the best of the red wines of Italy, Barolo, comes from Piedmont. It is a full-bodied, deep purple wine with a fine aroma, which ages well. Barbaresco and Freisa are other red Piedmontese wines of repute. Soave is an excellent white wine from near Verona.

Lombardy produces much ordinary wine, but none of quality except that of the Valtellina, which is almost all exported to Switzerland, where it is sold as Veltlinerwein. Orvieto, from Umbria, is a fine white wine of long repute. It may be sweet or dry, but although the dry is the better for keeping, it has not the quality of the sweet. The hills around Rome are covered with vines and some of the grapes are allowed to become infected on the vine with *pourriture noble* (see page 62). These of course make sweet wines, of the general type of Sauternes. It is rather more than doubtful if they are ever much superior to an average Sauternes, but they have great fame as the 'Castelli Romani' wines: Frascati and Marino are the best. A dry variety of each is also made. They are white and share with Montefiascone ('Est-Est-Est') the honour of being the best wines of Latium. From Southern Italy a number of famous, but not really very interesting, wines come: Capri, either pale yellow or red; Falerno, probably quite unlike Horace's Falernian; the Apulian Sansevero, a pale yellow dry wine; Savuto, from Calabria, a full red wine; Lacrima Cristi, perhaps more famous for its name than for quality, which to that eminent and outspoken connoisseur, George Saintsbury, 'suggested ginger beer alternately stirred up with a stick of chocolate and a sulphur match'.

A considerable number of dessert wines are made in Italy (apart from Marsala, which has already been treated in Chapter 7). Of the dry there are the Malvasia and Vernaccio of Sardinia, and Zucco secco; among the sweet are the Sardinian Girò and Monica, various muscatels (*moscati*), and the Malvasia of Lipari.

Malta

Remembering the proximity of Malta to Italy and the long-standing commercial relations between the two countries, it is surprising that more and better wine is not made on the island. There are many vines, it is true, but wine is made only in the south, on a coastal fringe. Irrigation is difficult in Malta, and spring and summer are hot and dry. The heavy rains of the early part of the year have drained off or evaporated away long before vines need water. The wine is all consumed locally and is coarse and harsh.

Germany
(German Federal Republic) (Maps 9, 10, 11; Plates 16, 17, 18)

When all is said and done, there are only two countries in the world which can make table-wines of truly superlative quality, and one of them is Germany; hock enthusiasts have been known to say that both of them are Germany. The great hocks are undoubtedly unique (as are the great Bordeaux and burgundies). Since many of them, and those the finest, come from the most northerly fringe of the European wine-zone, it is clear that they can only be produced by taking scrupulous pains at every stage of the grape-growing and wine-making operations. Phylloxera has reached this area only in the last few years as an invasion of serious proportions, and such scourges as *Peronospera* (page 57) and cold summers are the chief enemies of the wine-makers of the Rhineland. Some German wines have the tendency to be too hard and acid, just as the wines of the hot countries tend to be too fat and bland. A poor hock approaches cider in taste, but a good one is outstanding for delicacy. German wines are, so far as comparisons can be made, more expensive than French, and this unfortunate fact seems to be dependent on the restricted area of the vineyards and on the climatic difficulties. France has over three million acres of vines, Germany barely 150,000. Eastern Germany (the German Democratic Republic) has a few small vineyards near Dresden in the Elbe valley, and around Freyburg in the valleys of the Saale and the Unstrut. The wine is mediocre.

The vineyards of the *Rheingau*, the premier wine district so far as quality is concerned and the most northerly, lie on the north bank of the Rhine from Rüdesheim up to Mainz. Since the river is flowing almost westerly at this point, we are going east. At Rüdesheim (Plate 16) the vineyards are high up on the hill and were very badly damaged by Allied bombers aiming at Bingen; even now they have not recovered completely. A few miles further up-river is Geisenheim, where the vineyards, on the Rothe Berg, give better wine on the western slope than on the eastern. It is at Geisenheim that the most famous of Germany's institutes for wine research is situated. Next there is the flatter land where are Winkel and Östrich, both famous for their vineyards. Just to the north is the most famous vineyard of all, the Johannisberger-Schloss, at the sound of whose name the devout doff their hats, for a Johannisberger Kabinett wine is one of the great wines of the earth. A few miles east is the Steinberger, second only to Johannisberger. Probably no vineyards anywhere are tended with the care lavished on these two. Each has its own farm attached, to supply the properly accredited manure and straw needed for the vines, visitors change into special footwear before they are admitted; the whole is an artistic as well as a scientific triumph. It seems almost a sacrilege to submit the nectar which is produced to the carnal operations of human metabolism. These wines are rich in sugar, fairly high in alcohol, and have a bouquet which returns to the palate for long after; they are wines to tempt Rechab himself (and his son Jonadab). The wines of the other villages of the Rheingau are often fine – Vollrads and Hattenheim, Eberbach and Erbach, Hallgarten and Eltville, and the very-near-great Rauenthaler – but none is Johannisberger or Steinberger. For the past century the Johannisberger vineyard has been owned by the family of Prince von Metternich; the Steinberger is the property of the State, and the Rauenthaler is distributed among a number of small proprietors. All three together cover scarcely more than 200 acres.

These fine wines are produced by allowing the *Edelfäule* (page 62) to attack the grapes in the first place, and in the second by selecting only those bunches which are fully ripe, rotten-ripe, and efflorescing sugar. Such wine is labelled *Spätlese* (gathered late) or *Auslese* (selected). A further refinement is to gather only those grapes in the bunches which are bursting-ripe. The wine from these is called *Beerenauslese* (selected berries). A *Kabinett* wine is one of these 'extra-special' wines, the inference being that it is equal to that put aside for the proprietor's own 'Kabinett'.

The wine of the *Rheinhesse* is by general consent considered not quite up to the standard in delicacy of that of the Rheingau. It is 'decidedly milder and softer,' says Mr Morton Shand, the well-known connoisseur, 'and apparently lighter in taste'. Here the districts are Nierstein in the first rank, with Oppenheim, Laubenheim, and Bodenheim jostling for second place. The Rheinhesse is a region of loess and red sandstone, well known for its fertility; it is farmed in small vineyards – for there is little else but the vine grown between Mainz and Worms – and instead of being planted predominantly with Riesling, like the Rheingau, the Sylvaner is the principal *cépage*.

Further up the Rhine from Worms the vineyards are of little but local significance. However, away to the west is the plateau of the Haardt, known variously as the Palatinate and the Rheinpfalz *vignoble* (or *Weinland*). The *Pfalz* is the largest of the German wine regions, with about 40,000 acres of vineyards. The vines here get more sun than those of the other German vineyards and give higher yields. The predominant *cépage* is Sylvaner, with Riesling and a little Traminer, although there is a certain amount of black grapes grown (some

3,300 acres) for making red wine, which is not exported. The (white) wine of the Pfalz does not rival in delicacy those of Rheingau or Rheinhesse; it is milder and less acid, and matures early to a comparatively short life. The important towns – or villages – of the Pfalz *Weinland* lie along the so-called Winestreet (*Weinstrasse*) which runs north from Neustadt, through Mussbach (with Gimmeldingen and Koenigsbach a mile or two to the west of the Street), Deidesheim and Forst – these two producing the best Palatinate wines – Wachenheim, Durkheim, and so to Kallstadt: a total distance of about eleven miles. Both to the north and the south of this short stretch are grown *Konsumwein*, very good on hot days, but not worth exporting.

Flowing into the Rhine at the *Deutsche Eck* at Koblenz is the Mosel, which winds so as to flow at different places towards every point in the compass. The best vineyards face south, so they appear sometimes on the left bank, as at Wehlen, Brauneberg, Piesport, and Trittenheim, sometimes on the right such as those of Zell, Zeltingen, Graach and Bernkastel, and Thron (or Dhron). These are all white wines: red vineyards scarcely exist on the Mosel. Some ten million gallons a year of still wine is produced between Zell and Trittenheim and some one and a half million gallons of sparkling Mosel (ten million bottles). Mosel is a very variable wine; it may be full and luscious with a magnificent bouquet, like a good Bernkasteler, Piesporter, or Wehlener, or it may be very acid, when it is locally called a 'three-man wine' (*Dreimännerwein*: for it takes the forcible persuasion of two men to induce the third to drink it). Mosels mature quickly and are best drunk when four years old or thereabouts. Rhine wines, on the contrary, have an average life of some fifteen years and have been known to be quite genial at the half-century.

These are the best of the German wines, but there are more restricted *Weinländer* in the valleys of the Saar, the Nahe, and the Ruwer, while ordinary wines are made in Baden and Württemberg. Saar wines incline to be thin but often have a fine bouquet; the best seems to be the Scharzhofberger. The wines of the Nahe, of which the best are from Bockelheim and Kreuznach, are rather light wines with not much flavour. Ruwer wines, of which some 300,000 gallons are annually produced, like those from Luxembourg, are acid and hard, but fresh and fragrant; according to M. André Simon, the best is that of Casel.

1. Bullock-cart going out in the early morning to bring in the vintage. In the Médoc

2. Vines pruned back before the growing season starts. *Les Grandes Murailles* vineyards at Saint-Émilion

3. The ripe grapes. The Bordeaux method of training the vine on wire supports

4. The gathered grapes. In the Médoc

5. A modern press-house. Chapoutier's at Hermitage, in the Rhône valley

6. The vat-house of a great claret vineyard. Château Latour, in the Médoc

7. The vat-house of a cooperative in the Languedoc. Trausse-Minervois, Aude

8. The vat-house of a large Australian vineyard. Seppelt's winery at Nuriootpa

9. The great Sauternes vineyard, Château d'Yquem

10. Terraced vineyards. At Hermitage, in the Rhône valley

11. One of the most ancient of all vineyards. Château Ausone, with the town of Saint-Émilion

12. Chablis and five of its great vineyards. Centre, Les Clos; right, Blanchot; left, Valmur, Grenouille, and Vaudésir (Les Preuses and Bougros lie to the west, beyond Vaudésir)

13. One of the greatest of the claret châteaux. Château Margaux

14. The vineyards of 'Sparkling Saumur'. In the Loire Valley

15. Grapes for the sweet wines of Roussillon (the 'V.D.N.').
Banyuls, on the shores of the Mediterranean

16. A well-known hock vineyard. The Rüdesheim slopes, with the town of
Bingen, in the Rhine valley

17. The vineyards of Piesport. On the Mosel

18. A Steinwein vineyard. In Franconia, Germany

19. The terraced vineyards of the Valais, in Switzerland

20. A vineyard overlooking Lake Geneva. At Marsens in the Vaud, Switzerland

21. A typical Australian vineyard. Seppelt's Dorrien winery, in South Australia

22. The pergola method of training vines. In Madeira

23. The private cellar of the Château Margaux in the Médoc

24. A cognac vineyard on the banks of the Charente

26. Sherry: The *lagars* *Messrs G. G. Sandeman & Co. Ltd*

25. The *remuage* of champagne

27. Sherry: Transporting must to Jerez

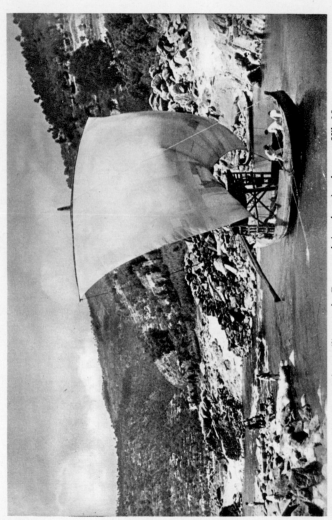

28. Port: A boat sailing up the Douro to bring the wine down to Vila Nova

29. Port: Vineyards, and the port of Pinhao on the Upper Douro

30. Brandy: Cognac stills

31. Whisky: A low-wines still and a wash-still

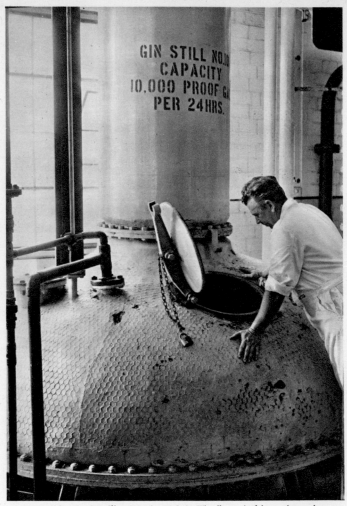

GIN STILL NO.16
CAPACITY
10.000 PROOF GA
PER 24 HRS.

32. Gin: A gin still at Peoria, U.S.A. The 'botanicals' are charged
through the manhole

Isolated and lonely in the sea of *Konsumwein* vineyards of Bavaria, by the old-fashioned town of Würzburg, stands a small *vignoble* which pretends that nothing has changed since the Middle Ages. A white wine is produced which is usually dry; it is sold in dumpy, broad-beamed flagons (*Boxbeutel*) with narrow necks (whose shape was borrowed by the Australians for some of their wine). Here the river Main writhes west to south, then north and again south, west once more, and then north through the Franconian countryside, and, enclosing the villages on its slopes – Iphofen and Ippesheim, Abtswind and Nordheim – grow the vines for Steinwein: Sylvaner, Riesling, and Traminer. It lives longer than any other beverage wine, it is a Rip-van-Winkle of a wine, which in a good year is said to resemble Chablis. 'It is a wine of noble breed and unsuspected strength of body,' says Mr Morton Shand.

The red wines of Germany, chiefly from Assmannshausen in the Rheingau and Ingelheim in Hesse, are exported in only small quantities (Britain took 460 gallons in 1954). Liebfraumilch is a white wine from no particular district, of reasonably good quality if it comes via a reputable importer.

Switzerland
(Maps 2 and 7; Plates 19 and 20)

Switzerland makes no great wines, but it is difficult to find wines which are more fresh and pleasant, more drinkable by those 'who don't care for wine'. They often have the slight latent sparkle which is more easily tasted than seen, and which is attributable to the malo-lactic fermentation (see page 86). Swiss vines are often grown on such steep-terraced slopes that it is surprising that they do not fall into the lake below.

A very large proportion of the surface of Switzerland is obviously as unsuited for the cultivation of vineyards as it possibly could be, but nevertheless scarcely a canton is without a few acres of vines: even Schwyz has its thirty acres. The main vineyard areas of Switzerland are (*a*) along the northern shores of Lake Geneva; (*b*) in the canton of Valais (Wallis), where are the highest vineyards in Europe; (*c*) in the southern Italianate canton of the Ticino (Tessin), and (*d*) on the shores of Lake Neuchâtel, although the wines of Zurich are not inconsiderable.

The finest white wines of Switzerland come from the terraced slopes of Lavaux, in Vaud, between Vévey and Lausanne. To the southeast of this district lies Le Chablais in the Rhône valley, and to the west, La Côte. The vineyards are all but continuous from Commugny in the west to Bex at the extreme south of the Chablais. The wines from the Chablais are rather higher in alcohol than those from the Côte and Lavaux.

Second in area and production only to the Vaudois vineyards are those of the Valais, high up in the Rhône valley, where the river runs south-west to Martigny before turning sharply to the north towards the Chablais and Lake Geneva. The vineyards are on the right bank and so have a southern exposure; even 'straw-wines' are made: *vin flétri*, sold as 'Valais malvasia'. Most of the wine of Valais, however, is fine table-wine: the white Fendant and the red Dole. Dole is undoubtedly the finest red wine of Switzerland. Each of the villages from Martigny at one end of the valley to Visp at the other has its cluster of vineyards above it on the hillside. From the vines of Visp, over 4,000 feet above sea-level, comes the so-called Pagan (*païen*) wine; Sierre, further west, gives the Glacier wine, bitter and white, which is stored for ageing high up on the mountain-top.

The wines of Neuchâtel are light, and more than any other show the sparkle ('the star'), so that they must be well iced. These are white, but the Neuchâtel red wines have an equally high reputation: the Cortaillod wines, labelled *œil de perdrix* (partridge eye), or *grain d'orge* (barley grain). Ticino wines have not the quality of those of Vaud, the Valais, and Neuchâtel, but a change is now being made from the old Bondola vine to the fine Bordeaux *cépage*, the *merlot*.

Swiss wines are scarcely exported at all and consequently it is not easy to purchase them in Britain.

Austria
(Map 2)

Before the First World War, Austria was one of the largest producers of wine, but since then she has lost the greater part of her vineyards to Yugoslavia, Hungary, Czechoslovakia, Romania, and Italy, so that now she is very low down on the list of producers (see page 24) and most of her wine is drunk within her own frontiers. Doubtless it contributes notably towards maintaining the proverbial Austrian gaiety. About 88,000 acres are planted with vines and almost all of this area is in the eastern part of the country. The north-eastern region, bordering on Moravia, produces most, but the finest wines of Austria come from further south, near Vienna and in the Burgenland.

From just west of Vienna come the flowery, delicate wines of Wachau. The vineyards of Dürnstein (or Durrenstein) and Krems are well known. Retz and Poysdorf, to the north, also make good wines. Nearer to the capital are the full strong wines of Sievering and Nussdorf: 'one has to bite them', it is said. Those from the nearby town of Grinzing are rather lighter and a little more acid.

It is from the south of Vienna, in Burgenland, the 'Wine quarter', that the two best Austrian wines come: Gumpoldskirchen and Voslauer. These are sometimes very fine indeed and in the days of Mozart and of Strauss were among the foremost attractions of Vienna. Gumpoldskirchen is a full, heavy, rather sweet white wine, which is very popular in Switzerland. Austrians will tell you that Gumpoldskirchen is not a '*Schoppenwein*', i.e. it is not to be tossed off in pints, as are the light country wines. Voslau is a village a little further to the south, and Voslauer is a red wine, milder than Gumpoldskirchen, but strong; we are approaching the large Neusiedler Lake and the climate is rather warmer than in the Danube valley.

Austrian wines are obtainable in Germany and Switzerland, but not elsewhere without much difficulty. It is a pity, for Austrian wines are made with an almost Swiss or German care. The wine school at Klosterneuberg, near Vienna, is internationally famous.

Yugoslavia
(Map 2)

The story goes that it was in Illyria, the eastern region of Yugoslavia, that Noah planted his vines. This legend is generally discredited. Nevertheless, there are vineyards in Illyria to this day. The principal wine-producing region of the country is in the north, in Slovenia (or Slavonia), although the wines of Istria and the Dalmatian coast have a high reputation. The vineyard areas of Lake Balaton in Hungary, of the Austrian 'Wine quarter' (*Weinviertel*) in the Burgenland, and of Slovenia-Dalmatia may almost be considered as one, trisected by the Treaties of Saint-Germain and the Trianon.

The climate of Slovenia, although somewhat central-European, is tempered by the sea breezes of the Adriatic and so has a touch of the Mediterranean about it. The summers are very hot, but cool, northerly winds sometimes blow down the corridor between the Apennines and the Balkan Mountains. These are the Bora winds, which become the Vardarac further south, and in Greece the Etesiae, in Turkey the Meltenie: St Paul's Euroclydon (Acts xxvii. 14). Slovene wines have long been famous: in the Middle Ages they were well known to the merchants travelling the long caravan route to and from the East; in the nineteenth century, Luttenberger (Ljutomer) wines contributed to the gaiety of Vienna. Many Yugoslav wines are named from the grape which produces them: the Riesling, the Pinot, the Sauvignon, the Sylvaner. The vineyards of Slovenia tend to cluster around Ptuj, where there is a wine-museum. Ljutomer wines have a very high reputation. They are particularly suave in taste and may have up to 16 per cent alcohol in fine years, such as 1945, 1947, and 1949. The white Haloze Pinot is a generally drier wine, although some Ljutomer wines are dry. At Maribor, the Sauvignon and Traminer wines are well known. At Radgona, on the very border of Hungary, dessert wines are made, such as the famous Tigermilk. The most renowned of Istrian wines, from between Fiume and Trieste, is the Kraski Teran, fermented on the skins for several months. Some think the best white wine of Yugoslavia is the Zilavka from the southern province of Herzegovina.

Yugoslav wines are produced by co-operative wineries. Collective farming has been only very partially successful in Yugoslavia; according to at least one authority 'it has failed', and the difficulties, due to 'bureaucracy without an efficient civil service', have been exacerbated by a run of five extremely bad harvests between 1948 and 1952. (In 1953, however, it was very good.) A considerable amount of Yugoslav wine is imported into Britain and is quite cheap. At the price it is reasonably good.

Central and Eastern Europe
(Maps 2, 12, 13)

Details of present-day methods of viticulture and vinification in Hungary, Czechoslovakia, Romania, and Bulgaria are hard to come by, and even before these states embraced communism, or were embraced by communism, accounts were scanty and untrustworthy. Broadly speaking, this part of Europe is geographically a single region, separated from the wooded plains to the north by the sweep of the Carpathians and their continuations, the Riesengebirge and the Erzgebirge, and by the Balkan Range and the Dinaric Alps from Mediterranean conditions. The great plain enclosed within these boundaries is traversed from west to east by the Danube, while a little to the north-east of its centre rise the Transylvanian Alps. Between these and the Carpathians lies the Great Pannonian Plain over which Hungary and Czechoslovakia spread themselves. To the south of the Transylvanian Alps lies the Danubian Basin: Southern Romania (Wallachia) and Bulgaria.

In all this area July is the hottest month, with a mean temperature of just over 70°; in January the mean is several degrees below freezing-point. These are means, not extremes, it should be noted. It is a typical continental climate. The rainfall is quite adequate in most parts: about twenty-five inches for the year, with a maximum of three to four inches in May and June.

CZECHOSLOVAKIA

Czechoslovakia, the most northerly of these states, with its Bohemian head jammed between the Riesengebirge and the Böhmer Wald and its tail nestling in the lee of the Carpathians, has its vineyards on slopes overlooking the great plains of grain and beet. They are principally in North Bohemia, in the Morava valley, and in the eastern tip of Slovakia. The vineyards of Bohemia are in the valley of the Labe (Elbe), where wine has been made since 1248 at latest. The Labe valley is broken hilly country between Prague to the south and the spa country – Carlsbad (Karlovy Vary), St Joachimsthal (Jachymov), and Marienbad (Marianske Lazne) – to the north. This is the most fertile part of Bohemia. The Moravian vineyards of Central

Czechoslovakia are on the slopes of a tributary of the Danube. Here it is low and gently undulating country, away from the river marshes, and the vines lie about thirty miles to the south and east of Brno (or Brunn) in a countryside devoted as much to cattle- and pig-rearing as to the ubiquitous beet and grain. Most of the vineyard area of the country is in the eastern part, in Slovakia. Here we are well down into the Danubian plain. Both social and agricultural conditions are poor (or were before 1939) in Slovakia. Houses are small and in clusters described rather as settlements than villages, without the gay colours of the Czech lands to the west. Much of the country is heavily forested and agriculture is primitive; the peasants are poorly educated and superstitious: it is the land of the were-wolf and the vampire.

HUNGARY

Hungary has for long been famed in the wine-marts of the world for its Tokay, a sweet wine made without fortification from over-ripe grapes. The village of Tokay or Tokaj itself is in North-eastern Hungary, on the river Tisa, a little place with only 6,000 inhabitants, not far south of the Slovakian vineyards. 'Imperial Tokay' is made from selected berries which have dried on the vine so that they burst and effloresce glucose. The must from them contains 30 or 35 per cent of sugar. It is added to must from ordinary ripe grapes in the proportion of 2 to 5 'Butten' (or *Puttonyos*) to the cask containing about 30 gallons. (One 'Butto' is about 30 pounds.) Fermentation is very slow in the cool cellars, but eventually a wine is obtained which contains between 10 and 15 per cent alcohol and the same amount of unfermented sugar and one or two per cent of glycerine: a luscious, expensive drink. A Tokay is specified by the number of 'Butten' to the cask. The furmint grape, all but peculiar to Hungary, is grown to make Tokay. From the same district comes the yellow fiery wine, Izamorodny (or Smorodni), which is also made from the furmint grape, in mediocre years when passulation on the vine is impossible. It has a fine aroma said to be reminiscent of 'fresh breadcrusts'.

The main vineyards of Hungary cluster around Lake Balaton in the south-west of the country, especially along the valleys of the little rivers which drain into the lake from all directions, but particularly into the north-east of the lake between Mecshety and Vorosbereny.

Much ordinary wine is made: Balatonfuredi is a fine dry white wine made from the Riesling grape. Many of the wines of Hungary are named by district and grape: Egri Rizling, Somlai Furmint, Mori Ezerjo, and Villanyer Rizling. (Mr John Brophy, in his charming book, *Ilonka Speaks of Hungary*, gives a very good summary account of Hungarian wines.)

ROMANIA

Romanian wines come from the southerly-facing slopes of the Transylvanian Alps, the Moldavian Plain to the east, and patches among the hills of Transylvania to the north. Romania's richest and largest vineyard area was in Bessarabia, the north-eastern province between the Dniester and the Prut, which passed to Russia in 1940 and so lost to Romania about 40 per cent of her production of wine. Wine is not a very popular drink in Romania; braga, the very small beer made from millet, is the common peasant drink. Nevertheless nearly a 100 million gallons of wine are produced annually.

BULGARIA

Bulgaria is almost wholly agricultural, with wheat and maize as the principal crops, but cultivation methods are primitive and yields are low. The Balkan range of mountains which runs east and west cuts the land into two all-but-equal parts: the Danubian plateau to the north and the Maritza (Mariza) valley to the south. The Danubian plain, divided from Romanian Wallachia only by the Danube, is a low chalk plateau with a covering of loess, and although partly open to the cold east wind from the Russian steppes and the Black Sea, is shielded to some degree by the north-curving spurs of the Balkan mountains along the river Pravadia. All along the Danube, but especially in the lee of the hills, are vineyards which produce wine of mediocre quality. There are very few towns in this region, but only largish straggling villages. The Maritza valley is warmer and the winters short and mild. Peaches and apricots, lemons, figs, and almonds flourish, as well as the grape-vine. There is much less rain than in the north and irrigation is necessary. Here the wines are better and have some ancient fame, for Plovdiv (Philippopolis), the central town, has a population of over 100,000 and has for many centuries been on the trade routes to the East.

GREECE (Map 12)

Greece has always grown large quantities of grapes, but for some centuries has dried the greater proportion and exported them as currants and sultanas. These are made from the small seedless grape, the corinth. The currant trade is a very old one; Hakluyt mentions that in 1534 Greek currants were part of the cargo of *The Holy Cross*. Almost all the wine made is either drunk in the country, or exported to France, Italy, and Germany for extending *vin ordinaire*, *vino da taglio*, and *Konsumwein*. The export of fresh grapes has assumed some importance in the last ten years or so. Much of the domestically-consumed wine is flavoured with sandarac, a resin obtained from the Aegean Isles and otherwise used for making varnishes (especially employed for coating lead pencils). This makes 'retsina' wine little sought after, since it gives the drinker the impression that the inside of his mouth has been flayed. Unresinated wine appears to be more popular than it once was, even in the rural districts; country wine is generally very acid and keeps badly, for the acid is acetic, the presence of which is due to crude methods of vinification.

Especially in the islands, several richer and more alcoholic wines are made for export and the luxury market. Not easily obtainable in Britain, they have some sale on the Continent, especially in Germany and Italy: Venice has been a good customer for the finer Greek wines since the fourteenth century. The most well known of these are *Mavrodaphne*, and *Samos* wine (Byron's 'Samian wine', which he three times demanded and then dashed down the bowl: *Don Juan* iii. 86). These are of the style of Madeira or Malaga: very sweet and with fairly high alcohol content. *Mavrodaphne* is the sweeter. *Santonin* is less heavy and rather lower in alcohol. The wines of Crete, grown on the narrow coastal plain in the north of the island, have no present importance.

Near and Middle East

TURKEY (Map 12)

Smyrna for long had a high reputation for its wines and its dancing-girls, but tastes change, and although much wine is still made at Smyrna (now named Izmir), it is not the best wine that Turkey can produce. As to dancing-girls, they fall outside the scope of the present volume, of course.

When Phylloxera struck at Western Europe, Turkish wines were imported by France and other devastated countries. Apart from this, a considerable amount of wine was sent all over the world, especially that of Bursa, on the Sea of Marmara. The red wine of Bursa had a high reputation. This trade ceased with the war of 1914–18. In 1943 a scheme of modernization of the Turkish wine industry, started in 1931, was making rapid strides, and by 1945 about thirty up-to-date wine-making establishments had been founded. Even now, however, only 3 per cent of Turkey's grapes go to make wine; 75 per cent become sultanas, currants or raisins, or *pekmez* (see page 91). More than one-third of the wine is made by the State, which produces all the spirits and liqueurs as well.

Most of the wines of Turkey are drunk within a year of making, as in all vineyard countries, but an increasing amount of *vins de garde* is made. Much of the land is unsuitable for viticulture or indeed for agriculture, but Turkey is underpopulated and about three-quarters of the people live off the land, although at a low standard. The country is very much underdeveloped. All the grain grown is consumed domestically; and cereals are the principal crop. Nevertheless, grapes are cultivated widely and good wine is made in various parts of the country. The white and red wines of Hasandede and Kalecik of the Ankara region improve on keeping, but the Çubuk wines made nearby are best drunk young. Further south, at Isparta, although most of the grapes are grown for eating, the good red wine of Siyah Dimrit is produced, with 14 per cent alcohol, yet not deficient in acid. In ancient Cilicia, Antep (Gaziantep) and Kilis give fairly good red and white wines, but those of Tarsus, famed in antiquity, are mediocre, for the grapes ripen by the end of July and the wines lack acidity and body. The best wines of Turkey are those of Elazig (Mezre, Mezere, Yeni-Harput), some 350 miles east of Ankara, deep in the mountains of Asia Minor. The best Elazig wine, called Bull's Eye (Okuzgozu), is so deeply coloured that after keeping it a year or two, the pigment forms a crust in the bottle. Both Okuzgozu and Bogazker (i.e. the strangler: it is sometimes too high in tannin) often contain 15 per cent alcohol. The wines of Thrace and the Marmara littoral are plentiful, and at Tekirdag, some seventy-five miles west of

Istanbul, much very ordinary wine is made. The good wine of this area is Papaskarasi, which is red, and fermented for a fortnight until quite dry.

The addition of resin to Turkish wines, at one time common, is now illegal and all but obsolete. Turkey exports no wines to Britain, and little elsewhere except to her immediate neighbours, but doubtless one day the rather stumpy and wide-necked bottles of Papaskarasi and Bull's Eye will appear on the English market.

CYPRUS

The wines of Cyprus, once so famous, are but the ghosts of themselves. Commandaria, formerly the analogue of a Johannisberger *Spätlese* or Château d'Yquem, is now described as resembling a mixture of 'inferior port, prune juice, and treacle'. The Commandaria vineyard, founded in the fourteenth century by the Knights Templars, made the wine from passulated grapes, which were fermented in earthenware jars of five or six gallon capacity. In the 1860s Thudicum found it still being made in the same way: a dull red wine, he said, 'a little sweet, with astringent by-taste, fiery, of great and peculiar flavour and a fine bouquet.' The flavour was derived from resins, clove, the scented Rhodus wood, and other constituents, which were tied in a bag and suspended in the wine. Much of the wine of Cyprus is made by the villagers for their own consumption by the methods of their forefathers: it is stored in rough earthenware jars which are sometimes of 200 gallons capacity, and transported in goatskins. Beer bottles are commonly used for transport and sale in small quantities. Cyprus wine of commerce has no very high reputation. The manufacture is concentrated in the Limasol district, where there are large concrete fermentation vats. The factories are at Mallia and Perapedhi. France imported a fair quantity before the Second World War for mixing. Egypt is the largest market: a small amount comes to Britain.

ISRAEL

Of the wines of ancient Israel nothing definite is known and until the end of the nineteenth century they were peasant-wines of no importance. However, after Phylloxera, which appeared in 1890, had been controlled the industry was organized and modern methods introduced. This revolution, powerfully encouraged by Baron Rothschild, consisted in the careful selection of the best varieties of French and Spanish vines, improved presses, refrigeration – necessary in this hot climate – precautions against vine-diseases, central warehouses, and the formation of export companies. It resulted in overproduction by 1905, and although the industry was reorganized, after the First World War production diminished steadily and became quite unimportant again. Recently it has been revived once more.

The soil is good. It is mostly a light sandy limestone, and although it needs irrigation, this is nowadays being provided, especially from the waters of Jordan. Israel is America's best customer for sprinkler and irrigation equipment. The chief vineyards are in the plain of Megiddo (Esdraelon) in the north and along the narrow coastal plain. French (aramon, carignane, carbernet-sauvignon, malbec, semillon) and Spanish scions are grafted on to American *porte-greffes* and the vines are normally pruned *en gobelet*, that is, in a compact bush. Besides the whole gamut of vine diseases known elsewhere, Israel vines are subject to peculiar maladies, such as the Jaffa Disease. The sirocco, here known as the *chamsin*, often burns the plants as in the North African vineyards.

Israel wines are named, it would seem rather irresponsibly, according to the *cépages* used or the type. Muscat, porto, 'Sauterne' are white; Alicante and Médoc are red. A few years ago it was announced that they would be available in Britain and elsewhere, but there is no sign of them, and it may be concluded that sales are confined to the Jewish communities.

LEBANON, SYRIA, AND JORDAN

Local wines of sorts are made in the more fertile parts of Syria, Lebanon, and Jordan, but agricultural methods are exceedingly primitive. Fertilizers are scarcely known and farm implements are usually of wood. It is only the coastal plain which is suitable for viniculture at present, although such tracts as the valleys of the Orontes, the Euphrates, and the Litani could be utilized if drainage and irrigation works were undertaken. Mr Fedden, in his recent book *Syria* (Hale,

1955), says that in the Bekaa valley, between Beyrout and Damascus, he found a 'quite good' *rosé* wine. This area is in Lebanon. In Syria, more arrack than wine is made, and the latter is scarcely drinkable.

ALGERIA, TUNIS, AND MOROCCO (Map 14)

If the Mediterranean between France and Algeria were rather narrower it would save the merchants of Marseilles, Sète, and Algiers an enormous amount of trouble, for then a pipe-line could be laid beneath the sea and the wine pumped north through it. Algeria makes almost ten per cent of the world's wine and nearly all goes to the French mainland, for mixing with the deluge from the Midi to make *vin ordinaire*. Algerian wines are made with the greatest care; the experts of Maison Carrée are for ever feverishly searching for new ways to make the grape yield half a drop more wine, for half a drop per grape means nearly a million more gallons of wine every year.

Behind the coastal plains and the low hills which lie at their back are long narrow strips of fertile land, somewhat elevated, with plenty of sun but barely enough rain. The most famous is the Plain of Mitidja, a closed slot some sixty miles long and ten miles across. This is the headquarters of the great French agricultural colony in Barbary. Further east is the Plain of Bone, of about the same size. These regions were well known to the Romans and, once the Carthaginians were subdued, supplied the imperial capital with a great part of its bread. After the Franco-Prussian war of 1870, France turned to her African colonies to regain her lost prestige and began to cultivate the fertile Barbary *tell*. French settlers ousted the natives and by the beginning of the present century some 300,000 acres were under vines; at present the total area of vineyards is about a million acres. The region is admirably suited for making wine, through not for making very good wine. The Atlas Mountains to the south protect the *tell* from the worst effects of the Saharan sirocco, and labour is cheap. The temperature is high, but if this causes difficulties in vinification, it also increases the sugar in the grapes.

The kind fairies who were present when Algeria rose from the ocean, many million years ago, missed only one gift: water. True, in the winter the weather is under the control of depressions which move along the Mediterranean from the south-west and bring 20 or 25 inches of rain, but rain in the winter does not interest the *vigneron*. It is August and September rain that he would like, but there is never an inch between the two months, and irrigation is a necessity. Consequently the Government has been obliged to undertake a vast programme of dams and canals. The ground beneath the soil is sandstone and so elaborate spillways of concrete are necessary. A new industry of armoured slabs and prefabricated, prestressed pipes has grown up in Algeria to supply them.

The wines are not fruity, with a taste one remembers long after, like a good claret or hock, but they are satisfactory for quenching the thirst.

French writers assert that certain Algerian wines, such as Royal Kebir, those of the Clot Fallet of Médéa, of the Côteaux de l'Harrach, of Mascara and Miliana, have a high and well-merited reputation on the English market.

Although there has been a tendency to emulate the Midi and to form co-operatives in Algeria, most of the vineyards are in the hands of large producers.

The principal vineyards of Tunisia are behind Bizerta. When the protectorate was formed, in 1883, large land-owning companies were formed to cultivate it and much was expected of the country. However, the results did not come up to expectations, and first cereals, then olives, began to replace the vines. Italian labour was imported. More recently vineyards have again increased. They are in much smaller units than formerly and many are owned by Italians.

Morocco produces insufficient wine for her own needs, and the wineries are owned principally by the Jewish community, which is large, for making their Vin Cachier. The vineyards are chiefly near Casablanca, Marrakesh, and Meknes. Near Marrakesh a reservoir as large as Lake Annecy has recently been dammed for irrigation, for water is almost as scarce here as in Algeria.

What used to be Spanish Morocco produces only a trickle of wine.

Russia
(Maps 12 and 13)

Within the confines of Russia, every variety of climate except tropical is found. The vineyard regions are naturally almost wholly confined to the most southerly parts of the country, but it is claimed that the agronomist Michurin has bred vine-strains capable of flourishing as far north as Moscow, that is, in latitude 55° 45' north, on the same parallel as Berwick-upon-Tweed and Lake Athabaska, and even in the Amur valley, north of the Gobi Desert (where a 'sound, pleasant wine' is made, so it is said). The wines of Russia are made in (a) Bessarabia, immediately bordering on Romania, (b) the southern Crimea, (c) areas north and south of the Caucasus between the Black Sea and the Caspian, (d) around the mouth of the Volga, and (e) in the Central Asian oases of Tashkent, Samarkand, and Bukhara. Minor vineyard areas are in the Middle Volga region of Kuibishev and a little further west, in the Voronezh district between the Volga and the Don. Although a number of indigenous *cépages* are used, much of the wine comes from pinot, riesling, aligote, semillon, cabernet and muscatel stocks imported from the West, and is called 'claret', 'burgundy', and so on.

The best wines come from the limestone slopes behind Yalta, on the south coast of the Crimea. This is the Riviera of Russia, with a Mediterranean climate: hot dry summers, mild winters, and about 20 inches of rain. Many fruits grow here which flourish nowhere else in Russia. The wines of Yalta are inclined to be full-bodied and rich; they have been famous since Russia annexed the Crimea at the end of the eighteenth century, especially that from the Massandra vineyards. They are made to resemble Madeira, port, and Tokay, although they mostly contain no more than 16 per cent alcohol. Poorer white table-wines, with between 9 and 11 per cent alcohol, are also made in considerable quantities. They resemble the *Konsumwein* of Rheinhessen and the Pfalz. The largest cellars in Russia are at Massandra and hold over a million gallons of wine for ageing, in cask and bottle.

The Crimean vineyard area extends eastwards across the straits of Kersch into the Kuban. Anapa is the chief centre, and riesling and cabernet stocks provide good white and red wine. Much 'Soviet Champagne' and brandy is also made between Anapa and Gelendshik.

The Bessarabian wines, once Romanian, are largely made from good French vines, planted during the nineteenth century. Much of the population has for long been Ukrainian and in 1940 Russia annexed the area: part became Ukraine and part the Moldavian Republic. Before that date this was the best wineland of Romania, and its champagne and brandy are still famous.

Between the Caucasus mountains and the Armenian highlands to the south is a region of broken country rising in places to over 5,000 feet, wherein are enclosed high valleys, like those of Kashmir and Bolivia. Here the winters are mild, for the icy winds cannot reach into these enclaves, and the summers are dry and sunny. Some open into the Caspian or the Black Sea, like the eastern Kura valley of Azerbaijan, just north of Baku, where cotton and tobacco cover the river plains and vines the slopes. In Georgia, in western Transcaucasia, is the valley of the Rion, with hot damp summers, where the wine is full and dark with much iron, drawn up from the deep red laterite soil. Between these two, in the centre of the Transcaucasus, lies Lake Sevan, more than 6,000 feet up, where irrigation is necessary to grow the vines and other fruits for which the district is famous. The best Armenian wines are from Lake Sevan, and the vines are the Garandmak and Mskhali for table-wines and the Voskeat and Chilar for sherry. These are apparently native *cépages*. Since Mount Ararat is near, perhaps Noah knew them. Armenian wines are sometimes very good, especially perhaps the sweet white ones, and there is a flourishing export trade.

The wines of the middle and lower Volga and of Voronezh are *vins ordinaires*.

The ancient cities of Turkestan – Bukhara, Samarkand, Tashkent, and Ferghana – once no more than clusters of caravanserais where the merchants from the Far East halted their camels on their journey to Europe, are now large industrial cities: Tashkent has over half a million inhabitants and Samarkand about 150,000. A vast system of canals has persuaded the two rivers of the region, the Syr Darya and the Amu Darya, to irrigate the land, and although the climate is extremely continental, with 'Siberian winters and Egyptian summers' the soil is the very fertile loess, and cotton, sugar-beet, and rice are grown, as well as many vines. The vineyards are extensive enough to supply all Russia with wine, but in fact 90 per cent of the produce goes for table grapes or is dried for raisins. The Central Asian 'Magarach' Institute publishes much experimental work on fortified wines, champagne, and rum, as well as a wide range of investigations on fermentation procedures, yeast strains, and the ageing and diseases of wines. This area is now divided between the Uzbek, the Tadjik, and the Kirghiz S.S.R.

Developments in Russia are chiefly concentrated on improving the quality and increasing the quantity of fortified and sparkling wines. Perhaps the Russian belief may be justified, that by the 1970s the production will be second only to that of France.

Persia
(Map 13)

Wine has been made in Persia from the most ancient times and was celebrated in poetry many centuries before Omar Khayyam. Some vines, said to be as old as Persepolis itself, grow on the mountain slopes near Shiraz. Their stocks are as thick as tree-trunks. Once the wines of Khurasan and Mazanderan were famous, but nowadays Isfahan wine bears the palm, although that of Tabriz is said by experts to be better. It is towards the north, on the southerly slopes of the Elburz Mountains, that vines grow best, for damp winds come occasionally from the Caspian Sea and irrigation is not such a problem as in the south. The making of wine is mostly in the hands of Armenians and Jews, and vinification methods have probably changed little in the past few millennia. Grapes are brought in by night, trodden, and the juice left to ferment for three weeks or so. Then the wine is strained into the large jars known as *qarabas* (or carboys) and sealed up with matting and mud for a few months. Upon keeping, the wine becomes paler and is said to resemble sherry. More often, however, sugar, raki, saffron, and hemp extract are added. There is no export trade.

India
(Map 13)

It may be that one day the assiduous workers of India and Pakistan will uncover sufficient information to enable a coherent account of the vineyards of early India to be pieced together. At present there are only the most exasperatingly exiguous fragments of information. Certainly wines of some sort were known something like twenty or more centuries ago. They were certainly used medicinally, and for religious sacrifices. Spirits may have been made from them. Whatever happened in the vineyards, wherever they were, under the Hindu dynasties of the first dozen centuries A.D., there is no doubt that the coming of the Muslims at the beginning of the thirteenth century enormously increased their importance. It is a little odd to read of the enthusiasm which the Grand Moguls showed for wine. However, Muslims are promised a paradise with 'rivers of delicious wine', and to the elect 'choice sealed wine shall be given' (Koran: Suras 41, 47). Akbar (1542–1605) encouraged wine-making in Kashmir, and Jahangir, his son (d. 1628), struck coins depicting himself brandishing a cup of wine. In the seventeenth century there were well-known vineyards also at Golconda, Surat, Kandahar, and Pegu (in lower Burma). Golconda was well known for its white wines.

In the nineteenth century the wines of Kashmir alone had any fame. A pleasant red wine, *opiman*, a white wine, *katchebourie*, said to resemble Chablis, and the poorer *kawaury* were exhibited at the Calcutta Exhibition of 1884. The vale of Kashmir, to which the fantasy of Shangri-la may owe something, is a valley among the Himalayas with the climate of Central Europe and the latitude (34° N.) of Los Angeles and the Atlas Mountains. It is some 5,250 feet above sea-level, so that while the winters are severe, spring and autumn are mild and delightful and summer warm. Already well known as a tourist and honeymoon resort, it is obviously moving towards its destiny as the Blackpool of *fin-de-siècle* trippers. The Bordeaux vines of the nineteenth century were devastated by Phylloxera in 1890 and American vinestocks were then introduced, with Médoc and Barsac scions. The orchards produced other fruits than grapes, and Srinagar apple brandy had considerable fame. The vineyards then occupied just under 400 acres, about twice the size of Château Lafite or Château Margaux. They were under State management but did not pay. The future of Kashmir wine is highly problematic since both India and Pakistan are inimical to alcoholic drinks.

Australia and New Zealand
(Map 16; Plates 8 and 21)

As prompt as Van Riebeck at the Cape, Captain Arthur Philip planted the first vines of Australia at Farm Cove near Port Jackson, now known as Sydney, in 1788, the year of the founding of New South

Wales. It was nearly half a century later before any further development took place. In 1824 James Busby arrived from Britain, wrote three books on viticulture and expended much enthusiasm, which at last resulted in the foundation of vineyards on the Hunter River and elsewhere. Commercial wine-making started about 1840, and in 1854 the first shipment of wine was sent to Britain – 1,389 gallons.

At present three-quarters of Australia's wine comes from the vineyards of South Australia. The river Murray, which divides Victoria from New South Wales and then flows down through South Australia to the Southern Ocean at Encounter Bay, is fringed with vineyards on both sides, and there are also many thousands of acres on the slopes of the hills between its lower reaches and Adelaide, on the Gulf of St Vincent. At the beginning of the century, South Australia made less than one million gallons of wine – about one-third of Australia's production; nowadays the figure is over twenty-five millions. On the slopes of the Lofty Mountains, which extend behind Adelaide northwards, are the *vignobles* of Morphett Vale, Reynella, where the vineyards date from 1838, McLaren Vale, Magill, where Penfold's have large holdings, with the Angaston 'Yalumba' vines of Smith and Sons, and Seppeltfield, Tanunda, and Nuriootpa of Seppelts further still, until Clare, the most northerly vineyard of South Australia, is reached.

By means of a series of locks, the waters of the Murray river are impeded on their way to the sea and constrained to irrigate the riverine vineyards of Waikerie, Renmark, and Berri, in South Australia, and also those extending along the right bank in New South Wales: Mildura, Swan Hill, Cobram, and so along to Corowa and Albury, which face across the river the irrigation vineyards of Rutherglen, Chiltern, and Barnawartha in the state of Victoria. Many of these vineyards in the Murray valley are run by co-operatives. Further south the Geelong vineyard once flourished, where Phylloxera first appeared on Australia's soil, and away to the northwest of Melbourne is Great Western, another of Seppelt's large installations, where sparkling wine was first made successfully by Irvine soon after 1887. The vineyards of Hunter River, Parramatta, and Minchinbury are near Sydney. Much of the vineyard area here specializes in light wines of the type of claret and hock, while the Murray river vineyards make the heavier and more alcoholic 'Australian Burgundy' class of wine.

Australian wine is the typical 'standard wine', dependable, full, high in alcohol, never bad but never great, lacking only delicacy and distinction of flavour. The Australian *vigneron* has the enormous asset of an equable climate; his difficulties are due to the exiguous water supply, the long haul to the world's markets, and the protective tariffs which prevent his wine reaching the large customers of the world. Australia is in one of the driest belts of the earth; her rivers are few and most flow only for a month or two in the year. The interior has no water; Tasmania has too much and is too cold; Queensland has fierce and often protracted deluges, but is too hot: good for the sugar-cane but bad for the vine. The rain of the south-east, where over 90 per cent of the vineyards are sited, comes from the anticyclones driving in from the Tasman Sea, and deposits on the hills to swell the Murray and its tributaries. Snow is very rare indeed and in many places has never been seen. The tropical cyclones, the 'Willy-Willies', never reach the vineyard areas, but very hot, dry winds (the 'Brick Fielders') sometimes come scorching out from the interior. Many vineyards have never known Phylloxera; the only areas now considered to be prone to it are some just south of Sydney and a patch on the Murray (Rutherglen and Corowa). Australia finds that the Cabernet Sauvignon, the Malbeck, and the Palomino, the great wine-grapes of Europe, are not well suited to climatic (and economic) conditions there, and the Frontignac, the Riesling, the Hermitage, the Pedro Ximenes, the Semillon, and the Rosaki (or Waltham Cross, a table variety) are the most-grown *cépages* in the east. In Western Australia, Cabernet Sauvignon is grown for claret-type wines, Semillon for both sweet and dry wines.

Australian vines are widely spaced: there is no need to conserve the warmth, and by planting at anything from 8 to 10 feet to 14 feet between rows it is easy to employ mechanical cultivation. Some of the vines are trellised nowadays and lorries pass between the rows at vintage-time – in March and April – to carry away the grapes piled into them.

All the larger wineries and many of the smaller ones propagate their own pure yeast strains for fermenting in the concrete vats, which vary from 1,000 to 2,000 gallons in capacity. As in most of the warmer *vignobles* of the world, where the grapes ripen rapidly and fully, it is common practice to add tartaric acid and tannin. Even so, Australian wines mature very rapidly in cask, and are bottled early. Imported wood must be used for the barrels: local woods are unsuitable.

The vineyards of Western Australia are chiefly close to Perth, the State capital, some 1,300 miles distant from Adelaide. This *vignoble* differs in several respects from those in the east, and if Australia ever breaks into the fine-wine market, it may be with West Australian wines. The soil, which is all alluvial, varies from the light and sandy clays to marls of heavier consistency, and the grape-varieties suitable for each type of soil are selected so that a single vineyard may give dry, claret-type wines in one part, and port-type wines only a short distance away. The vineyard area extends to the foot of the Darling Ranges, but cultivation does not extend up the hillsides. The climate is often compared to that of the French Riviera. The rainfall is about 34 inches, nearly all of which falls in June, July, and August. Perhaps Western Australia has the best climate in the Commonwealth for growing the wine-grape – at least in the Swanland district. Differences in soil and exposure in the area allow a remarkably wide range of wines to be made, of quality outstanding among the standard wines of the world. Unfortunately, the cost of transport overseas of fine wines is prohibitive, and the local palate is uneducated. The greater part of the wines are produced by two large British-owned companies, but small *vignerons* make a certain amount for local consumption.

Australian viniculture and vinification have the reputation of being at the very least as efficient as anywhere else in the world. The Commonwealth laws concerning food hygiene are very strict, and from the technical point of view no criticism is possible of Australian wine-making. No *vignoble* can change its soil or vary its climate. If in some corner of the Swan River vineyards a great wine were produced, it is doubtful if it could make headway in the world's markets against the centuries-old reputation of the great clarets and hocks, the vast French publicity-potential, and the strongly entrenched and largely justifiable prejudice of the connoisseur.

The bulk of Australian wines is made by large companies, such as Seppelt, Penfold, Emu, Hardy (Tintara), and so on, but there is a considerable number of small growers – many of Slav extraction in Western Australia – who sell their grapes to the large companies for vinification.

New Zealand is one of the smallest wine-producers of the world, but it has the distinction, perhaps unique, of more than doubling its output since the war. About half a million gallons are now made on the average, by two hundred wine-makers, but scarcely a half of these *vignerons* depend solely on wine-making for their livelihood. Most of the grapes are grown either near Auckland, or in the Hawke's Bay district, both in North Island; the climate here is excellent for vines, especially perhaps in the drier Hawke's Bay region.

South Africa
(Map 15)

The grape vine has been grown at the Cape for just three hundred years. The land near modern Cape Town was settled by the Dutch in 1652; in 1655, with commendable promptitude, the first vines were planted. Van Riebeck, the Governor, obtained vines from Holland, which were presumably French and German stocks, and also from Spain, Italy, Brazil, and elsewhere. The first wine was made, as soon as the vines were mature enough, on 2 February 1659. The oenology of few countries is so well dated and documented. The wine-making industry languished somewhat until 1688, when French Huguenots settled in the districts behind Cape Town, and by the early eighteenth century South African wines, especially that of Constantia, were famous throughout Europe.

The Cape vineyards are all in the western part of the province within 150 miles of Cape Town: around Cape Town itself, Paarl, Stellenbosch, and Malmesbury on the seaward slopes and coast south and west of the Drakenstein Mountains, around Tulbagh, Worcester, Robertson, and Montagu in the Little Karoo between the Drakenstein and the Langeberge, and between Oudshorn and Ladismith, in the gentle depression between the Langeberge and the Swartberg ranges. The first area differs in many respects from the second and third and is known as the Coastal Belt, in contradistinction to the others, both of which lie in the Little Karoo. Throughout, the soils vary so much that generalization is difficult. By suiting the *cépages* grown to the exposure, the soil, and the micro-climate of the particular district, wines of a wide variety of types may be made. Robertson is the largest producer in Cape Province, with Worcester close behind, then Paarl and Stellenbosch running together next.

Cape sherry has some distinctive quality, but none of the beverage wines are outstanding when compared with French or German wines. They are reliable, for the climate of Cape Province is reliable, unlike that of Bordeaux, Burgundy, or the Rhine, but they are just 'standard' wines and no more.

The best red beverage wines come from the Constantia district, near to Cape Town itself, although in this region the vineyards are giving way to the demands of housing for the workers of the city, and in any case produce more table-grapes than wine-grapes. The more full-bodied red wines of South Africa come from near Stellenbosch and Paarl. Paarl wines are generally fuller-bodied than those from Stellenbosch. Bordeaux grapes such as Cabernet Sauvignon and some of the old Rhône *cépages* are used. It is perhaps in the field of the red beverage wines that South Africa may one day establish herself in the fine-wine market.

Although some white wines of better quality are produced near Stellenbosch and Tulbagh, there is little of interest in the white wines of the Cape, and this is not altogether suprising. There is too much sun, with a consequent loss of delicacy in flavour and aroma of the wines. The high temperatures have the additional effect of causing the wines to finish maturing before they have developed their best qualities: the curse of the warmer *vignobles*, and largely due to low acidity in the must. The best white wines come from districts where the weather is the arch-enemy: the Rhine and Mosel, Burgundy, and Sauternes. In spite of the inferiority of Cape white to the red wines, four-fifths of the wine made is white.

For countries like South Africa and Australia, the hope for the future seems to be to establish fortified varieties, of port, Madeira, and sherry types, for the lack of delicacy in the flavour and bouquet of their wines then becomes of little or no importance. Almost half of Cape wines are fortified – 47 per cent to be exact. South African sherry-type wines are establishing a name for themselves and are satisfactory for almost all but the connoisseur. In the beginning of the nineteenth century, between a quarter of a million and a million gallons of wine were exported annually. These passed as Madeira: unfortunately the market for Madeira-type wines is comfortably saturated by wines from Madeira nowadays. Nevertheless, approaching three million gallons of wine are exported each year from the Cape now: a good deal more than pre-war (under two millions in 1938). Just about half of this comes to Great Britain, and Scandinavia, Holland, Germany, and the Commonwealth countries take the rest.

Most of the wine-producers of South Africa have organized themselves into the K.W.V. – the Ko-operatieve Wijnbouwers Vereniging: the Co-operative Wine-Growers Association, a limited company. This was originally founded in 1918, and after the inevitable early troubles with the selling side of the industry and with independent growers, the Government conferred considerable powers on the Association, which in fact controls the growing, vinification, and distilling trades. It has some five thousand members.

Wine is cheap in South Africa: four shillings is the price of a bottle of a good-quality Cape red or white.

America

Over 10 per cent of the world's wine is made in America and of this more than half comes from the Argentine. All but a very small proportion is consumed either in its country of origin, or at any rate within the continent. Chile is the only American country which exports wine to Europe. This situation would probably be changed if the dollar area were enlarged, by some miracle, to include European countries. Nevertheless, it is generally agreed on all sides that America makes no great wines, and it is extremely doubtful if any really fine wines are produced. The most that can be said of Chilean wines is that they are good value for their price in England. Ecuador, Colombia, and Venezuela are the only countries (with the exception of the toy republics of Central America) which have no wine vineyards.

The United States produces a wide range of wines, which are made with the greatest care and under strict control. Like Australian wines, they are typically 'standard' wines, using the phrase in the special sense described on page 21. They are made for a public which above all others in the world insists on having a product which shall be predictable in quality.

THE UNITED STATES (Map 17)

The first attempts to cultivate the vine in North America were made as early as 1564, forty-three years before the colony of Jamestown, Virginia, was started. Planting began seriously over two hundred years later, in 1767, when a company of Franciscan friars established themselves in California. They domesticated the wild grapes of the district; they imported vines the progeny of which are still grown ('Mission grapes'), though not to produce very good wine.

Until 1848, California was Mexican, and only fifteen years before this date the Mexican Government secularized the missions, when the production of wine ceased for all practical purposes. Later, although Longworth in Ohio tried to cultivate French and Madeira vines in the United States, progress was slow. Longworth's experiments were a failure. Others introduced European vinestocks with rather more success, and by 1860 California was producing about 200,000 gallons of wines of various types, but it was the Ohio River region which had the name of the Rhineland of North America. This was before the overproduction slump in the 1870s. By 1875, many of the vineyards were abandoned. In 1879 interest revived, largely because the great influx of European immigrants was clamorously demanding *vin*, *vino*, and *Wein*. Between 1881 and 1888 the vineyard acreage increased more than four times. By the mid-1890s, California was producing 20 million gallons of wine a year, and Ohio was nowhere. Of this wine, two-thirds was drunk in California itself and most of the rest was consumed by nostalgic and thirsty European immigrants in the other states.

Nevertheless, a certain amount was exported even then, and 'Californian "Big Tree" Burgundy' was widely advertised in Great Britain. For burgundy, this was remarkable, for it had nearly 15 per cent alcohol, a figure which is more than rare in Burgundian burgundy.

Production advanced slowly until 1919. On 18 October 1919, Congress passed the eighteenth Amendment to the American Constitution. This, popularly known as the Volstead Act, forbade 'the manufacture, sale, or transportation of intoxicating liquors within, the importation thereof into, or the exportation thereof from, the United States and all territory subject to the jurisdiction thereof, for beverage purposes.' Its passage was followed by a considerable increase in the consumption of alcohol, for it stimulated the production of home-made (grape) wines, which Joslyn and Amerine, the American experts, consider mostly contained about 13 per cent alcohol. 'Bootleg' (i.e. illicit) spirits were also drunk in considerable quantities. America was 'dry', and in 1929 the Great Depression started.

In the next presidential election, F. D. Roosevelt was elected with an overwhelming majority. He was inaugurated in 1933, and in the same year, the Volstead Act was repealed on 5 December. The effect of repeal was that home-made wines continued to be made at first in almost the same quantity as during the Prohibition period, that is, about 35 million gallons; the quantity produced before Prohibition was negligible. Commercially-made wine increased from 38 million gallons in 1934 to about 100 million gallons six or seven years later. Another striking change was the increasing preference for dessert wines compared with table-wines: the consumption per head in 1940 was two and a half times that in 1934. Dessert wines form three-quarters of the total made.

Although wine is made in twenty-nine of the forty-eight states, California is by far the largest producer. Nine-tenths of North American wine is Californian. New York State is a very poor second. The quondam 'Rhine of North America' produces only a very minor amount indeed.

California has a climate which is not well suited for growing grapes to make the finest wines. There are rather too many years when the sun scorches the grapes, so that the wine lacks the finest flavour. This difficulty is important chiefly in the making of light table-wines, since fortification has a tendency to conceal the scorched taste, which may indeed contribute desirably to the taste of some American dessert wines. Nevertheless, even in making dessert wines, certain varieties of grape are avoided because of their tendency to scorch.

In spite of this disability, Californian wines are certainly the best still table-wines made in the United States, for it is the only state in which *Vitis vinifera* varieties flourish. The difficulty is merely that in the Californian climate the finest varieties do not give of their best. In the other twenty-eight wine-producing states *Vitis labrusca* is grown, and this gives a foxy taste to its wine (page 50). It is illegal in

California to use grapes from any other state in making Californian wine, even mixed with Californian grapes. The Fingers Lakes production of sparkling wine is dealt with in chapter 6, and dessert wines in chapter 7.

In California, the chief wine-making districts are those ranged along the Sacramento and San Joaquin rivers, that is, in a strip some 200 miles long and 60 miles inland from San Francisco. Of the Californian total of 100 million gallons annual production, almost half comes from the San Joaquin valley and nearly all of this from Fresno and Tulare counties.

The scale of the operations has been indicated in chapter 4. It is true that the quotation on page 63 refers to one of the largest wine-producing establishments in the world, with a capacity of 80,000 tons of grapes a year and a wine-storage capacity of over fifteen million gallons. There are between three and four hundred 'wineries' in California, most of them on a very much more modest scale than the installation of the Roma Wine Company at Fresno. In some smaller ones, the vine-growing and the making of the wine are carried out by the same company, but in the larger concerns the grapes are bought from individual growers.

In the large concerns, the making of the wine is controlled by chemical and biological testing, although this is of necessity supplemented by tasting. There is no doubt that most of the wine of California is made under ideal conditions. That none is 'great' is to be attributed in the first place to the climate, and perhaps to some extent to the soil, and also to the large scale and the standardization of the conditions under which it is produced.

There are a great many types of American wines, and the names given to them are in many cases misleading and confusing to those used to European nomenclature. Like a number of other non-European producers, such as Australia, Chile, and the Cape, European names are used for wines which only distantly resemble their namesakes.

Californian *claret* and *burgundy* are usually somewhat lower in acid than true claret and burgundy and higher in alcohol. American *burgundy* is darker in colour than European. Californian *Chablis* distantly resembles the lower grades of Yonne Chablis but is rarely made from the European Pinot. *Sauterne* (without the 's' in the singular) may be a dry white wine in America; it may, on the other hand, be sweet. In the latter case it is usually described as Haut Sauterne. Californian *Tokay* is not at all like the Hungarian wine: it is fortified, and is not made from furmint grapes. Riesling, Mosel, and hock are white wines without much body, somewhat acid. Californian *barbera* is a rather heavy-bodied red wine with plenty of tannin. Zinfandel is one of the few American wines which sell on a name of their own: Zinfandel is made nowhere else. It is a dry red wine of peculiar flavour and bouquet. Aleatico is sweet and *rosé*.

In southern and eastern states, where the wine is made from Labrusca grapes, or at least contains Labrusca, names follow the varieties of vine used: Concord, Delaware, Catawba, or Norton.

Although the most distinctive American light wines have been named in these paragraphs, there are others, less well known and less easily specified: in California alone sixteen red and twenty-five white wines are sold under the names of grape-varieties or (European) districts. This does not include wines named from Californian wine-districts, although these usually have the name of a grape variety also attached, or of a European district also, such as Livermore Chablis or Livermore Burgundy, from the Livermore valley.

Besides the 200 odd million gallons produced by California, some three million gallons of foreign wine are imported each year.

CANADA (Map 17)

Canada has a small wine industry centred in Ontario which produces between four and five million gallons a year.

Canadians like to think that wine was made in their country by Europeans before Columbus discovered America. Norse explorers described a country, 'Vineland', in which the wild grape proliferated and with Noachian enthusiasm they set to and made wine. The Canadian Wine Institute think it was 'probably crude'.

Early in the seventeenth century the ubiquitous Jesuit missionaries used wild Canadian grapes to make sacramental wine. By the nineteenth century, the domesticated Labrusca vines of the eastern United States were introduced into the Niagara Peninsula. In this area 95 per cent of Canadian wine is still made. It is some forty-five miles long, stretching by the shores of Lake Ontario from just beyond Hamilton in the west to Niagara and Crystal Beach in the east. The chief centres are Niagara Falls, Welland, London, Grimsby, and St Catherines.

As is usual in the newer wine-countries, the vines are spaced about eight or ten feet apart so that mechanical cultivators and transport vehicles can move freely between the rows. The vines are on trellises and it is chiefly the Labrusca grape varieties which are cultivated, with some French strains also. Concord and Niagara are the chief *cépages*.

The vineyards cover about 20,000 acres and the annual production is more than four million gallons. Ontario is one of the most important fruit-growing areas of Canada, and its chief fruit is grapes, most of which are made into wine. Canada makes 'Sauternes' and 'Rhine wine', which are white, 'claret' and 'sparkling burgundy', 'champagne', and 'sherry', 'port', and 'Concord sweet' dessert wines, besides sweet and dry vermouths.

Vinification methods are mostly of the Californian type, although some firms keep to more traditional methods. It is upon the strictly hygienic conditions of their wineries that the Canadian *vignerons* particularly pride themselves. Only about a dozen firms have fermentation cellars, and they buy the grapes from the two to three thousand grape-growers. There are no co-operative selling organizations as in Europe and South America. The wine companies support a Wine Institute in Toronto which organizes the interests of the trade.

Mexico (Map 17)

Mexico is an arid country, generally unsuitable for viniculture. Moreover, from prehistoric times, before the Huaztecs had been conquered by the Aztecs, *pulque* had become the alcoholic drink of the country (see page 259) and wine takes a subsidiary place.

Both in the western states of Sinaloa and Nayarit, and in the central region (Aguas Calientes and Michoacán) vines are grown and wine is made. The land in the west, sloping down from the Sierra Madre to the Pacific Ocean and the Gulf of California, produces dates, figs, and olives, as well as vines. This horticultural intrusion into a land which only supports maize, wheat, beans, and chile with difficulty was the result of the settlement by the Jesuit Fathers after 1590. Nowadays all the land is in the hands of large owners.

In the central states of Mexico, the *pulque* industry is supreme: the *maguey* flourishes on poor soil. Vineyards are scattered and not large. Although most Mexican wine is poor, some is at least the equal of that from California.

South America (Map 18), with about 13 per cent of the land area of the world, produces rather more than 8 per cent of the wine. This is worthy of notice, since by far the greater part of the continent is within the tropics, and in fact four of the ten vineyard areas of the continent lie between 12° and 23° south.

The wines of Peru and Chile come from oases west of the Andes, those of Bolivia from an inland valley 400 miles south-east of Lake Titicaca. The plains in western Argentina provide 60 per cent of the wine of South America from a series of vineyard areas stretching from Tucuman in the north to Neuquén, 800 miles away to the south. The wine of Paraguay is grown on the divide between the plains and the eastern plateau, around Villa Rica. Brazil and Uruguay both produce wine from grapes grown in valleys in the plateau.

Most of the wine of South America is drunk within its own boundaries, in the great cities of Buenos Aires, Rio, and São Paulo, but Chilean red and white wines are exported and, for their price in Great Britain, are not to be despised.

Argentina

A great dry belt runs across Argentina, so that much of the north-western part of the state needs irrigation to support agriculture. A few streams flow down from the permanent snowfields of the Andes and where these emerge they are fringed with oases of fertile land. Alfalfa (lucerne), which feeds the great herds of range cattle, is the largest crop, but most of the wine vineyards of the country are here also, at Mendoza, San Juan, and San Rafael. Further north, on the edge of the sugar-cane district of Tucuman, are smaller areas, at La Rioja and Catamarca (see map 18). Rainfall is very slight in this area: less than 8 inches at Mendoza and only 3½ inches at San Juan, but by running irrigation ditches between the rows of vines, the grapes are prevailed upon to fill and ripen.

The Mendoza wine is commonly called *chica*. It is not highly alcoholic (6–8 per cent alcohol, or even less), and resembles some of the wines of Southern Italy more than anything else. Some is champagnized, in a somewhat rough and ready fashion.

There are 250,000 acres in the vineyard oases south of Tucumán, and two-thirds or more of the wine of the Argentine is produced here: over double the amount of wine made in California, which is the second-largest *vignoble* of the American continent.

The Mendoza vineyards fell into overproduction about twenty years ago and many growers uprooted their vines and planted orchards. Most of the *vignerons* are Italians, of whom more than 20,000 immigrated since the late nineteenth century. It is in fact to these experienced viticulturalists that Argentina owes her wine industry. Pears, especially at San Rafael, which was hit very badly, peaches, apples, plums, cherries, and apricots are now grown extensively in this area, although there are still vast vineyards.

A better-quality wine than the Mendoza *consumo* is made further south in the Rio Negro oasis, around Neuquén. This land was undeveloped until 1910, when vineyards and fruit orchards were planted. Vineyards now occupy 17,000 acres in the Neuquén oasis. The combination of tree-fruits and grapes is very convenient, for in north Patagonia the cherries ripen in December, peaches and plums in January, leaving the labour force free to attend to the grape harvest in February and March.

The Burgundian Pinot and the Cabernet Sauvignon from the Médoc are grown for red wine, and for white the Graves grapes, Semillon and Sauvignon blanc.

CHILE

Although Chile produces only one-third as much wine as Argentina, the quality is generally superior, and some is exported to Europe: in 1952 to the value of over four million pesos.

Here the wine-grape takes precedence over the table-grape, and Sauvignons and the Sylvaner are principally grown. Two areas are given over to vineyards, one just north of Valparaiso and Santiago, that is, just over the Andes from Mendoza, and the other some four or five hundred miles south, at Talcahuano, in the same latitude as Neuquén.

It is only in these regions that the vine is cultivated intensively, although almost every Chilean *hacienda* has its own vineyard. Chile is one of the most unaccommodating regions in the world for agriculture. It forms a narrow strip, at most 250 miles wide but more than ten times as long, hemmed in between the Andes, which in many places are over 20,000 feet high, and the Pacific Ocean: about the width of England but stretching from the latitude of Carlisle to that of Timbuktu. Communications between north and south are difficult and costly. The northern 600 miles, the Atacama, is one of the most barren places on the earth; no rain has ever been known to fall on it. It daunted even Pizarro. South Chile, 1,000 miles long, is a labyrinth of precipitous fjords, a region of almost continuous storms, the landscape constantly hidden by cloud and driving rain. It is overgrown with dense forests, and the rainfall is so heavy that trees cannot be cleared by burning; it is uninhabitable. Tierra del Fuego is its tip, by far the most southerly mainland of the world.

The vineyards of Chile are in the central region. The land in these areas is very fertile and water supply is ample, but modern methods of cultivation are scarcely used at all. There is very little mechanization, and cultivation is carried out by tenant-workers (*inquilinos*). Most of the land is in large *haciendas*, more than half of which are over 12,000 acres; the largest contains 618 square miles.

BRAZIL

Brazil exports no wine, but makes for her own consumption about fifteen million gallons each year, and imports much in addition from Portugal, although her wine imports are diminishing rapidly.

There are two wine-producing areas, a northerly one in São Paulo province, almost equidistant from Rio de Janeiro and the city of São Paulo, and a southerly, on the uplands behind the great lagoon, Lagoa dos Patos.

São Paulo province is intensively planted with coffee, and the vineyards, at Pinhal, lie just to the west of the plantation area. They are on the slopes of a 2,000-foot *cuesta*, which is characteristic of this region of land rising in huge steps of diabase to the Great Brazilian Escarpment. The soil is a reddish clay, *massape*, which is very fertile.

Further south, in the province of Rio Grande do Sul, there are more extensive vineyards high above the valley of the Jacui. Here more than 80 per cent of the wine of Brazil is produced. This is one of the many districts where immigrants from Europe have formed little colonies within the United States of Brazil. It is one of the phenomena of the growth of Brazil from its population of about four million early in the nineteenth century to more than eleven times that number nowadays, that hordes of settlers from Europe have made a new home for themselves within her $3\frac{1}{4}$ million square miles: Italians, Portuguese, Spaniards, Germans, and Poles, and also Japanese. Many of the settlements have flourished vigorously and expanded over quite extensive areas. A considerable proportion are not employees of large estates but small landowners, and they have impressed their European way of life, and especially a European architecture, on the districts in which they have settled.

The vineyards of Rio Grande do Sul are managed by an Italian colony which is centred around the two towns of Caxias do Sul and Alfredo Chaves (Veranopolis). The vineyard area around Caxias is the most populous part of southern Brazil; besides the cultivation, cattle- and hog-rearing occupy some of the inhabitants. On these pleasant hills, summer is the rainy season, but the balance through the year is fairly well maintained, and on descending to the coastal plains at Pôrto Alegre, the maximum rainfall is in winter (that is, in June and August). Although generally the weather is hotter than in the tropical Amazon forests, sometimes waves of cold air come north from the pole and shrivel the vineyards. A smaller amount of wine is made also by Italians further north, on the hills behind Blumenau.

They are not high class, or even good enough for export, these wines, but they can compete with imported wines within Brazil, and are drunk as the *consumo* throughout the country.

URUGUAY

Like Paraguay, Uruguay is not an agricultural country, yet it produces about eighteen million gallons of wine every year. The vineyards of Uruguay are almost all in the department of Montevideo, which besides the wine sells about 100,000 tons of table-grapes. As well as Portuguese grape-vines, the Gamay of Burgundy is also grown. Drought is not the main enemy of the *vigneron* as it is in Argentina, although in some years a long dry spell will reduce the crop very considerably. The normal rainfall in the vineyard area is just under forty inches, spread evenly throughout the year, and the temperature variation is normally between 50° in July and 72° in January and February, towards vintage-time. Nevertheless, the variations from year to year make the crop as unpredictable as in European vineyards.

Locusts are more destructive than in neighbouring Argentina, and descend in hordes from the north, consuming everything green in their path, down to the very weeds.

PARAGUAY

Only about one per cent of Paraguay is cultivated, but the country is self-supporting except for wheat. The vineyards date back to the early seventeenth century, when the Jesuit missionaries brought vines and cultivated them for wine. Wine and tobacco were the chief products of the thirty-two missions which they established, and they were so successful that the large landowners, finding them serious competitors in the markets, arranged for their expulsion in 1767.

Paraguay had fewer European settlers during the nineteenth century than most of the eastern states. However, a few Germans came in during the seventies and it is to their *mestizo* descendants that Paraguay owes her small wine production, which amounts to only 150,000 gallons a year. The vineyards are about a hundred miles south-east of Asunción, the capital, on the low hills just below the plateau which covers inland Paraguay in these latitudes. The heavy deciduous forest has been cleared, and the vineyards run up the western-facing slopes. Villa Rica is the local town and the grapes are sent in to the wineries there for fermentation and treatment.

PERU

Although the wines of Peru were known in Europe in the sixties and seventies of the last century, the industry has not grown sufficiently to export any notable quantity, and the three million gallons which are produced nowadays each year remain inside the American continent. All of Peru lies well within the tropics, and north of Lima, at 12° latitude, there are no vineyards.

Behind Lima, however, at Ica and Pativiloa, although cotton and the sugar-cane are the main crop, the vine flourishes and wine is made. Southern Peru, just short of the arid Atacama, contains a smaller *vignoble*, in the valley of Moquegua. The wine here is shipped out through the nearby port of Ilo. The table-grapes, which are of very high quality, conveniently ripen when North American grapes are unobtainable. Most of the land hereabouts must be given up to subsistence crops, for the hard dry ground is not fertile, and it is the vineyards of the mid-Peru oases which supply most of the wine of the country.

The mid-Peru vineyards in the Lima district suffer greatly from the low rainfall, which is usually less than two inches (for the year). This is nearly as much as Western European countries average each month. There are a few streams, but their water is meagre and the ground is so steep that it soon reaches the ocean and is lost. Many simply disappear in the sandy soil: of fifty-two which leave the mountains, only ten reach the coast. The floods which come down in mid-summer, between December and March, are only a memory a month or two afterwards.

The Incas, long before their discovery by Pizarro in the sixteenth century, had constructed irrigation works on a magnificent scale. (See chapter 4 in book 1 of Prescott's *History of the Conquest of Peru*.) These the Spanish conquerors allowed to fall into dilapidation, so that they became choked with silt and vegetation. Between 1932 and 1937 the Peruvian government built new aqueducts and even tunnelled the Andes to catch some of the tributaries of the Amazon and divert them. Something like 100,000 acres were irrigated. The Incas had terraced the hillsides into *ardenes* in just the same way as the Mediterranean is cultivated and these terraces are still a feature of the Peruvian vineyards.

Although the chief meteorological difficulty of the Peruvian *vigneron* is drought, there are years when the contrary is the case in this coastal region. The sea off Peru is cold through the winter: about 60° is normal. Every year, in December, northerly winds from the equator blow down warm water which spreads as a film on the surface of the cold ocean. Every year it comes, just before Christmas: it is known as *El Niño*, the Christ Child. Until March, the sea is superficially warm, and the air is moist. Then the temperature falls again and for eight or nine months the sea remains cool and the earth without humidity. Occasionally, the warm current of surface water is much stronger than usual and *El Niño* travels further south and stays longer. The temperature of the sea rises greatly, not merely in the surface layer, but below. The atmosphere becomes very damp indeed and enormous masses of cumulus shut out the sky. Then the rains come. More rain falls in a few days than is seen for many years: in 1925, one of Peru's freak years, more than six times as much rain fell on Trujillo in three March days as in the previous seven years. Such deluges as this destroy the houses, which are of baked mud, built for a rainless climate; roads and bridges are undermined and collapse, the irrigation ditches become choked and gravel and stones spread over the vineyards. This is just about vintage-time, and the vines, heavy with grapes, are battered to the ground.

Such years of disaster came to Peru in 1939 and 1932 as well as 1925, and earlier, in 1918, 1891, 1884, 1878, and so on back to Inca days. Wine of those years is very poor in quality and very small in quantity.

Methods of vinification employed in Peru vary from the very crude to the reasonably controlled. In some places the vintage is trodden and left to ferment without even troubling to keep the *sombrero* of skins under: when it sinks of its own accord the fermentation is considered to be about finished. In many of the *bodegas*, however, the grape-juice is tested for sugar content, and is sulphured to kill off any bacteria; when fermentation begins, the temperature is watched so as to ensure that overheating does not take place, and the wine is run off from the skins less than 48 hours after fermentation has started. The wines are rather strong – nearly 13 per cent alcohol on the average – but practically all are adulterated by addition of alcohol, or water, or both. Strong, crude, sweetish, and acid wines are the rule.

BOLIVIA

Bolivia is a country with so many natural disadvantages that it is not surprising that only a little wine is made and none of that exported.

Ten per cent of Bolivia is a high plateau from 5,000 to 20,000 feet above sea-level, and on the plateau live three-quarters of the population. Only the northern part has enough rain for agriculture and the difficulties of transport are immense. It is at Tarija that the wine-grapes are grown, and there they are subordinate to crops of olives, pears, peaches, and apples. Like many of the *haciendas*, the vineyards are still worked under something like the old feudal system of Europe: the Indians work for three or four days a week and in payment are given small holdings. A gradual change is now taking place to a system of small holdings, and some Indian communities till the ground in a sort of co-operative system. Much of the cultivation is still with wooden ploughs and conditions are in other ways very primitive indeed.

The Bolivian *peon* is a heavy drinker, but *chicha* is his drink. This is an alcoholic beverage derived from maize which was made in Inca times (and has no connexion with the Argentine *chica*).

CHAPTER 9

HOW TO DRINK WINE

To appreciate properly a first-class wine is not easy. Years of experience are necessary and they must be attended with enthusiasm and application. It is quite a serious study, although with superb compensations. At the end of the apprenticeship you will find yourself speaking a strange language: you will evaluate the *sève*, the breed, of a wine by deciding how *capiteux*, how *charnu*, how *fruité* it is. Your closest friends will tell you that you are trying to cage the ineffable; everyone else will say that you are a pretentious fool, and unless you happen to be gifted with considerable powers of introspection and great honesty of mind, they will be correct.

It is great fun learning, however slowly, to distinguish the various wines by their taste, their bouquet, and their colour, and educating one's palate to distinguish a poor wine from a good one, and a good from a better. It is not difficult to detect acidity, tannin, or alcohol in a wine, to decide that it has body or lacks it, or to distinguish the bouquet of a Rhine wine from that of a claret. It is when one tries to go beyond this point that the ground beneath one's feet becomes boggy, and one finds it difficult to form a judgement and harder still to communicate it. You will do well to read what Mr Warner Allen has to say on this subject (*Natural Red Wines*, chapter 2), for no writer comes nearer than he to communicating the bases of judgement of the connoisseur.

In some years, when the weather is favourable in a vineyard region, the wines will be generally good throughout. This was the case in 1945 and again in 1947 in all the *vignobles* from the Douro to the Rhine. However, even in bad years some good wines are made. They are very difficult to sell at a good price, however fine they are, for all amateurs of wine carry little cards which tell them that 1930 or 1931 or 1951 was a poor year and so they refuse to buy the wines of those years. It is a constant source of irritation and financial loss, to *vignerons* and merchants alike, that their customers rely so blindly on these little cards. They have been heard to execrate the whole system of '*les grands millésimes*'. As Poupon and Forgeot (*Les Vins de Bourgogne*) say, this cataloguing of the years is too simple: it is only the *general tendency* which is recorded. Much depends on the age of the vines, the orientation of the vineyards, and whether they are sheltered or not, the soil, the care taken in cultivation, the date of the vintage, and so on. Luck also plays its part.

In 1935, the *vignerons* of Var in Provence awaited the best date for vintaging. From the middle of September the sugar in the grapes rose from 16 per cent to 18 per cent, and then on the thirtieth of the month to 19·2 per cent. This would give them a wine of 11·4 per cent alcohol, and some *vignerons* gathered their grapes, remembering that a bird in the hand . . . Most held on for the good Provençal sun of early October. On the fourth of the month there was a deluge which lasted for seven hours. The water was immediately sucked up by the thirsty vines and the next day the sugar in the grapes was down to 16 per cent again, diluted by the water. This is equivalent to only 9·5 per cent alcohol in the wine. For Provence, where wines are expected to be *capiteux*, it meant low prices. Many cut their losses and harvested, others held on for another week. At the end of that time there was sugar enough to give wine with over 10 per cent alcohol, but the very tenacious, who waited longer, saw the vineyards drenched again and their wine contained only 9·5 per cent. The little *millésime* cards give Provence a wine below average for 1935. The average alcohol content of Provençal wines is about 10 per cent, so that it depends from whom you bought your wine that year whether you got poor wine at 9·5 per cent alcohol or fine stuff at 11·4 per cent – or average at 10·2 per cent. (The alcohol content is not everything by a long way, but it is a very fair index of quality.)

Much depends on the *cépages* grown. In Anjou the spring of 1935 promised well and it was hoped and expected that the fine and abundant vintage of 1934 would be equalled if not surpassed. But by the end of June there had been 170 fewer hours of sunshine than in the previous year, and flowering was ten to twelve days late. July and August were hot and dry and some leeway was made up; nevertheless, ripening was eight or ten days late and in September there were sixteen days of rain; also the temperature was low. The first ten days of October were cold and rainy too, and the vintage was gathered hastily. The red vines gave only 380 gallons to the acre compared with 550 in 1934 and the muscadets (one of the most important red vines of Anjou) were 50 per cent lower than in the previous year. Moreover, the wine from the muscadets had only 8·7 per cent alcohol, while the finer cabernets gave wine with 10·2 per cent.

In the same year, a little higher up the Loire, in Touraine, the growers of Vouvray and Tours made 5 per cent more wine than the average, but, like their neighbours in Anjou, the alcohol was low. Burgundy, not far to the east of Touraine, made rather good wines in more than average quantity in this same year of 1935, but both quality and quantity of Bordeaux were poor, in Médoc, Graves, Saint-Émilion, and Sauternes alike. It was an excellent year on the Douro, further west still, and very good on the Mosel and the Rhine, east of Burgundy. All the same, some 1935 ports and hocks were poor and some clarets very good. The *millésimes* record no more than a general tendency.

As to the integrity of a wine, it has already been explained (page 96) that in France the regulations of the *Appellation d'Origine Contrôlée* are a safeguard against your buying a bottle of mixed Algerian and Andalusian wine but paying for a Richebourg. Much wine is exported to Britain in barrel and bottled here, however. Some English importers put *Appellation Contrôlée* on their labels, but in fact you are relying on their honesty, for the term has no legal force in this country. At one time more commonly than at present, it was usual to purchase wines bottled at the vineyard: 'estate-bottled wine', paying 50 per cent or more premium for them. Nowadays one is more likely to save one's money and rely on one's wine-merchant. The final guarantee of an estate-bottled wine (which always has a picturesque label and a legend such as *Mis en bouteille au Château*) is on the cork, which may be stamped YQUEM. LUR–SALUCES. MIS EN BOUTEILLE AU CHÂTEAU, or some similarly glorious text. Nowadays it is generally recognized that wine imported into this country in cask and bottled here is in no way inferior (and is often superior) to that bottled abroad.

In buying wines it is important to have a reliable wine-merchant. If you cannot find locally one who inspires you with confidence, it is

wise to write for their lists to the large merchants and buy from them.*
Wine-lists are an interesting study, in any case. The range of prices
will surprise those who have seen only restaurant and hotel lists.
They will notice that it is possible to pay eight or ten pounds for
a bottle of a superlative German wine, but that one may get a
bottle of fine wine for twelve or fifteen shillings. A bottle contains
just under a pint and a half (1·35 pints). Half-bottles of most
wines can be purchased at sixpence or a shilling more than half the
price of a bottle. Since hotels and restaurants charge exactly double
the retail price for wine, it is obviously advisable to drink wine only
at one's own table. Wine-merchants usually seem to make a comfort-
able living selling by retail, but hoteliers are dissatisfied with less than
three or four times their profit.

A half-bottle, which is modestly sufficient to accompany a meal for
two, costs about six shillings if it is a good Bordeaux or burgundy.
This compares not unfavourably with the cost of an afternoon run in
the car, or the price of forty cigarettes. Hocks and Mosels are only
slightly more expensive unless of superlative quality.

Bottles of wine must be stored lying down, so that the bubble of
air within the bottle is clear of the cork; if the cork dries out, air will
carry *Acetobacter* and other organisms into the bottle and consume the
wine before you. Your cellar may be as extensive as you like, or a
wooden box as small as a foot by three inches (for one bottle makes a
cellar). It must be cool and free from perceptible vibration. The ideal
temperature is between 50° and 55°. Dampness within reason is unimportant, but darkness is best; bright sunshine brings a lingering
death.†

By tradition, wines of Bordeaux, Burgundy, Champagne, and
Germany each have their own bottle shape (Fig. 4); by the caprice of

* The Army and Navy Stores; Berry Brothers; Hedges and Butler;
Justerini and Brooks; Layton's; Loeb; Saccone and Speed, all of London;
Harvey's and Avery's of Bristol; Baty of Liverpool; Lupton of Manchester,
and C. A. Rookes of Stratford are all well-known names. This is a random
selection.

† It is considerably cheaper, and certainly great fun, to import your wine
from France in barrel (280 bottlefuls), half-barrel or quarter-barrel, and bottle
it yourself. All the details of price and practice are given in Mr Edward Ott's
book, *From Barrel to Bottle*, and there is the Wine Lovers' Society of 21, Park
Hill, Moseley, Birmingham, 15, which advises its members on this subject.

Burgundy

Hock
Mosel

Champagne

Bordeaux

Steinwein

Fig. 4. Wine Bottles

amateurs, enthusiastically supported by the glass manufacturers, with the bovine acquiescence of those who are especially prone to suggestion, each wine is drunk from a differently-shaped glass (Fig. 5). Professional tasters and those who like wine for its own sake employ the *tulipe* for all still wines. Glasses should be colourless, so that the natural colour of the wine is not falsified, and they should be plain without any ornament so that the clarity of the wine may be seen. The walls of the glass should be thin so that the contents are easily warmed by the hand in order to increase the aroma, and the shape should be that of the *tulipe* so that the aroma is retained in the glass. The traditional sherry-taster's glass is also shown in Fig. 5. Wine-glasses are never more than two-thirds filled, in order that the aroma may not be dissipated as soon as it leaves the surface of the wine.

Red table-wines are served at room-temperature, white are cooled (though not frozen), as are sparkling wines and, generally speaking, the fortified aperitifs and dessert wines, excepting port: the temperature for serving port is optional.

Red table-wines, vintage port, and very old wines of any colour (unless they are sparkling) should be decanted before serving. It is as well to have a piece of dry and well-rinsed muslin or a filter-paper at hand to deal with the last of the bottle, which, especially if of port or old hermitage, can be extremely difficult. Decanting is carried out a few hours before serving. The bottle is stood upright and left over-night so that the sediment will slide to the bottom. After wiping the outside of the neck, it is uncorked with great care, and then the inside of the neck is wiped, still taking pains not to jar or knock the bottle. Now, without trembling or allowing any worry to enter your mind, pour gently and steadily into the decanter. When the first trace of sediment appears in the stream flowing through the neck, stop. It is necessary to view the stream in the neck with a light behind it – best a candle, or a bare light-bulb – in order to be able to detect the first sediment. The lees may be filtered – not that the sediment does any harm except to the appearance of the wine. Some red table-wines need to be aired for an hour or two before drinking for, fresh from the bottle, they have a 'bottle-stink'. Wine not drunk the day it is opened loses its highest qualities, but to drink wine on the second day, although undesirable and to be avoided, does not count as one of the deadlier sins.

Vouvray · Anjou · Alsace

Brandy · White Burgundy · Red Burgundy

White Bordeaux · Red Bordeaux · Sherry Sampler

Fig. 5. Wine Glasses

There are rules of correlatives in choosing wines to accompany a meal; at one time these were very strict, but with the recent spread of civilization, or merely democracy, they have been somewhat relaxed. Red wines, generally speaking, don't go well with fish or eggs, and certainly not with oysters, but they do with roasts or poultry. Champagne, or sherry, or hock, or Mosel can be drunk throughout a meal. A sweet white wine is best with melon, or with the sweet, or dessert. Dry white wines go with fish or hors-d'œuvre, and any wine with cheese. Never follow a fine wine with a poor one, or a heavy wine with a light one. These rules will be found to be based on common sense. Nevertheless, it is also common sense to drink any wine with anything, if you like it that way. Before a meal a dry sherry or Madeira; after, an oloroso, malvasia, V.D.N., Malaga, Marsala, bual, or verdelho, or, of course, a port, or a fine brandy.

The most important, perhaps the only important, fact about drinking wines is that you should try everything at least twice and then make up your mind, and your cellar. Try to be tolerant, for tolerance is nowadays considered a civilized virtue, and the drinking of wine is one of the techniques of civilization, and always has been (see chapter 3).

RECENT GREAT VINTAGE YEARS

Claret: 1953 1952 1947 1945 1943 1934 1929 1928 1924 1920 1904 1900

Sauternes: 1953 1952 1949 1947 1945 1942 1937 1934 1929 1928 1924 1921 1916 1914

Red Burgundy: 1953 1952 1949 1947 1945 1929 1923 1921

Hock: 1953 1949 1937 1934 1929 1921 1920

Mosel: 1947 1945 1937

Champagne: 1953 1949 1947 1945 1938 1937 1934 1928

Port: 1950 1948 1947 1935 1934 1931 1927

*

'There are no good wines: there are only good bottles.'
Albert Thibaudet

Part Two

SPIRITS

CHAPTER 10

INTRODUCTION

WINE has innumerable good qualities, which it would be tedious to enumerate here. It has one or two disadvantages, however. Unless it is carefully made and properly stored it does not keep, and it is bulky to transport, for nearly nine-tenths is water. If the alcohol content can be doubled, the difficulty of keeping disappears, and the amount of water which must be carried about with it is of course reduced considerably. If all the water could be abstracted and a pure wine-essence obtained, this would keep for ever (although it would evaporate very rapidly) and the bulk would be very greatly reduced: to perhaps one-seventh or one-eighth. By adding water again the original wine would be reconstituted. It is unfortunately not possible to do this without profoundly changing the taste, and the principal attraction of wine is its taste.

Nevertheless, it is possible to remove a great deal of the water and still leave a liquid which is considered by a fair proportion of the world's population to be eminently drinkable. The only process for carrying out this operation which is actually used is distillation, and the product is a brandy. Besides wine, other weak alcoholic drinks such as beer, cider, and the fruit wines can also be concentrated similarly to give one or other of the spirits.

The process of distillation crept into technology almost imperceptibly and it seems to be quite impossible to determine the date or place of its invention. The operation itself is exceedingly simple: to heat a liquid until it boils and turns to vapour, and then to catch the vapour and cool it again so as to recover the liquid. Aristotle, a couple of centuries before Christ, mentions that pure water could be obtained from sea-water but does not describe just how to do it. Later writers, Dioscorides and Pliny, both in the first century A.D., seem to have known of distillation, but are equally reticent about details.

It does seem to be fairly certain that distillation was practised in Europe in the ninth or tenth century, and the evidence for an earlier date is considered to be unreliable. It is thought that the Moors brought the invention west, and it may be that some ingenious Arab of Damascus or Baghdad really invented it some time before A.D. 900, or it may have come from further east. At some unknown early date the Arabs had used distillation for extracting perfumes and had built a flourishing trade in these commodities, which were almost necessities for those who could afford them, in those insanitary days. The distilleries were first at Sabur and later at Damascus. By the twelfth century Salernus was writing about distillation, and a hundred years later Albertus Magnus gave a description of the process. By 1500, a full account was published by Hieronimus Brunschwygk.

The wine-shippers of the Gironde found distillation useful to save transport charges in the Middle Ages, and distilled liquids became especially popular in the sixteenth and seventeenth centuries. The Irish Gaels seem to have been making *uisge-beatha* from a barley beer some time in the fifteenth century or earlier.

The problem of the distiller is to separate alcohol from water. Alcohol boils at 78°C. and water at 100°C. At first sight, one might think perhaps that if the distiller warmed up his wine to 78°C. and kept it at that temperature, the alcohol would all boil off, leaving the water behind, for water does not boil until 22° higher. If this were so, all he need do is to condense the vapours coming off first and he would have pure alcohol. (Not that he wants pure alcohol.) However, water gives off vapour even at ordinary temperatures; if it did not, nothing once wetted would ever dry until it was heated to boiling-point. At the boiling-point of alcohol, water has a very strong tendency to vaporize, and so the vapour coming from the still is a mixture of water and alcohol. There is a higher proportion of alcohol in the vapour than in the liquid, and by condensing fractions of it separately, some distillates – the early ones – will contain a much increased alcohol content.

In the distillation of Charente wine to make brandy, the distiller starts with wine of about 8 per cent alcohol content and obtains a main distillate with 20 per cent alcohol. He redistils this and gets a fraction with about 60 per cent alcohol: this is the spirits he wants. It is extremely important, especially to the brandy- or whisky-distiller, that the taste of his particular spirits shall be retained; this must stay with the spirits-fraction. However, there are substances, such as methanol and fusel-oil, which are undesirable. A little fusel-oil contributes to the normal taste of whisky and brandy, but more than a very small amount is nauseating. It happens that the methanol in the wine, which comes from the pectin of the grapes, passes over first of all in the distillation, that is with the first fraction of the alcohol-water mixture. Fusel-oil is predominantly in the still-residues and in the higher-boiling fractions.

In making gin, it is undesirable that any taste but that of alcohol shall be present, for the flavour of gin is carefully inserted afterwards. So the gin-maker adopts a different method from most other spirits-distillers. He wants a so-called 'neutral' spirit, which whisky distillers call 'silent spirit'. Some rum-makers also make an almost neutral spirit and then put in the taste and aroma afterwards.

Unless neutral spirits is being made, the still used by distillers is often the very simple type known as a pot-still. This is merely a hemispherical copper pot with a cover shaped to a tube, through which the vapours pass to the condenser, where they are liquefied by cooling. Most of the best brandy and some whisky is made in pot-stills. There is a great waste of heat in these stills, and the tube carrying the hot vapours from the still is usually surrounded by a chamber through which the cold wine is circulated, so that it shall be warmed before entering the still. This chamber is called the *chauffe-vin* in the Cognac district (see Plate 30).

Various elaborations of the old pot-still are in use in the French brandy industry. The *chauffe-vin* is the simplest improvement; next is a bulbous excrescence on the vapour-pipe just above the still. In this, with the large cooling surface, the heavier fractions tend to condense and drip back into the still, while the light fractions which need to be cooled to a much lower temperature to liquefy, pass on. A further complication is to divide the still itself into two chambers, so that the vapours leaving the lower chamber bubble through the liquid in the upper and partly recondense. It is only when the liquid in the upper chamber is sufficiently hot that any but the light fractions will escape, to pass the gauntlet of the cooling-bulb on the vapour pipe.

About 1830 an Irishman named Coffey invented a still which is quite different from the pot-still, and is still called the Coffey still, after him, or sometimes a patent-still. (Some at least of the credit should go to French engineers, who were inventing patent-stills at a great rate from about 1820 onwards.) In this, very little heat is wasted and, moreover, it gives the distiller a much closer control over his product and enables him to recover more of the desirable constituents of his wine. Furthermore, the throughput of spirit is greatly increased, and the distillation is carried out continuously. In the pot-still, when the charge of wine has been exhausted, the still must be emptied before a new charge is admitted from the preheater.

A diagram of the Coffey still is shown in Fig. 6. It consists of two columns, sometimes of wood held in an iron framework. Each column is divided horizontally into a number of compartments. The left-hand column in the diagram is called the 'analyser', the right-hand one the 'rectifier'. Steam is blown into the bottom of the analyser and passes upwards from one compartment to the next. Wine trickles in at the top of the column and collects for a short time on the plates separating the compartments, where it is warmed by the rising steam. By the time it reaches the bottom of the column it has been stripped of all its alcohol, which passes upwards with the steam and out at the top of the column. The stripped liquor, together with some of the steam which has condensed, flows away to waste at the bottom.

The hot alcohol vapours, together with uncondensed steam (and the minor constituents of the wine which give it flavour: the 'congenerics'), leave the top of the analyser and are led to the bottom of the rectifier. The rectifier is divided horizontally by a number of perforated plates and the vapours flow through them and bathe a zig-zag pipe which passes across each compartment. This pipe contains the cold wine on its way to the top of the first column, the analyser. The wine is cold when the pipe enters the column at the top, but it is warmed by the ascending vapours, which are gradually cooled. The heat is transferred from the vapours to the liquid through the wall of the pipe. The vapours begin to condense; the first drops of liquid which condense are mostly water and the high-boiling part of the wine – the fusel-oil. Next the main fraction liquefies on the pipes and drops on to the perforated plates. Lastly, at the top of the still, the light fractions condense, or if they are very light, pass right through as vapour.

By putting a plate which is not perforated at some point in the rectifier, a fraction of any desired composition can be collected. This is run into the finished distillate tank; it is 'spirits'. The first fractions

ANALYSER   RECTIFIER

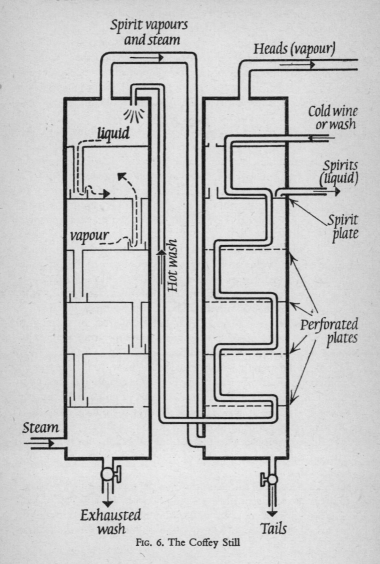

FIG. 6. The Coffey Still

are collected in a special tank and fed into the top of the analyser column to make sure that they contain no alcohol, and the residue from them joins the waste at the bottom.

Continuous stills of this kind are very flexible in operation, for conditions can be changed by altering the steam entering the bottom of the analyser, or the volume of wine being pumped into the pipe at the top of the rectifier, or the position of the blind plate in the rectifier.

It is illegal to distil spirits in Britain without obtaining approval from the Excise Department and a licence, which costs ten pounds unless you wish to distil more than 50,000 proof gallons a year, in which case the cost goes up *pro rata*.

In Britain and the Commonwealth and in the U.S.A. the alcoholic strength of spirits is always stated as so much over or under 'proof'. The origin of this practice is obscure and its operation ridiculous. In France and Italy the alcohol content is stated as per cent by volume, and in Germany as per cent by weight. The American practice differs from the British.

The Customs and Excise Act of 1952 says: 'Spirits shall be deemed to be proof if the volume of the ethyl alcohol contained therein made up to the volume of the spirits with distilled water has a weight equal to that of twelve-thirteenths of a volume of distilled water equal to the volume of spirits, the volume of each liquid being computed as at 51°F.'

This, translated into plain English and transferred to meaningful units, is: 'At 51°F., proof spirit contains 57·06 per cent alcohol by volume or 48·24 per cent alcohol by weight.'

The alcoholic strength of spirits sold in Britain is '30° under proof', which is the same as '70° proof'. That is to say, it contains 70 per cent of proof spirit, or just about 40 per cent alcohol by volume or 33·3 per cent by weight. A bottle of spirits contains just over 10½ ounces of alcohol.

Absolute (100 per cent) alcohol is 175·1 proof.

The duty on spirits is £10 10s. 10d. a proof gallon, that is 24s. 7d. a bottle. In 1840 it was 3s. 4d. a proof gallon, in 1855 it was 8s. 0d., and in 1914, 14s. 9d.

In the U.S.A. proof spirit contains 50·0 per cent alcohol by volume, and spirits are sold at various strengths between 86° and 100° (U.S.) proof, Scotch whiskies at 86° or 86·8°, domestic at 86°, 90°, or 100°. The Federal Excise Tax is $10.50 a proof gallon, State taxes a further $3.18.

CHAPTER 11

BRANDY

So long as no Scotsmen are within earshot, it may confidently be said that brandy is the king of spirits. All the same, there are inferior brandies, and it may be as well to take a rapid conspectus of what the term 'brandy' can include.

Brandy is the spirit distilled from grape wine; fruit brandies, many with special names, like slivovitz and jambava from plums, kirsch from cherries, and so on, are obtained from fruit wines, or in the case of applejack and Calvados, from cider. The word brandy, first used in the seventeenth century, was originally *brandwine* or *brandewine*, from the Dutch *brandewijn*, that is, burnt (or distilled) wine.

Of brandy, fundamentally a French spirit, there are subdivisions. There is *cognac*, which is a brandy of especially high quality made only in the French *départements* of the Charente and Charente Maritime, although the term is sometimes used outside France as synonymous with 'brandy'; this would be illegal (at least as basis for a sale) in France. Another sort of brandy, usually admitted not to be *quite* of the quality of cognac, is *armagnac*. It is made in certain parts of the *département* of Gers, near the town of Condom. Its quality is high and the name is legally protected in France; some prefer it to cognac. Besides these, brandies are made all over France, and in other countries, from the *marc* remaining after the wine has been pressed out (see chapter 4). In France this brandy is known as *eau-de-vie-de-marc*, as distinct from *eau-de-vie-de-vin*; in Germany it is called *Tresterbranntwein*, in Italy and California *grappa*, in Portugal *bagaceira*, in South Africa, *dop-brandy*. Spirit can also be distilled from the lees of yeast, etc., remaining in the casks after racking. This is *eau-de-vie-de-lie* in France and French Switzerland, *Hefebranntwein* in Germany, Austria, and other German-speaking regions.

French Brandy

COGNAC

Immediately north of the Bordeaux district lie the *départements* of the Charente and the Charente Maritime, and almost exactly in the centre of the combined area of the two *départements* is the little town of Cognac, with nearly 18,000 inhabitants. It is a pleasant place on the south bank of the Charente, with pleasant landscape paintings in its museum, and an ancient castle, that of the Valois, overlooking the slow river. Its life, like its name, is cognac. Cognac even fills the castle of the Valois, for the edifice has been used for the past 160 years as a storehouse by the firm of Otard. Hennessy's and Martell's also have their cellars within the confines of the little town.

The cognac district extends in all directions from the town, and those motoring south by the N10 to Bordeaux, Biarritz, or into Spain through Hendaye traverse some seventy-odd miles of it from Ruffec through Angoulême to Cavignac, where the Bordelais commences. Besides Cognac itself, the chief centres of the district are Segonzac and Jarnac. These are mere villages, neither with more than 4,000 inhabitants. The area under vines in the whole cognac district is 150,000 acres, but there are subdivisions of this. Only grapes grown in the area may be made into cognac, and to a connoisseur there are seven grades of cognac. The vineyard areas corresponding to these are, first, the Grande Champagne, centred on Segonzac and extending north to the Charente river and south for about an equal distance; secondly, the Petite Champagne, which forms an arc only a few miles wide semi-circling the Grande Champagne to the south; thirdly, the Borderies, a small area to the north-west of the town of Cognac; the area of Fins Bois encircles these three and includes Angoulême and Saintes; outside this again is the belt of the Bons Bois; lastly, between this circle and the coast are the sub-districts of the Bois Ordinaires and the Bois Communs: La Rochelle and Rochefort lie in this part of the district.

The region has for long been well known for its brandy, and references in eighteenth-century literature to the spirits from La Rochelle, the shipping port, are legion. It was in 1909 that the district in which cognac could be made was defined. In 1936, when the *Appellation Contrôlée* decrees were passed, the specification of districts, grapes, and method of distillation took its place with that for armagnac and the various wines.

The only grapes which may be employed are the Folle blanche, the Saint-Émilion, Colombar, and five others, The Saint-Émilion is the principal grape now employed. The soil here is alluvial with a calcareous tendency, for the headwaters of the Charente flow through the Jurassic limestone. The Folle blanche is not a sweet grape suitable for eating; its wine is hard and rather acid, with low alcohol content (rarely above 8 per cent). The Saint-Émilion is little better, though the Colombar wine may contain up to 11 per cent alcohol. Intermediate between the Bordelais and Touraine in climate, the Charente region has a well-distributed rainfall, but snow is not common. There is less sunshine than in the Gironde, and it is the dull skies which lower the sugar of the grapes; the Saint-Émilion grape gives wines which are quite up to the average in alcohol and more full-bodied than other Bordeaux wines only a few miles to the south, in their home country.

Phylloxera hit the Charente hard and replanting with American stocks proceeded cautiously. Only scions from the indigenous Folle blanche and other grapes were used, and this accounts for the maintenance of the high reputation of cognac.

The wine is made off the skins, in the white wine manner, in the Charente, and pressing is gentle in order to avoid introducing inferior taste and odour, which is associated with the pectins and tannins from the cells of the grape skins. Sulphur dioxide is not used, and a short rapid fermentation is carried out to leave low residual sugar. The resultant wine is not racked off the lees before distillation but run straight into the stills.

The cognac pot-stills have changed little over the years, in order that there shall not be the slightest change in the character of the cognac (Plate 30). As the Bureau National de Cognac modestly says, 'you cannot improve on perfection'. The design of the stills can be plainly seen from the illustration, which shows the bulbous partial condenser above the still, the *chauffe-vin* behind, and the condenser capped by a hood. Stills are not always in pairs with a common flue like this, but it is a not unusual arrangement. It is necessary to have very good cooling on the condenser, or some of the prized aroma is lost, and distillation is carried out slowly for the same reason.

With a charge of 200 to 250 gallons, boiling-point is reached in two or three hours after the first runnings have been taken off, and heating is kept steady until distillation of the hearts is almost ended. About seventy-five to eighty gallons of the main fraction, the *brouillis*, are collected at an alcohol content of 20 to 25 per cent. The still residue (*vinasse*) contains very little alcohol.

The mixed *brouillis* from three primary distillations is distilled again into three fractions: a very small amount of 'heads', which is mixed back with the next lot of *brouillis*; the main heart fraction, which takes another ten hours or so to come over; and the tails, which amount to forty or fifty gallons and still contain 16 per cent or more alcohol: this also goes back to the next *brouillis*. The main fraction (*bonne chauffe*) has just over 70 per cent alcohol in it, that is, it is about 25 per cent o.p. (British), or 40 per cent o.p. (U.S.).

Cognac is blended by year and district, and aged in oaken casks. It is fortunate that just east of the Charente lies the forest of Limousin, and the flavour of cognac is to some degree attributable to the oaks of the forest. The best cognac is matured in cask for as long as twenty years. Unfortunately the loss in keeping spirits in wood is very high, mostly by the slow percolation of the spirits through the pores in the wooden casks. On the average it amounts to over a quarter of the volume during the course of maturation.

A good armagnac is a very fine brandy, although not up to the best cognacs. The vineyard area around Condom is zoned like that of Cognac and produces about one-fourth as much brandy. The best armagnac is Grand-Armagnac, the next grade Fin-Armagnac, and the third Petit-Armagnac.

OTHER FRENCH BRANDIES

When a Frenchman wants a really first-class brandy, he asks for *un fin* or *une fine champagne*. But for ordinary drinking at the end of a meal, or between meals, there are the much cheaper local *marc* brandies, made in every wine region from the fermentation murk. Comparatively little *eau-de-vie-de-vin* properly so called is made except in the Charente and Gers, but some of the *marcs* are very good indeed. Not to put too fine a point on it, there is some considerable rivalry upon the relative qualities of the various *marcs*. However, it is more than probable that Marc de Bourgogne takes the palm.

Burgundy *marc* brandy is not produced in large quantities: less than half a million gallons a year. It is usually made during the winter when the *vigneron* has his wines safely stored in the *chais* and another season's worries are laid to rest. The solid mass of skins, stems, and pips, called *gennes* in Burgundy, has been hard packed into casks or a vat and covered with a mortar of clay to keep out *Acetobacter*. He has occasionally inspected it and filled up the cracks which formed as autumn turned to winter and the *gennes* dried. Then it is dug out and water added, the whole mixed up into a slurry and slowly fermented.

A still is set up in the village and the *marc* wine is distilled under supervision of Government inspectors. It is only just about (British) proof in strength as it comes from the *alambics* – the old alchemical word is still used – and goes for ageing to the oak barrels. Before sale, it must be inspected by an official Tasters' Commission, and is sold at 44 per cent alcohol (44° French).

In Burgundy also a little *eau-de-vie-de-lie* is made, a highly aromatic brandy much esteemed by village connoisseurs. The annual production is no more than 40,000 gallons: *fine bourgogne* is the designation.

Bouilleurs de cru account for a sizeable proportion of French brandy production, in fact for such an amount that an extremely vigorous campaign has been carried on for a number of years to limit the privileges of the *bouilleurs*. During the Napoleonic wars, the French government allowed growers of vines to distil a certain amount of spirit for their own domestic consumption. It needs only a moment's thought to see how easily such a privilege can be abused and how difficult it is to control its operation. Half a century ago about a million people claimed the right to distil for their own use. In early 1954 the number was about four millions; each was allowed to make nearly five gallons of brandy, that is, twenty-five bottles or so. A decree passed in 1953 limited the privilege somewhat, and another in the following year reduced the numbers of *bouilleurs de cru* to between two and a half and three millions. The *bouilleurs* control an extremely strong caucus in the National Assembly, for every *bouilleur* has a vote. Against them are ranged the cognac-makers' lobby, and the temperance reformers: an interesting combination. In many rural districts a perambulating pot-still of the simplest design goes from village to village distilling wine for smallholders. The illicit distillers, not inconsiderable in number, use home-made stills, which are constructed from copper sheet and pipe. In the distillation of wine, and more in the distillation of *marc*, the first fractions which come over contain much methanol, and methanol is poisonous. Unless the first fractions are rejected, the *eau-de-vie* tends to become *eau-de-mort*, and amateur distillers are inclined to be careless and ignorant. Methanol is added to spirit in Britain to make methylated spirit, which is nauseous and attracts none. Methanol, which comes from the pectin in the grapes, occurs in minute quantities in all spirits.

In most parts of France outside the Charente basin, a higher degree of rectification is needed in the distillation, otherwise an unpleasant *goût du terroir* passes into the brandy. In the Rochelle district, just north of the Charente, where spirits have been made for several centuries, a pot-still with a rectifying head of a characteristic local design is used: the 'Alambic des Iles'.

Brandy was made in Languedoc even before the district set up as wine-maker on the large scale. It was used for *vinage* (see page 84) to improve weakly wines. The spirit produced was known as *Le Trois-Six de Montpellier*. The origin of the name, like those of the cognate *Trois-Cinq* and *Trois-Sept*, is obscure. The common explanation is that three parts of *Trois-Six* and three parts of water were mixed to give (about) six parts of ordinary *eau-de-vie*. (There is a slight shrinkage on mixing spirits and water.) Three parts of *Trois-Cinq* with two parts of water would give five parts of brandy; and similarly with *Trois-Sept*. As *eau-de-vie* contains 50 per cent alcohol, this is impossible with 3/7, and more than unlikely with 3/6. Thudicum believes that *Trois-Sept* contained about 94 per cent alcohol, *Trois-Six* about 84 per cent, and *Trois-Cinq* about 78 per cent. Montpellier, Sète, and Béziers still make spirit *à viner les vins*, but the old names have all but died out. The modern Midi brandies are not much used for drinking neat, for after Phylloxera the *vignerons* unwisely grafted inferior scions on the American *porte-greffes*.

Commonwealth Brandy

SOUTH AFRICAN BRANDY

South Africans are in general spirit-drinkers; after all, their forebears invented gin and whisky. A higher proportion of the wine made is distilled to brandy than in any other country in the world (except possibly Peru, for which complete statistics are not available).

The brandy district is chiefly the middle and eastern stretches of the Langeberge slopes, an area about a hundred miles long starting some seventy miles north-east of Cape Town. The chief centres are Worcester, Robertson, Montagne, Swellendam, Barrydale, and Ladismith (which is to the north-east on the Broodswarteberge slopes). The industry has a fairly venerable history and some firms still in existence are over a century old. At one time muscat species of grapes (Muscat of Alexandria, Hanepôot, used for dessert wines in the U.S.A.) were used for distilling, but the muscat flavour persists in the brandy, and nowadays the cognac grapes, Folle blanche, Saint-Émilion, and Colombar (here as elsewhere often called Colombard), are used.

The vintage is made early, before the grapes have fully ripened, for Cape sunshine is a good deal stronger and longer than that of the Charente valley. Irrigation is necessary; the rainfall is low and the rich alluvial Bakkweld beds of the region dry out easily. Wisely enough, the distillers parallel cognac practice: they do not sulphur, and lees and wine are distilled together in pot-stills not unlike those used for cognac. Wines which are rejected go for high-rectification in patent stills to make neutral spirits.

South Africa now produces over four million gallons of brandy – three and a half times as much as in 1938 – and exports about 10 per cent of it; a considerable amount goes for fortifying her dessert wines, which constitute almost half of her total wine production. Drinking brandy, that is, brandy not used for fortification, matures at least three years in wood. Most of the brandy is made by members of the K.W.V. (see page 183). Government supervision is strict and prices are fixed by law for the wholesale disposal of brandies, which are divided for this purpose into three grades according to the method of making them, whether from wine, wine and *marc*, or from *marc* and water.

The chief importers of South African brandy are Scandinavia and Canada, Malaya and West Africa, and Western Germany. Britain takes only 2 per cent of the exports – about 14,000 gallons a year. In South Africa, domestic brandy sells at about 10s. 6d. a bottle retail.

AUSTRALIAN BRANDY

Australia is not a spirit-drinking country like South Africa, and although it needs spirits for fortifying its dessert wines, as the Cape does, the production of brandy is only about one-fifth of that of South Africa, that is, rather under a million gallons.

The earliest wine-distilling in Australia seems to have been carried out at Renmark in South Australia, near the Victoria border, and was started in order to find a use for the Gordo Blanco grapes, which had been originally planted in large areas along the Murray River for drying to make raisins. The advent of the seedless grape (the Californian Thompson Seedless) threw tons of unsaleable Gordo Blanco grapes back into the hands of the *vignerons*, and in order to use them up, a co-operative society was formed at Renmark to go into the distilling business. The spirits made were sold to firms making dessert wines, in spite of the fact that the Gordo Blanco is a muscat with its tenacious flavour. The manufacture of sweet white wines fortified with their own spirits became the principal business of the co-operative distillers of Renmark. The same course of events was followed at nearby Berri and Waikerie and also over the border at Mildura in Victoria. The difficulty in finding a market for the fortified wines, at first considerable, was overcome when Britain allowed Imperial Preference. The comparatively small amount of brandy made for drinking as such is distilled, almost all in South Australia, in pot-stills of the Charente type. The Doradillo grape is largely used nowadays for drinking-brandy; it is probably identical with the Spanish Jaén grape. Fortification spirit is generally made to a higher proof by rectification.

Canada and Malaya take the major part of Australia's brandy exports and much of the rest finds its way into made-up cocktails. In Australia, domestic brandy sells at twenty shillings to twenty-six shillings a bottle: just about half the price of imported cognac.

Brandy of the U.S.A.

Brandy takes second place among spirits in the U.S.A. Nevertheless, California alone makes more brandy than France. It was in California that brandy was first made in America, by the Jesuit missions. Crude pot-stills were employed there as early as the seventeenth century, but only small amounts of spirits were made, and the production had no commercial significance at all until 1843, when a distillery was built by Sutter, and it was not until the 1870s that the business became a success.

California, which makes four-fifths of the U.S.A. production, has over a hundred distilleries. As in Western European countries, three types of brandy are made: spirit for fortification; beverage brandy of high quality; and *marc* brandy, here called *grappa* or *grappo*.

The grapes used for Californian brandy are various, and Folle blanche, Saint-Émilion, and Colombar are not among them. Even Mission grapes are still used, though muscat, alicante, and zinfandel are more common. The larger firms use yeast cultures for the fermentation, but most of the smaller ones still rely on the natural yeasts from the skins. It is not uncommon to add ammonium salts and phosphates to the vat to stimulate the yeasts and so cause a rapid fermentation. Few pot-stills are employed nowadays, although some small distillers use them. The usual still is an elaboration of the old Coffey still, a many-chambered duplex still, which has a throughput of about 120 gallons an hour. The main fraction is collected at 70 or 80 per cent alcohol and is diluted with pure water to 60 per cent for storage. Ageing is carried out in white oak casks which have been well-seasoned (an important point) but not charred. Ageing in charred casks tends to produce a spirit which may be mistaken for whisky. Caramel is used for colouring. The ageing is carried out in the naturally warm rooms of the Californian summer (110°F.), but apart from this, artificial methods of quick ageing are rarely employed.

In the other states making brandy, New Jersey, New York, Washington, Oregon, Connecticut, etc., pot-stills are commonly used, but continuous stills are slowly replacing them.

Grappa is made from pressed *marc* (pomace), which is stacked so that a certain amount of fermentation goes on in the dry: this results in special and characteristic flavours in the *grappa*. After a few months the stack is broken up and mixed with water and wine lees and distilled in a pot-still. The heart of this distillate is then transferred to a continuous still of the Coffey type and again distilled to give a distillate of about 80 per cent alcohol or lower. This is diluted with water before bottling.

For fortification, spirits are made by distilling to give a neutral distillate of more than 95 per cent alcohol in two column stills of basically Coffey type, the columns being commonly thirty or forty feet high and five or six feet in diameter with perhaps fifty plates, each of complex construction so as to separate the water and congenerics.

European Brandy

SPANISH BRANDY

Spanish brandy, most of which is made in the Jerez district, is exported to South America, and to Cuba and Mexico. That retained for domestic sale has a high reputation, and many think it ranks with any brandy but cognac and armagnac.

GREEK BRANDY

Greece is quite an important brandy producer in her own sales area, the Levant, and Greek 'cognac' may be found all over the Continent and even in Australia. It is almost all made from white grapes; local varieties are used: Savatiano, plump grapes which are allowed to become very ripe so as to increase the sugar, that is, the alcohol, together with two *cépages* which are less sweet but, being highly flavoured, supply the congenerics which give Greek brandy its characteristic flavour and aroma. Most of these groups are grown on the mainland (Attica and the southern Peloponnese) and on Euboea, and the distilleries are at the Piraeus. The wines contain 12 to 14 per cent alcohol, extraordinarily high for brandy-wine. They are distilled in Charentais-type stills for the first distillation and in pot-stills fitted with rectifying columns for the second. The stills are steam heated. The brandy is aged for three years in casks containing 400 gallons, and, as in the U.S.A., the temperature is allowed to rise in the maturing-rooms. Rain-water is used to bring down the alcohol content to between 40 and 45 per cent.

Greek 'cognacs' (as they are persistently described) have the faint but unmistakable flavour and odour due to the Rodites and Phileri grapes, and although many inferior brands are sold, at their best they are good. The chief cause of the inferiority of the poor ones seems to be the inclusion of musty grapes in making the wine, and the consequent necessity to rectify too highly in the distillation: in keeping undesirable tastes out of the brandy, desirable congenerics are also excluded. Greek brandy made on the island of Chios is flavoured with resin and then called *Masticka*. *Ouzo* is brandy with added aromatic compounds which are sometimes put in the wine before distillation. Neither can on any count be included among the fine spirits.

OTHER EUROPEAN BRANDIES

In every vineyard in Europe some brandy is made, but in most cases it is drunk locally or at least not exported from the country of its origin. German brandies have a mediocre reputation; and Italian spirits are little better: much of the brandy in Italy is highly rectified and goes to the making of the innumerable liqueurs. Yugoslavia makes little grape-brandy and that little is consumed locally. Her fruit brandies are well known, of course. Russian 'cognac' is said to be of fair quality, 'not particularly fiery, but with not much body'.

South American Brandy

Brandy made in most of the vineyard countries of South America is of no more than local interest, but Peru has for long made a spirit, called *pisco*, whose reputation extends all along the west coast of the continent, as far north as California. The manufacture started in the early days of the *conquistadores*, or perhaps in the second generation of the Spanish settlement. It appears that Don Geronimo de Cabrera, who founded the town of Ica, then called Valverda, began distilling the wine from grapes grown in the district. He was a man who liked his *aguardiente*, and employed the natives of the district, of the *pisco* tribe (from the Quechua word for 'bird'), to make jars to store and transport it. These were small earthenware containers of the shape of the ancient Greek amphoræ. They were coated internally with the wax of the wild bees to make them spirit-tight. They also became known as *piscos*, and the trade, which became important even in the seventeenth century, gave its name to the port from which they were shipped and to the district, which in fact are both still called Pisco. By 1640, *pisco* (the brandy) was well known and much liked by the European immigrants who began to come over soon after Pedro de la Gasca had pacified the country.

Nowadays about half a million gallons of *pisco* are made in the Ica district and sent by rail to the sea at Pisco, where it is shipped north as far as San Francisco, south to Valparaiso and Concepción de Chile. It is made in pot-stills of primitive construction, and pains are taken not to lose the traditional taste and odour of beeswax.

Spirits are also made at Chincha, without the aid of beeswax, from grapes or *marc* (*Aguardientes de Chincha*). They have a wider range of alcohol content than *pisco*, which rarely contains less than 43 per cent or more than 46 per cent, while Chincha spirits may have as much as 55 per cent – one-third as strong again as the brandy, whisky, gin, and rum of Western Europe.

The Maturing of Brandy

Fine wines mature in bottle; spirits mature in wood. Inferior wines and spirits do not improve at all on keeping and may deteriorate. The fact is that most of the possible chemical reactions between the constituents of brandy, or other spirits, take place in the still, for chemical changes are much more rapid at high temperatures. So that a bottle of spirits kept for a century is just the same as it was when it was bottled, unless it has lost by evaporation, or the cork has rotted. On the other hand, wine can change because change is implicit in it: when fresh it is incomplete.

The action of the wood on brandy is in general an exchange between the brandy and the wood, some of the more volatile constituents of the brandy escaping through the pores of the wood, some of the tannins and other (obscure) constituents of the wood dissolving in the brandy. A list of the noteworthy researches on the maturing of brandy runs to hundreds or thousands of items, but it is probable that on the balance what happens is that in the early stages of the maturation in wood, there is a gradual increase in the substances dissolved and that these react with the brandy slowly thereafter. Meanwhile there is considerable loss of brandy through the wood, and more alcohol than water is lost because alcohol passes through the pores more readily than the water. Air meanwhile comes in through the pores and reacts by oxidizing some of the constituents, both those originally present and those absorbed from the wood.

Fruit Brandies

Fruit wines when distilled give fruit brandies, and although these are most often made at the northern edge of the vine-belt, in Normandy and in Central and Eastern Europe, a considerable amount is also produced in Yugoslavia and the U.S.A., and in Alsace, all of which are within the vineyard area. There is no reason why spirits should not be made from elderberry wine or parsnip wine, but in fact the only fruit brandies of any importance are those from apples (that is to say, cider), from plums, and from cherries, although apricot brandy is also common in Central Europe.

The best known apple brandy is *Calvados*, made in the French *département* of the same name. Applejack, the U.S. apple brandy, is the American equivalent. The fruit brandies are made in a very similar manner to grape brandy. Applejack is said to have been made in the United States in the seventeenth century. The first distillation of the cider gives a main fraction with about 30 per cent alcohol, and the second distillation then produces a heart fraction with about 60 per cent alcohol. This is diluted for ageing to just over 50 per cent and run into oak barrels, where it is kept for between three and six months before bottling. The belief that apple brandies are made by congelation (compare page 84) is a legend: no more.

Of all the plum brandies made in the orchard regions of continental Europe and the U.S.A., only one has a reputation outside its native country. This is the Yugoslav *slivovica* (*sljivovica; slivovitz; sliwowitz*). The fruit used is that of southern Yugoslavia, Bosnia, where large areas are planted with pozega plums, which are particularly large and sweet, rivalling grapes in the latter respect (and surpassing them handsomely in the former). The district has been well known for its plum brandy for at least seven centuries. Trees are not cropped for *slivovica* until they are twenty years old, and when the fruit is crushed for fermentation a proportion of kernels is included in order to introduce the peculiar, slightly bitter taste. Pure yeast cultures are used in the larger factories and the fermentation is carried out in large glass-lined tanks. Continuous stills are used to give a distillate of about 23 per cent alcohol content. The second distillation produces a spirit with 40 per cent alcohol or higher. The smaller producers use simpler equipment: wooden fermentation vats, and pot-stills. The spirit is aged in oaken casks, often of 400 gallons capacity, for at least three years. It is sold in Britain at 40 per cent alcohol (70° proof) and 50 per cent alcohol (87° proof). A much smaller amount of *klevovaca* is also made in Yugoslavia. This is *slivovica* to which juniper berries have been added in the first distillation. It is sold in Britain at 70° proof (40 per cent alcohol).

Kirsch is the cherry brandy of west-central Europe: Alsace and the Vosges country in France, the Black Forest area of Germany, and Switzerland. The products differ somewhat and none should be confused with the syruped liqueur sold in Britain as cherry brandy. Well-ripened morella cherries, and in France wild cherries (*merises*) also, are crushed and the mash fermented in wooden vats for five days. In Alsace where the kirsch of highest repute is made, some proportion (about a third) of the stones is crushed with the fruit, as in making *slivovica*. The glycoside amygdalin is extracted from the kernels by this means and decomposes to give glucose and a compound which further breaks down to give an almond-tasting oil and hydrocyanic (prussic) acid. There is only a very small amount of amygdalin in the kernels and even smaller amounts of oil and acid are formed from it, but they are sufficient to impart the required flavour. (This is an instance of the frequently observed fact that the presence of minute quantities of a substance is often beneficial and attractive, although large quantities would be intolerable. The principle is well known in the formulation of perfumes.)

The liquid drawn off from the fermented cherry-mash is distilled in pot-stills; steam rather than direct-firing is most often employed. It is collected at just under proof (50 per cent alcohol; 12° under British proof; 100° U.S. proof). Blending with neutral spirits and with prune distillate (*Zwetschgenwasser*) and the addition of almond essence are not unknown in making inferior varieties. The detection of sophistication in these fruit distillates, including grape brandy, is rarely a simple matter; chemical analysis for the dozen or so main constituents very seldom reveals any significant differences between the various brandies, and it is usually necessary for the analyst to search for likely additives and to conclude with a probability rather than a certainty.

CHAPTER 12

WHISKY

IT is only a matter of three or four generations ago since whisky, like golf, was almost solely a Scottish pastime, although it is true that Irish whisky pre-dated Scotch. Whisky is now spread uniformly over the Anglo-Saxon world, and is increasing in popularity in some Latin countries.

Although 'whisky' and 'whiskey' are used almost interchangeably in the ordinary way, trade usage in Britain favours 'whisky' for Scotch and 'whiskey' for Irish. In the U.S.A. 'whiskey' is the commoner spelling for both; in Canada, on the other hand, all is 'whisky'. The word derives from the Gaelic phrase for 'water of life', *uisge-beatha*. The French feel that brandy is also the water of life, *eau-de-vie*; in Italy, it is *acquavite*; in Scandinavia, the most popular spirits are called *akvavit* by the Danes and *aquavit* by the Swedes and Norwegians. (Some Swedish brands are also called *akvavit*.)

Scotch whisky, like vodka, *Kornbranntwein*, *tiquira*, and *kava*, is a spirit made from starch. Among them, it is the universally-acknowledged aristocrat. In fact the position is: cognac and whisky first, and the rest nowhere. Just as cognac is inimitable, so no imitation of Scotch whisky would deceive even a lifelong teetotaller. Attempts have been made to produce whisky elsewhere – Australia, for instance. Soon after the war finished in 1945, a sort of whisky was made in Denmark and sold in Britain to the adventurous. It was drinkable, although there was fusel-oil in the taste, but its relationship to Scotch whisky was so distant that it would have been better labelled with a less reminiscent name. Whisky is made in the U.S.A. and in Canada, but the method of making differs in a number of respects from that used to produce Scotch. There is no doubt that if a colourable imitation of Scotch whisky could be made outside Scotland, it would be made.

The uniqueness of Scotch whisky, which is unquestioned, is something of a mystery. The whisky experts attribute it to the peculiarities of the barley or of the burn-water used to make it, or to the virtues of the peat used to provide the fuel for the drying of the germinating grain, or to the shape of the pot-stills used to distil the spirit, or, in their more romantic moments, to the very air of Scotland, which, as no one would think of denying to a Scotsman, is unique.

The making of wine is, broadly speaking, a single-stage process: fermentation. The making of brandy is a two-stage affair: fermentation and distillation. But in the making of whisky three processes are necessary, for the raw material of whisky is grain, and in particular the starch in the grain, which must be converted to sugar before fermentation to give the alcoholic liquid which is distilled. Starch will not ferment with yeast.

Considering whisky made in Scotland, Ireland, the United States, and Canada there are several varieties, distinguished from one another by the various methods used in their manufacture and by the grains they are made from.

There is first of all the malt whisky made in the Highlands and on the west coast of Scotland. Pot-stills are used to distil this. A small amount of pot-still malt whisky is made in Ireland also.

In Scotland and Ireland, grain-whisky is made. All the Scottish grain-whisky is made in distilleries south of St Andrews with the exception of that from the Montrose distillery in Angus.

Rye whisky is made in the U.S.A. and Canada.

Bourbon is made in the U.S.A.

Scotch malt whisky is the heart of Scotch whisky and is mostly blended with grain-whisky to suit the modern palate: malt whisky is too heavy in flavour for the Sassenach and the Lowland Scot.

Malt Whisky

Four types of malt whisky are made in Scotland: Campbeltown, Highland, Islay, and Lowland. Campbeltown malt whisky comes from three distilleries all within ten miles of Campbeltown in the Mull of Kintyre; ten distilleries on the island of Islay produce the Islay malts. Highland malt whiskies are made in about eighty distilleries, mostly concentrated in the counties of Aberdeen, Banff, Moray, Nairn, and Inverness: that is, north and west of Aberdeen, east of Loch Ness.

There are, however, three on Orkney Mainland, two near Fort William, one at Tobermory, one at Skye, and three more around Pitlochry. Malts of the highest fame are those made in the valley of the Spey in Moray and Banff. Lowland malts all come from the waist of Scotland, between Edinburgh and Greenock.

In the vine, the starch produced by photosynthesis from the carbon dioxide of the air is turned to sugar by the agency of enzymes in the plant, and the pulp which forms within the grape-stones is the food on which the seeds draw for their sustenance until their roots are ready to use the humic and other materials from the earth. The grains of cereals also secrete enzymes to make the starch of the grains available to the germinating seed by turning it to sugar. These enzymes, generally lumped together under the name of *diastase*, form in that part between the embryo itself and the rest of the grain, so that they can take the starch and pass it through to the embryo after saccharifying it.

As the grain ripens, the amount of diastase increases, and as the grain begins to shoot, it continues to increase until much more has been formed than is necessary to saccharify all the starch available. It is at its maximum when the tiny plumule which will become the stem of the new barley-plant is about as long as the grain. This takes somewhere between nine and fourteen days, depending upon the type of barley.

The distiller takes advantage of all this to obtain the enzymes to saccharify his grain by the processing known as *malting*, in much the same way as the brewer. Malt is almost all made from barley. The grain is first cleaned from dust and grit. It then passes to tanks where it is soaked in cold water which softens the grains. The next operation is the malting. The wet grain is spread out on the malting-floors and allowed to sprout. Its temperature is kept at about 75°F. and it is periodically shovelled back and forth so as to prevent it overheating. When malting has proceeded long enough, the sprouted grain is conveyed to the adjoining kiln, where it is heated gradually. The object is to stop growth but not to destroy the activity of the enzymes. The green malt is spread on perforated floors while a peat fire beneath slowly heats them to the correct temperature, about 125°F. or perhaps a little higher. This temperature is reached in three or four days.

The malted barley is now dry; it resembles ordinary barley in appearance, but has the reek of the peat fire about it. It has swollen a little – about 6 or 7 per cent, and it contains enough enzyme to saccharify much more starch than is actually present. Next, it is matured for some weeks in bins, then ground up finely. The grist which is produced is mixed with hot water in tanks called *mash tuns*. Here the temperature is still of great importance, for the starch must be turned to sugars by the diastase and extracted by the water. It is stirred constantly and kept warm with steam-pipes or the injection of live steam. Mashing is most commonly carried out in instalments; often four separate mashings are made on the grist. The amount of water – pure water – needed to supply a distillery is very great, and may amount to ten or more times the volume of proof spirits produced. This is the reason why most distilleries remain sited beside Highland streams of pure mountain-water.

The mash tun has a perforated false bottom, and when all the sugar has been extracted, the sweet liquor, the *worts*, is drawn off, leaving the grain-husks in the tun. These, known as *draff*, are used as cattle-food. The next stage, the fermentation, carried out in *fermenting backs*, is in general like the fermentation of grape-must. The vats hold between 2,000 and 10,000 gallons. The sugar present is not only glucose and fructose, however; sucrose is also present (that is, ordinary table-sugar, such as is obtained from cane or beet). No yeast is present, of course, and the enzymes of malt are not those which are capable of carrying out the alcoholic fermentation described in chapter 4. The worts are cooled to about 70°F. and yeast added. Cooling coils are fitted in the backs to control the temperature. Fermentation takes two or three days; the alcoholic liquid, known as *wash*, contains perhaps 10 per cent alcohol, and is something like very strong beer.

Scotch malt whisky is twice distilled in copper pot-stills (Plate 31). The stills are of the simplest type, without *chauffe-vin* or other complications. They are of much larger dimensions than the cognac stills and have a capacity of several thousand gallons (up to 10,000 according to the size of the distillery). In the first, the *wash-still*, is a rotating chain, the *rummager*, which continually scrapes the bottom of the still and prevents suspended solid material from sticking and burning, and besides burning, causing irregular boiling and 'bumping'. Stills are direct-fired, with coke or peat. All the alcohol is driven off in the wash-still; distillation is continued until only water is left. The *low wines*, as the distillate is called, are collected in copper worm condensers cooled with water. From 10,000 gallons of wash some 3,000 to 3,500 gallons of low wines are collected. The residue in the still, *pot-ale*, is run to waste or used as a fertilizer.

The low wines, which contain about 20 per cent alcohol, are distilled again in smaller stills, the *spirit-stills*. There is no need for a rummager in these, but otherwise they resemble the wash-stills. The first, light fractions which come over, the *foreshots*, contain alcohol together with various secondary constituents. They are added to the next batch of low wines for redistillation. The next fraction is whisky, and to determine the point at which to change from collecting foreshots to collecting whisky is not a decision to be taken without long experience. The whisky fraction as collected is usually between 11 and 25° o.p. (over proof), that is, it contains between 63 and 71 per cent alcohol. When it has been decided that all the whisky has come over, a third fraction, the *feints*, is collected. This contains about 25 per cent alcohol, as well as fusel-oil and other substances. Like the foreshots, it is returned for mixing with the next batch of low wines. The residue in the spirit-still, amounting to about half its charge, is turned into the drains. These spent lees probably contain desirable flavouring substances, but fusel-oil and other nauseating materials are also present, and so the baby must be thrown away with the bath. It is, however, a small baby.

In many Lowland malt whisky distilleries, three distillations are made in order to obtain a finer definition of the product. In Irish malt distilleries also, three distillations are made in pot-stills, which are larger than the Scottish; some contain 20,000 gallons of wash. Soap is sometimes added to the wash-still to prevent frothing, and charcoal in the low wines still absorbs some of the less desirable compounds. The whisky fraction in Ireland usually contains about 70 per cent alcohol.

Grain-whisky (Patent-still Whisky)

In fifteen distilleries, mostly near Glasgow and Edinburgh, grain whisky is made. All whisky is made from grain, of course, but the term 'grain-whisky' is in common usage reserved for spirit made with little help from malt, and distilled in a patent-still of the Coffey type. It has very much less flavour than a malt whisky and the two types are blended to give ordinary Scotch.

The long chains of the starch molecule can be chopped up into their sugar units by boiling starch with acids, without help from enzymes, and much of the sugar in wort for patent-still whisky is produced in this way. The procedure is to mix an unmalted grist, that is, ground grain, to a mash with water, then to add sulphuric acid diluted with water, and finally to heat the whole with steam slowly, while the mass is being agitated. When the process has proceeded, not to completion, but to some intermediate point, the acid in the partly saccharified mash is neutralized by adding milk of lime and powdered chalk. The sulphuric acid is thereby removed by combination and forms a sludge of calcium sulphate. The neutral mash is then cooled somewhat, usually to about 145°F., and malt at a temperature some 20° lower is added; the conversion to sugar now proceeds to completion, and one has worts almost identical in composition with malt worts. It has comparatively little of the constituents contributed by the malt, naturally.

Fermentation of grain worts is usually carried out in larger vats than in the case of malt worts, but there is no essential difference. The fermented worts are distilled in a Coffey still or some variant of it (see page 209). The steam and worts inputs, and the position of the blind plate in the rectifying column, are adjusted to give exactly the product required, with the aid of many years of experience.

Whisky as it comes from the still, whether pot or patent, is an unattractive beverage. It has no colour and it is harsh in taste. The colour of whisky is scarcely at all due to extraction from the casks it is matured in; caramel is added to produce a fairly standard and popular shade.

The blending of malt and grain-whiskies is more than a mere mixing. There is some interaction between the constituents which tempers the crudeness of the taste. However, the amelioration takes place chiefly during the ageing period, when the whisky is stored in oak barrels in unheated warehouses for several years. Scotch whisky must be matured for at least three years before selling, according to the provisions of the Customs and Excise Act of 1952. The casks are usually old sherry casks, and there seems no doubt that the whisky takes from the oak of the cask some constituents, and loses others to the wood. The legal minimum of three years is always exceeded in practice and eight or ten years would be nearer the truth. After twenty years in wood, whisky usually tends to deteriorate. Once bottled, whisky changes no more, and to keep a bottle of whisky does no one any good, except one's heirs.

Irish whiskey is produced in Dublin, Cork, Tullamore, and Kilbeggan by five distillers (John Jameson, John Power, B. Daly, John Locke, and Cork Distilleries). Very little patent still whiskey is made and the product from the pot-stills is not blended to the degree necessary to obtain such a highly standardized drink as Scotch. In Eire the legal maturing period is five years, though a considerably longer period than this usually elapses. It may be noted that in the Republic, the strength of the whiskey is rather higher than in Britain, the measures are somewhat larger and the duty a little less. The Irish whiskey industry is on a considerably smaller scale than the Scotch. It is scarcely necessary to point out that comparisons between the quality of Irish whiskey and Scotch whisky should be left to the Scotch and Irish.

Most of the whisky produced is exported to the U.S.A. Scotland sends abroad about twelve million proof gallons a year (equivalent to about 180 million bottles) and Ireland about half a million bottles. About four million proof gallons of Scotch are consumed in Britain annually. These amounts are very much less than that produced in the U.S.A., which is considerably the largest whisky-producer. More than one-half of Britain's whisky exports goes to the U.S.A. and about one-fifth to the Commonwealth countries. The two principal foreign importers of Scotch whisky are Venezuela and Mexico, both of which, by an interesting coincidence, have a fairly large resident population of Anglo-Saxon oil-drillers.

American Whisky

American (and Canadian) whisky, whether rye or bourbon, is made by the same general method as Scotch grain or patent-still whisky, but the differences in detailed procedure are considerable.

Rye Whisky is made by malting rye or barley, and saccharifying a further quantity of rye with the malt.

Bourbon Whisky is made in the same way but from the action of a malted wheat or barley on a maize mash. (Maize is commonly referred to as 'corn' in the U.S., of course.)

There is considerable variation in practice in the U.S.A., but the larger distilleries mostly cook the grain-grist with water under pressure to begin with. Then it is mixed with the malt which converts the starch to sugar. Acid mashing is not common in the U.S.A.

Fermentation with added yeast is carried out with or without the addition of 'spent beer', the residue from the stills. In the first case the whisky is 'sweet mash whisky', in the second, 'sour-mash whisky'. Comparatively little 'sour-mash whisky' is made nowadays. There are no pot-stills in the production of American whisky: only patent, continuous stills are used. The wort is called 'beer', and this is pumped, without separating from the 'draff', at about 6 per cent alcohol, through heaters to the top of a column which is rather like the analyser column of the Coffey still, but complicated by a piping system which allows some of the liquids condensing on the plates to be returned to the column for rectification. The column is arranged so that the lightest and the heaviest fractions are removed continuously. Only about 2 per cent of the alcohol originally present in the beer is lost.

American whisky is not aged in old sherry barrels, like Scotch, but in white oak barrels which have been charred internally. This practice of charring, traditional in the American industry, is said to date from the days when old molasses barrels were used. The taste imparted by the charring of the oak became a desirable characteristic and charring was, and is still, continued. Bourbon is aged in unheated warehouses, like Scotch, rye in heated rooms.

Most U.S. whisky – two-thirds of all the domestic manufacture – is 'blended'. Straight whiskies are first mixed to obtain the desired balance of flavour and bouquet, and then neutral spirit is added: this dilutes the bouquet and flavour but does not affect the balance. Blended whiskies in the U.S.A. are therefore light-bodied, with a smaller proportion of congenerics than Scotch or Irish: that is, less taste and aroma.

CANADIAN WHISKY

Canadian whisky is somewhat light-bodied, so that the taste of rye or of 'corn' (read 'maize') does not dominate. Nevertheless, no neutral spirit is used in making Canadian blended whiskies. In Canada, the age of the youngest whisky in the blend is indicated on the label. Canada's licensing laws are peculiar to Canada. All Canadian whisky is made under government supervision by private concerns, and almost all is made by two companies.

Maturing of Whisky

The taste of whisky is to a great extent due to the presence of the combinations of acids formed in the fermentation with the higher-boiling alcohols, that is, to the esters. It is this same class of chemical compounds which contributes so greatly to the taste of wine, but in the case of grain spirits such as whisky, the higher alcohols, the fusel-oil, are in considerably greater quantity. Some of the fusel-oil, which is formed in the fermentation from the proteins of the grain, combines in the course of the distillation with the acids present, many of which are produced by oxidation of some of the higher alcohols themselves. The whole subject is very obscure in spite of investigations which have been carried out, chiefly by American chemists (Valaer, Tolman, Liebmann, and others).

Maturing in part continues, far more slowly, the changes which started during the distillation, but the principal changes are those due to interaction with the wood of the casks. So far as these are reflected in chemical analysis, however, it seems that the changes are very great indeed in the first month but thereafter are slow and subtle.

The innumerable methods which have been suggested, and often patented, for quick-maturing whisky may be dealt with fairly summarily; none seems to be employed in practice. Oxidation is doubtless an important factor in ageing, and rapid methods of oxidation are patented with fair regularity. Exposure to rays (ultra-violet usually) is another popular line, and so also is electrolytic treatment. A further method, which is rather one of imitation ageing than accelerated ageing, is to make an extract of oak-chips and sawdust and to dope the whisky with it.

The Drinking of Whisky

Whisky, not being a drink in which Latin nations are interested, has no particular position in the gastronomical curriculum. It is drunk, neat or diluted with water or almost any soft drink, with meals or at any other time.

In Britain the price at present is 36 shillings a bottle, or, when the contribution to the Exchequer is deducted, 11s. 5d. a bottle. Compared with wine it is not dear, calculated on the alcohol content, for it contains quite three times as much alcohol as the average claret, burgundy, hock, or Chianti, and as a foreign wine carries an Exchequer tax of 2s. 2d. a bottle, the equivalent price for a bottle of foreign wine should be 5s. 8d. a bottle. This is below the average price of even the most ordinary wines, and less than half the price of a really good one.

The story of the early rivalries between the large whisky distillers is told in Sir Robert Bruce Lockhart's book, *Scotch*. The combination took place in 1925 of the five largest Scotch whisky distillers: John Dewar ('White Label'), John Walker, James Buchanan ('Black & White'), John Haig, and Mackie ('White Horse'). They now form parts of the Distillers Company.

CHAPTER 13

RUM

Until about a generation ago, rum was considered to be a rather 'low' drink (from the social point of view) and its consumption was almost wholly confined to sailors. When cocktails became popular in the 1920s, however, it became a popular ingredient of mixed drinks, and nowadays, encouraged by the efforts of West Indian shippers, it is drunk with soda water, lemon (or other fruit-juice), milk, Coca-Cola, or bitters, as well as in cocktails. It has always been one of the ingredients of punch (page 268).

Rum is the spirit of the sugar-cane. It is almost all made in the West Indies and the mainlands around the Caribbean Sea, that is to say, in Jamaica, Puerto Rico, the U.S.A., British Guiana, Hispaniola, Cuba, Trinidad, the Virgin Isles, Brazil, Mexico, Martinique, and Bolivia. A little is produced in the East Indies and in Madagascar, and some in South Africa and Queensland.

The raw material is generally a mixture of the by-products from the extraction of sugar from the cane. At the factory, the cane is cut up and crushed between rollers, either wet or dry, and the residual *bagasse* again crushed to express all the juice. The liquid is warmed almost to boiling-point and then cooled and separated from the sludge which settles out. The sugar solution, very dark in colour, is treated with lime and heated again. A thick scum forms; this is removed: it is used for rum. The liquid is evaporated and then cooled. The sugar deposits and is separated off and purified. The dark liquid remaining, molasses, is evaporated further to obtain more sugar, but it becomes increasingly difficult for the sugar to crystallize out and the molasses is used for fermentation to make alcohol for industrial purposes, and to make rum.

The thick liquid molasses is diluted with water and mixed with the scum from the liming and 'dunder', which is the residue left in the stills from the last distillation: 'dunder' looks rather like pea-soup. This mixture is allowed to ferment for a few days. The methods vary widely. In some rum distilleries the mash is allowed to sour by itself; that is to say, by the aid of the natural yeasts. In this case, *bagasse* is usually added to the vat. In other distilleries yeast is supplied, either a bakery yeast, or a brewer's or winery yeast. In some of the more modern factories, a pure-culture rum yeast is used; this is natural yeast, cultured so as to free it from stranger yeasts. Pure-culture yeasts are considered to give a better-flavoured rum. Before fermenting, a little acid is added to the mash to counteract the effect of the liming of the juice.

The distillation is carried out in pot-stills in the older factories. In the more modern distilleries improved types are used, of course. Different firms distil to different strengths, from only just over proof (57 per cent U.K., 50 per cent U.S.A.; see page 212) to almost pure alcohol. It is usually stored at this strength and diluted before bottling. It is water-white, or nearly so, for the colouring matter of the molasses does not pass over but remains in the still.

The ageing of rum is important. The best rums are kept in cask for three years or more, some for very much longer. Rum is considered to continue to improve for twenty years in good oak casks. Colour is taken up from the casks and, as in the case with wine, some changes between the various constituents of rum take place and result in an improvement in the taste. More than in the case of other spirits, the constituents which give the characteristic aroma and flavour to rum are higher esters (see page 93).

Ageing is sometimes hastened in various ways, especially by treating with charred oak chips, and caramel is frequently added to impart or improve the colour.

Although the U.S.A. is an important producer of rum, most still comes from the islands of the West Indies. So far as Britain is concerned, only rums from the Commonwealth are obtainable – Jamaica, Barbadoes, Trinidad, and Demerara. France principally imports Martinique rum. The other producers are in the dollar area and the cost of importing their rum into Europe is too great.

Sugar became common in the world's markets because the sugar-cane could be grown so easily and abundantly in the West Indies. Before the sixteenth century, sugar was somewhat rare and very expensive. It was the Portuguese of Northern Brazil who first began to export it to Europe in quantity. By the latter part of the sixteenth century, production moved to the French islands of the Lesser Antilles – Martinique, Antigua, Guadaloupe, etc. During the eighteenth century, planting advanced to the Greater Antilles – Cuba, Hispaniola, Jamaica, and Puerto Rico. For a time Haiti was the chief producer, then Jamaica replaced it. The rise of beet-sugar and the abolition of slavery damaged the industry severely and nowadays more sugar is made from beet than from cane.

Wherever the sugar-cane is grown, rum is made; it is an obvious and lucrative outlet for products which would otherwise be wasted. For every hundredweight of raw sugar made, three gallons of rum may be produced, and the latter is the more valuable product.

Jamaica Rum

Jamaica, which was the first commercial producer of rum, is still one of the most important. The sugar estates are in the south of the island and extend in a narrow strip from Kingston, the capital, westwards for about thirty miles. This district has been under sugar-canes ever since the eighteenth century, when the island was a more important colony of Britain than those on the North American continent. At that time, and until about 1805, sugar was the one product of Jamaica. Nowadays bananas occupy twice the acreage of canes. Nevertheless, more than a sixth of the cultivated land is under sugar. Unlike bananas, which are chiefly grown by a large number of planters banded together in a co-operative selling organization, sugar is produced by a few large plantations (almost all by eight companies) and each of these has its own distillery. Each distillery, with its slightly different method of manufacture, produces a characteristic product, although differences are now disappearing.

All the estates, except those in a very small area at the extreme eastern tip of the island, need irrigation, for it is unfortunate that the north of Jamaica, where rainfall is abundant (over 100 inches) is less fertile than the southern plains of St Catherine, which have less than thirty inches. With the exception of these southern coastal plains, most of Jamaica is a high limestone plateau of up to 3,000 feet elevation.

The cultivation of the sugar-cane and the production of rum have changed greatly in Jamaica in the last half-century. Before 1914, full-bodied and highly-flavoured rums were made; nowadays the cocktail fancier prefers a less exotic-tasting drink, and a milder product is consequently supplied. The flavour of rum is almost wholly due to the presence of esters, and the higher esters have a stronger flavour and aroma, and a greater persistence of flavour and odour. Since the war, Jamaica rum contains an average of about one part in five hundred of esters, but thirty or forty years ago there was ten times as much, although a low-ester rum was always made: 'Common Clear Rum', it was called.

In the latter part of the nineteenth century a certain amount of very high-ester rum was made in Jamaica for the Continental market, chiefly for Germany. It had about one part of esters, mostly heavy esters, in twenty or thirty parts of rum. High-ester rums are made by keeping the mash more acid than usual, and allowing the fermentation to continue for much longer, up to a month. The Continental rums were not consumed in Europe. They were mixed with neutral spirit, made from potato or grain mash, and let down with water. The product was somewhat fiery but had sufficient of the flavour from Jamaica to pass, so it was shipped to darkest Africa as 'rum', as 'Jamaica Rum'. When the same material with the same designation began to reach England in sizeable quantities, the Jamaican shippers took action. To make matters worse, the shippers of Hamburg and Flushing began to omit the high-ester material from Jamaica as an ingredient and substitute an ester from their chemical factories which, with the help of a little colouring matter, distantly simulated Jamaica rum. In 1891 a Customs order was made confining the term 'rum' to spirits coming from the West Indies and Demerara. Anything with the flavour of imitation about it was to be labelled honestly, 'Imitation Rum'. In 1899, 44,000 gallons were imported under this designation, but the trade was dying, and by the end of the 1914–18 war, only a few hundred gallons came into Britain.

Fairly highly flavoured rums are still produced, but only in minor quantities. Jamaican is the most highly flavoured rum, with the possible exception of the Martinique product and some minor rums. It contains three or four times as much esters as U.S.A. rum, for instance, and above five times as much as Cuban. Jamaica rum is highly prized by many, and rums are made in other places to try to imitate it. Arroyo in Puerto Rico ferments a not-too-acid mash for a short time (a total of twenty-six hours) in two stages, the first with a pure yeast culture and the second with a bacterial ferment, and then distils very slowly indeed to allow the esters to form.

Jamaica has probably the most stringent regulations concerning rum production. It may not be distilled above 88 per cent alcohol (55° overproof) and only pure water and caramel from burnt sugar may be added. Government inspectors regulate the ageing in bond. Rum is diluted with water before bottling according to its destination; for the English market the product is let down to 37 per cent alcohol (35° o.p.). Legally, it is required to have aged for three years in cask before bottling.

United States Rum

The United States is the world's largest producer of rum, which is made in a few large distilleries in the eastern states and Kentucky. As the molasses has to be transported from the south, no 'dunder' or scum is included in the mash, only 'blackstrap' molasses.

Fermentation and distillation methods differ widely between the different firms, and even the time of fermentation may vary between two and twelve days. In some distilleries the rum is taken over into the receivers at 60 per cent alcohol or less (120° U.S. proof), in others at 95 per cent. Sometimes the product is redistilled or treated with charcoal. For ageing in warehouses it is reduced to 100° proof (U.S. – 50 per cent alcohol). If of very high proof it may not be aged but merely diluted with water and coloured. Ageing, in new charred oak barrels, takes place for anything between a few months and four or more years. Some is quick-aged (with oak chips) and sold as light-bodied rum.

U.S. domestic rum is generally rather heavy-bodied but tastes raw compared with the Jamaican or Demeraran product.

In Vermont a certain amount of rum is made from maple syrup.

Before the Eighteenth Amendment was passed in 1919, a special rum, 'Old New England Rum', was made in considerable quantities for blending and flavouring. It resembled Jamaica rum more than anything else. Ageing developed in it an excellent bouquet and it was much prized. Since 1933, the year of Repeal, production does not seem to have been taken up again.

The New England rum industry dates back to the early eighteenth century. In those days, New England made rum from molasses shipped from the West Indies, which were supplied with slaves brought from Africa in the ships of Boston which, on the east-bound trip of their triangular voyage, took the rum to European and African customers: the 'New England Triangle'. When, later in the century, the British Crown imposed taxes on molasses shipped north, the indignation of the colonists was extreme, and economists are inclined to rank it among the principal causes of the unrest which led to the 'Boston Tea-party' of 1773 and consequently to the secession of the colonies from the British Crown.

The U.S.A. imports most of the Puerto Rican rum production as well as considerable quantities from Cuba, Jamaica, and the Virgin Islands.

Puerto Rico Rum

Puerto Rico, a small island, even smaller than Jamaica but with half as many people again, is the second-largest producer of rum in the world. Like Jamaica, all but the coastal strips are mountainous. Nevertheless, the population density is extremely high (530 to the square mile, about double that of Jamaica).

The island has had an unfortunate history throughout. The first white settlement, in 1508, brought strange diseases besides the sword, and the native population of just under 100,000 was reduced to 4,000 by 1515. The Spaniards abandoned the island because there was no labour. Negro slaves were later imported and sugar-cane plantations started on the coastal strips. In the eighteenth century the island was fairly prosperous, although this scarcely benefited the natives, who were all dead. Many immigrants from the poorer provinces of Spain – Galicia and Asturias in particular – entered the country in the early part of the nineteenth century, and they were joined by Spanish-Americans from the countries of South America, forced to fly from their homes by the revolutions. By 1845, there were almost as many whites as Negroes. The great slump in cane-sugar due to competition from the beet plantations of Europe about this time caused overwhelming unemployment and consequent starvation to Spanish settlers and Negro slaves alike. In 1873 the Negroes were freed but not fed. The island remained destitute, with a fairly large population on the verge of starvation.

In 1898, American occupation brought many advantages. Roads were built, yellow fever and other diseases were stamped out, education was greatly improved, and methods of agriculture brought up to date. By 1940, the population had almost reached two millions. Most of the inhabitants are still living at a very low level of subsistence, however, for the sugar-plantations are almost all owned by absentee owners. Legally, no plantation may be larger than 500 acres, but in fact most of the sugar-plantations average 40,000 acres. Sugar is overwhelmingly the principal crop of the island and cane-plantations need only a small labour force except in the harvest season. It was to take advantage of the large amount of surplus labour that rum manufacture was started in 1935.

Before 1935, various spirits had been made, concoctions of imported rums with alcohol, wine, sugar, molasses, prune-juice, and other ingredients.

Present-day fermentation for rum in Puerto Rico uses a mash based on blackstrap molasses, with ammonium salt added as a yeast food. In order to prevent bacterial growth, some acid is usually added also. Fermentation commonly takes between four and seven days.

Puerto Rican rums are unusually light in flavour, for the short fermentation-time does not encourage their development, neither are materials added, as in several other parts of the Caribbean, to introduce flavour. They are exported to the U.S.A. chiefly, but also to the large cities of South America. Currency difficulties prevent any but inconsiderable amounts from leaving the dollar area.

Demerara Rum

Demerara, which gives its name to a grade of sugar and to a kind of rum, is a district in British Guiana around Georgetown, the capital.

The Guianas are not prosperous colonies of their respective parent nations. Cultivation is confined to the coastal strips and is carried out on only a minute proportion of the area – about a fifth of one per cent in British Guiana. The only agricultural products of any note are sugar and rum.

The labour for the sugar-plantations and the rum distilleries is a mixture of Negroes and natives from the East Indies. The white inhabitants are almost all of Portuguese descent.

The molasses remaining after the brown Demerara sugar has crystallized out is diluted with water, and a little ammonium sulphate and acid added to stimulate the yeasts and discourage the bacteria, respectively. Fermentation is completed in less than two days.

Distillation is carried out to a high alcohol content (about 90 per cent) and the product is then shipped in bulk for blending. Additions commonly made to Demerara rum are various and interesting. They account for the unusually fruity taste and odour, and include plums, raisins, and spices. At one time raw meat was put in the casks both to absorb certain impurities and to impart 'a certain distinctive character'. A considerable amount of caramel is added to give the characteristic deep colour, and this also has some influence on the flavour. After these additions have been made, the rum is rested for three or four days and fined with isinglass (see page 82). Then, after ageing, which may take from a few months to a few years, the rum is ready for sale.

Cuba Rum

Cuba, the largest island in the Caribbean, is almost as large as England and ten times the size of Jamaica. It is larger than the rest of the West Indies together. Unlike almost all the smaller islands, more than half the land is flat enough for mechanized agriculture, and the soil is fertile. The climate is ideal for tropical crops and it is the largest cane-sugar producer in the world. Three-quarters of its trade, both import and export, is with the United States.

In the earlier days of Spanish occupation, from the sixteenth to the middle of the eighteenth century, Cuba was chiefly grazing-land, divided into large cattle estates. Sugar-cane growing began to become important and to replace ranching in the nineteenth century, when competition from beet-sugar was increasing in severity. Nevertheless, by the time the sovereignty of Spain ceased in 1898, almost half the agricultural land was devoted to sugar.

For some years afterwards Cuba remained a sort of protectorate of the United States, and in 1903 a treaty between the two countries gave Cuban sugar preference on the United States market, the largest sugar market in the world. In the first years of the twentieth century, Cuba was rapidly modernized with the help of more than a thousand million dollars of American money.

The sugar-cane is grown all over the middle of the island, which is essentially a one-crop country. About 80 per cent of the exports are sugar and rum. The plantations, mostly owned by North Americans and Cubans, are small, but the sugar refining and the distilling of the rum is carried out on a comparatively few large estates. The cane loses 2 per cent of its sugar each day it is delayed after cutting, and the small planters are in effect employees of the large refining companies.

The seasonal labour demand is partly met by the temporary immigration, during the harvesting season, of many thousands of Haitians and Jamaicans. They come in December and depart in June.

In the rum distilleries, molasses alone is almost entirely used. The rapid fermentation takes three days and a special yeast culture is employed. Distillation from the fermented mash is usually carried out in continuous stills to a high alcohol content. Much of the flavouring material is removed by filtering through sand and charcoal. The product is then re-flavoured lightly with sugar, wine, fruits, bay leaves, and 'special ingredients'. Cuban rum is mostly sold pale – 'white Cuban rum' – a golden colour. There are two classes; Ron Carta and the slightly heavier Ron Oro. (*Ron* is Spanish for rum.) A certain amount of Cuban rum is coloured with caramel. Daiquiri rum is a high-class product with a characteristic flavour.

During the last thirty years, the sugar industry of Cuba has lost some of its original prosperity, owing to competition from beet-sugar, lobbying by the cane-growers of Louisiana, and the faulty economics of the producers.

Barbados Rum

Barbados is a small island, about twice the superficial area of the Channel Isles, with the extraordinarily high population density of 1,163 per square mile: more than twice that of Puerto Rico, four times that of Jamaica. It was established as a British colony in 1625 and its population is over 90 per cent Negro. Cane, which is the chief crop, is planted from seed and, after cropping once, is uprooted and maize, bananas, cotton, or yams planted on the ground for a year, when cane returns. The island is of coral, and great shelves of the coral limestone mount to a height of 1,100 feet. Barbados rum is about medium-bodied. The distillation of the fermented molasses is carried out with high rectification to over 90 per cent alcohol, that is to an almost neutral spirit. Formerly a surprising mixture used to be placed in the still with the fermented liquid: lime, soda, vegetable-roots, coconut-shells, and so on. An equally interesting mixture of flavouring materials is used to bring the neutral spirits into a drink with the required taste: sherry, Madeira, spirits of nitre, bitter almonds, and raisins.

Other Producers

A little rum is made in Mexico from simple cane-juice. The product is very light-bodied, and as no flavouring ingredients are added, there is little character in the drink.

Trinidad, Antigua, South Africa, Brazil, Bolivia, and other parts of Central and South America all produce rum in smaller quantities. It is mostly consumed locally, or exported to nearby markets.

There is sometimes a certain amount of confusion in the matter of South American rum, which is normally referred to there as *aguardiente de cana*, 'cane-spirit', often translated as 'cane-brandy', and so assimilated to brandy. *Aguardiente* is properly to be applied only to rather inferior spirits. Rum is made in limited quantities in most of the sugar-cane districts of the South American mainland. The Bolivian product, made in the rainy forest-slopes just east of La Paz known as the Yungas, has a high local reputation (see map 18) and is shipped out of the country in fair quantity. Peruvian rum is made in the valley of the river Marañón, on the border country with Ecuador. Facilities for transport are very poor in this area and most of the cane grown there is made into rum, which is more economically transported than molasses, which is apt to ferment during the long and hot journey down to the coast.

Jamaica and U.S.A. rums are the only ones with the flavours proper to them, the flavours formed during the fermentation or formed in the distillation. All the others are rectified to approach a neutral spirit and then flavouring materials are added.

In Russia, rum is made from cane grown around Tashkent, in the Uzbek S.S.R. (Turkestan). Normal in acids and fusel-oil, its ester content is several times higher than even Jamaica or 'New England' type rums.

The substances which give rise to the aroma and the flavour of rum are known as 'congenerics', that is, substances formed along with the alcohol. Whether true congenerics, or added later, those which cause the characteristic odour and flavour are esters, acids, or higher alcohols. Reference to chapter 5 will show that these are also among the important minor constituents of wine. It may be noted that glycerine, which is present in the vat, cannot appear in spirits (unless it is added after distillation) for it does not boil off with the water, alcohol, etc., but remains behind in the still. It is difficult to give an account of the effects on taste of the three classes of congenerics; there are other minor ones which contribute. Esters are generally sweet-smelling, somewhat fruity; the higher alcohols form what is known as fusel-oil, and have in themselves a repulsive, nauseating taste and odour. Acids vary very much in taste, and some are so weak as acids that they do not have the sharp taste of vinegar or tartaric acid. In any case they are all present in very small amounts. Jamaican and the 'Old New England' type rums are comparatively high in esters and fusel-oil, and both modern U.S.A. and the New England products are high in acids. Puerto Rican rum is fairly high in fusel-oil. The total amount of all three congenerics varies from two parts in one thousand for modern 'white' Cuban rum to six times this for pre-Volstead rum of New England. True-run Jamaican has about eight parts per thousand, and the U.S.A. average is nowadays about five or six parts.

A very considerable amount of rum is drunk in the world. Of that which comes into commerce, the U.S.A. produces about two million gallons a year on the average, Jamaica rather under half that; Puerto Rico's production is somewhere between. These amounts are far below those of brandy and whisky.

The war of 1939–45 had violent repercussions on the rum trade of the West Indies. Before the war the demand had been rising, but when the war came, the U.S.A. not only needed more spirits, but as much of the distillery capacity was turned over to making industrial alcohol for war purposes, there was so much the less of it. Puerto Rico, Barbados, and Trinidad all decupled their output. Jamaica was not so lucky, for much of her output had gone to Germany before the war. However, she lost nothing, for Canada and the U.S.A. took all she could send them, at the new prices. When, after the war, the whisky-stills returned to making potable spirits, the West Indies found itself with surpluses and unemployment. Skilful lobbying by the Puerto Rican plantation owners who lived in the U.S. brought the island rum freedom from duty in the U.S.A. Puerto Rico continues to flourish, and the profits it made during the war have been used to convert the island to a Welfare State on the most up-to-date models. The British islands, not so skilful, not so lucky, keep down unemployment by shipping surplus labour to Britain.

CHAPTER 14

GIN

GIN is not one of the great spirits of the world, but it is the most popular. It has been drunk fairly steadily for nearly 300 years in Britain, ever since Dutch William succeeded to the throne of Great Britain, for gin is a Dutch drink. More gin is drunk in the U.S. than Scotch whisky, and about five times as much as all types of brandy – domestic, imported fruit, or grape.

Gin is diluted alcohol carefully and deliberately flavoured with plant extracts. There are no congenerics in gin, using the word in its proper sense; the secondary constituents of gin, which give it its taste and odour, do not come from the same source as the alcohol. In brandy, whisky, most rum, and most of the minor spirits, the flavour, although considerably modified by the fermentation and the distillation, is due to the grapes, the grain, the cane, the palm-tree, or the rice, the apples, or the cashew-nuts; in gin it is added, like a profiteer's title.

The original, and still the principal, added flavour is that of juniper, and it is from the first syllable of the Italian equivalent (*ginevra*) of this word that the drink get its name. It was once called 'geneva', and is sometimes still referred to on occasion as 'Geneva' by the illiterate, although it has no connexion whatever with the Swiss city. Nevertheless, in South America it is sometimes referred to as 'Ginebra' (Spanish for Geneva city).

In the eighteenth and early nineteenth centuries, the most surprising constituents were added to spirits to give them 'kick' and taste. Oil of vitriol (sulphuric acid) and oil of turpentine were commonly, not exceptionally, added. Sabine in *The Complete Cellarman* of 1811 makes 'British Gin' by taking 'spirits (one in five); one pennyweight oil of vitriol; one pennyweight oil of juniper; one pennyweight oil of almonds; half pint spirits of wine, and 2 lb. lump sugar. Dissolve the sugar in 6 quarts water and simmer half an hour, constantly skimming it and when cold, add the spirits of wine and oils and put it to your spirits.' This would sell, he says, at 9s. 4d. a gallon.

Far more toxic concoctions than this were being sold in England in the first half of the eighteenth century. In those days a rating in the Navy was issued with half a pint of spirits a day, and far more alcohol was being consumed per head than nowadays. The duty on French wines and brandy had been increased greatly by William III, and gin, which could be made very cheaply, replaced them. In one of the largest parishes in London, say the Hammonds, one house in five sold gin. It was sold from stalls and barrows in the streets. Wages were often paid in gin. Fielding said, 'some swallow pints of this poison within twenty-four hours.' The Government, although reluctant to take action, was urged by petitions from the towns of Bristol, Salisbury, Rochester, Manchester, and Norwich to do something, and in 1729, retailers were obliged to have a licence costing £20. In 1736, the cost of the licence was increased to £50, and the tax, which had been 5s. 0d. a gallon, to £1. These laws were ignored and informers were terrorized. Between 1734 and 1742 the sale of gin increased by 40 per cent. An act in 1743 reduced the taxes in the hope that gin would only be sold legally, and it became illegal for retailers to distil. This had little or no effect, and in 1747 an Amending Act once more allowed London distillers to sell by retail.

It was at this time that outside the gin-shops could be seen the often-quoted notice, 'Drunk for 1d., dead drunk for 2d., straw for nothing', and young children were among those lying drunk in the kennels. In 1751, Hogarth painted *Gin Lane* and Fielding wrote *An Inquiry into the . . . late increase of Robbers*; in the same year new legislation was passed, and by 1760, about thirty-five years after the matter had become an open scandal, there was a considerable fall in the consumption of gin. One of the most effective provisions of the 1751 Act seems to have been the forbidding of grocers and keepers of jails and work-houses from selling spirits.

The recipe of Sabine, quoted already, was fifty years after this, and gin-drinking was very common amongst the poorer classes for half a century after Sabine.

During the latter part of the nineteenth century and up to the present day, gin distillers have prided themselves on using the same methods as those used for many generations. In the U.S., however, scientific methods are being used increasingly, though not by all firms. Since the base alcohol of gin does not contribute to the flavour or aroma, because it is distilled to a high proof, almost any source may be employed. Nevertheless, in the U.S., Britain, and Holland, the three chief gin-making countries, grain alcohol is used almost exclusively. In Britain between 1939 and 1953, the alcohol was obtained from molasses spirit, and some U.S. gin is still made from the sugar-cane. It is difficult and expensive to free cane-spirit from all taint of molasses, and what the Americans describe as the consequent 'harsh top notes' are not liked in Europe. Grape alcohol is too expensive, and alcohol from potato starch, even when highly rectified, retains its overtones.

Maize and rye are the grains chiefly employed, together with malted rye. In Holland, where the chief centre is at Schiedam, a mixture of malted and unmalted rye, without maize, is often used. The fermentation procedure does not differ notably from beer-vatting for whisky and the other grain-spirits, but distillation is always carried out in patent-stills in Britain and the U.S.A. to give a highly neutral spirit. In Holland pot-stills are sometimes used, but in that case three or four rectifications are necessary. The neutral spirit made in Holland has long been well known as 'moutwijn' (i.e. maltwine).

This neutral spirit is then redistilled in pot-stills of a special design (Plate 32) and the plant materials are placed in the still with the alcohol, which extracts the essential constituents and takes them over with it as it vaporizes. The exact composition of the 'botanicals' used is 'jealously guarded', and consists in Britain of juniper berries, coriander seed, orange-peel, cassia bark, angelica, liquorice, and orris-root; in America juniper berries and coriander seed form the largest proportion, with cinnamon bark, angelica root, lemon-peel, cardamom seed-capsules, and caraway seed. Something like 5 lb. of the mixed botanicals are used for each hundred gallons of proof spirit.

The juniper berries, the principal botanical used, contain one or two per cent of oil; the amount in unripe berries is greater than this but has inferior, turpentine-like flavouring qualities. The best berries come from Italy and Yugoslavia, but some are imported from the Austrian Tyrol and Germany. The coriander seed comes from Morocco, the cinnamon from Ceylon, South Germany supplies the angelica, Spain and Southern Italy the oranges and lemons; the cardamom is brought from Mysore and the southern plains of India, and the cassia from Indo-China (or once was).

'Cold compounded' gins are made more simply by adding essential oils to neutral spirit, and taste like it. London Gin is merely an unsweetened gin, and may be made in Peoria, Illinois (more in fact is made there than anywhere else in the world). Sweetened Gin, known in all languages as Old Tom (or sometimes as 'Old Ginebra' in Spanish-speaking countries), is made by adding sugar-syrup (or glycerine) to gin. Sloe Gin is made by steeping bruised sloes in gin, usually with added sugar.

One of the marks of great wines and spirits is the capacity to improve on storage; the great clarets live for forty years, waxing in excellence all the time; sherries take years to gestate, ruminating in their great *soleras*; 'no one drinks a port under twenty years'; Madeiras live almost for ever; in wood, cognac and whisky lose their rawness and become fine and round. But gin should not be kept long, for the essential oils oxidize and become bitter and rancid. The quality of gin, like that of other spirits, can be estimated to some degree by pouring a little in the palm of the hand, rubbing gently to get rid of most of the alcohol and then smelling the high-boiling-point secondaries which linger longest. Gin is rarely adulterated and then only with water.

The sale of gin has increased yearly since the war; most is drunk in the summer, largely in long drinks like gin and tonic water and in simple cocktails like gin and lime, etc.

CHAPTER 15

OTHER SPIRITS

THE minor alcoholic spirits, like the less eminent members of the hagiologies, are innumerable and obscure. Only a proportion have been described in print, and such descriptions as exist are often contradictory, or even not self-consistent.

Any vegetable product which contains sufficient starch or sugar can be used as a raw material for making spirits: a great many have been. The methods of carrying out the transformation naturally vary from village to village and from generation to generation. The Mexicans have for generations distilled the fermented sap of a cactus; and Indians have for generations distilled the fermented sap of plants; in India also, flowers are fermented and distilled and this has been going on since the first whisky was made in Ireland; the up-to-date African ferments Lyle's Golden Syrup and distils it in a home-made still.

In Europe, especially in the cooler countries, spirits are made from potato or grain starch and distilled to fairly high proof, so that something not far removed from neutral spirits results. Some, like *Vodka*, have an almost non-existent flavour. Vodka is made chiefly in Russia, Poland, and Finland from a rye-malt, or sometimes potato starch. The method of manufacture appears to resemble that by which grain-whisky is made, but the rectification is far higher, and the spirit is finally filtered through charcoal, so that any flavour which might have escaped the rectifier is absorbed by the filter. The addition of small amounts of herbs or herb-extracts, which is occasionally carried out, brings the drink almost to a sort of gin, and *Akvavit* (Danish and Swedish) and *Aquavit* (Norwegian and Swedish), which are flavoured with caraway seed, are of this type.

Kornbranntwein (which is German for 'corn-brandy') is in fact a slight variant of patent-still whisky and might reasonably be classified as German whisky. The Latins, who are not as sensitive as Gaels to the special character of whisky, do so describe it.

Before venturing into the troubled seas of oriental spirits it may be mentioned that although *aguardiente* (which may be translated as 'ardent water') is the word used in Spain generically for spirits, *aguardiente alemana* is not *Kornbranntwein* or a faintly flavoured potato spirit, but a medicinal concoction of jalop root, turpeth root, Aleppo scammony, and 90 per cent alcohol which is normally prescribed by the more forthright Spanish doctors in a vehicle of syrup of senna.

When one reaches the Levant, or even the Balkans, the distinction between different spirits begins to lose its outlines. The same name is given to a variety of distilled liquors. Even in Greece, the name *ouzo* is given not only to brandy flavoured with aromatic compounds (page 223), but also to a neutral spirit (made from grain or wine) with aromatic flavouring, which may be of the most various description.

The wilder Tartar tribes of Turkestan and the Steppes, especially before their conversion to more conventional ways a hundred years ago, used to make a crude spirit, *Araka*, by distilling fermented mares' milk. Since koumiss contains only negligible traces of alcohol, it is clear that sugar, either in the form of grape-juice or perhaps lactose, the sugar of milk, was added to the milk before fermentation. Grapes for wine are now grown in Uzbekistan (see page 175), and it is more than probable that it was must, either fresh or evaporated, which was added. The distillation was carried out in earthenware pots and the vapours passed through wooden pipes into the cooled receiver. The efficiency must have been remarkably low, and it is understandable that, as recorded, two or three distillations were necessary. The product was described as very potent.

Raki is a Balkan spirit which may be a plain honest brandy distilled from wine which has been fermented to complete absence of sugar, or incompletely so that some sugar is left; it may be made from wine-lees (i.e. *eau-de-vie-de-lie*); it may be a *slivovitsa* from plums; it may be a wine-spirit to which 'essence of cognac' and sugar have been added (in this case it is a sort of liqueur); it may also be made from molasses, grain, or potatoes, although this could not be described as raki, in Bulgaria at least, since 1934. Mastic, a resin obtained on the Aegean island of Chios, is imported and added to raki to make the drink called *mastika* in the Balkans outside Greece (see page 168), although *mastika* may also be made by distilling wine – or fruit-brandy, with aniseed. Egg-raki (or *cognac a l'œuf*) is a spirit, diluted to be about equivalent in alcohol content to a fortified wine (18 per cent alcohol by volume), containing a considerable amount of egg-yolk.

The word *raki* is derived from the Arabic *arak*, a word which in various forms is current throughout Asia to mean spirits (Turkish, *raki*; Mongolian and Manchu, *ariki*; Japanese, *raggi* – although this last term seems to be applied to an undistilled alcoholic drink made by adding sugar to rice and fermenting).

Arak originally meant sweat, or juice. *Arrack* (or *arak*) is the most protean of all spirits. It is made throughout the East, and also in Europe; in Europe it is a component of some of the ready-mixed cocktails bottled and sold under emotive names; in Asia it is drunk neat. Arrack was originally made from the juice of the coco-nut palm, which was fermented and distilled. Later, malted rice was added to the juice before fermenting. The resulting spirit was also called arrack. Alternatively, molasses and malted rice were fermented and distilled, the spirits retaining the name unchanged. The spirit from mahua flowers is also called arrack. Whether the same name has been applied to any other of the various Indian spirits is obscure, except that it has almost certainly been used for date-spirit. Mr J. B. Milton mentions that he has encountered an arrack based on petrol. It seems clear that arrack was originally distilled from toddy, the fermented juice of palm-trees, and that now the name is commonly applied, in Europe at least, to a spirit from rice and molasses, but in India it has a wider and vaguer signification.

Although a considerable number of species of palms give a sweet sap which can be fermented to give toddy, it is principally the palmyra (*Borassus flabellifer*), and to a lesser extent the nipa, which are actually used for making spirits. The palmyra or true toddy-palm grows wild all over the East, and everywhere it is cultivated: it is one of the most useful plants of Asia. Some ten million of the trees form forests in the Tinnevelly district, in the Tamil land of South India: the leaves are used for thatching and fencing, for fans, sunshades, and baskets, the fibres are used to make brushes and ropes, the juice is evaporated until it becomes the dark-brown crystalline sugar known as *gur* or *jaggery*, the sugar of the East. This is the chief use of the sap, but considerable quantities are everywhere fermented to give toddy. The trees are tapped by cutting, like rubber-trees. In Tinnevally the palmyra is the chief crop; except for senna, almost the only one. A native distillery company in 1905 found it economic to build a light railway to take the palmyra-juice down to its factory at Kulasekhara-patnam, after failing, because of premature fermentation, to run it down through a pipe-line.

In northern Ceylon also (at Jaffna), the palmyra is intensively culti-vated for spirit-making. Distillation, as may be imagined, is carried out in somewhat crude apparatus, and the product is described as having a cinnamon flavour when fresh. It 'might pass as an aperitif', says Spate. Upon keeping for a very short time it smells of ammo-nia, and worse: the smell of arrack and toddy is one of the basic components of the oriental odour which greets every traveller at Eastern ports (others being rancid coco-nut oil, ghee, and Asian tobacco).

The best arrack, it is said, comes from the East Indies ('Batavian arrack') and Jamaica. In these parts rice is a component and molasses replaces the toddy. In Jamaica the rice is steeped in water in large vats with slow agitation so as to allow the grain to sprout and malt. After a time the water is run off and the molasses or toddy is added. Fermenta-tion proceeds without addition of yeast; there are enough enzymes in Caribbean air to start fermentation. Javanese arrack owes at least part of its flavour to the teak containers it is aged in, and some to the fermentation starter which is used. This is a partly-malted rice preparation which is made up into small balls, known as *ragi* or *raggi* (presumably to confuse etymological researchers). Since little rice but this *raggi* is employed, Javanese arrack is almost indistin-guishable from rum, for the source of the sugar is overwhelmingly molasses.

The mixing of rice and toddy to make a combined spirit is doubt-less due to the great economy in land which can be effected by plant-ing palms along the raised bunds which separate the flooded paddy fields. The combination seems to be as old as Indian civilization itself. Nowadays it is particularly characteristic of the coastal parts of Bengal, and of Cochin (in the extreme south-west of the peninsula). Extraordinarily high population densities are possible by this economy (up to 4,000 a square mile). There are two main paddy crops (Aman in the winter and Bhadoi in the summer) and the palms can be tapped at any season.

Rice spirit (*sura*) is mentioned in the ancient Sanskrit literature ('The Institutes of Manu') written some 1,500 years ago, and if *sura* really was a distilled drink, the birth of distillation applied to drinks must be pushed back to an earlier date than is usually attributed to it. Some native arrack has as much as 70 or 80 per cent alcohol – almost twice the content of commercial West European spirits – but all the same its intoxicating effect has often been enhanced by infusing hemp leaves and poppy-heads in it. Datura has for centuries been administered by murderers in arrack. Either the seeds of the *Datura* (*stramonium*) were steeped in the spirit or a more laborious method was used: the seeds were burnt on a fire and the smoke caught in a reversed earthenware pot which was then filled with arrack. The effect of datura is to drive one literally and permanently insane.

Arrack was once produced in Germany in considerable quantities by Firma Winkelhausen from molasses and rice. It was often known as *Reisbranntwein* (i.e. rice-brandy). It was made by malting the rice with warm diluted molasses for twenty-four hours, then adding more dilute molasses, leaving for three days and putting in some neat molasses. After fermenting for eighteen days, it was distilled. German arrack contained between 50 and 60 per cent alcohol, and the esters and fusel-oil were rather high (compare page 235). It is especially necessary, in making spirit from rice, to be careful to reject the fore-shots, for a toxic low-boiling fraction is present; more even than in the case of other spirits.

The nipa palm (*Nipa fruticans*) is less frequently used in the Middle East for making spirits. It is a low palm with a dense mass of leaves and the juice is commonly made into *gur* or toddy. In the Philippines, it is more frequently employed for making the fermented juice, here called *vino de nipa*, and for producing spirits (*aguardiente de palma*, or *aguardiente de nipa*).

Mahua spirits are unique in being made from flowers, although they are by no means unique in being called arrack; the native names of *madhvi* and *daru* are also used. Mahua spirits have been known from ancient times. Various species of the genus *Bassia* are employed, especially *B. butyracea*, the butter tree. This is a large deciduous tree growing at elevations of up to 4,000 feet in the Western Ghats between Travancore and Kanara (that is, from behind Goa southwards). Enormous clusters of cream-coloured flowers form in spring, before the leaves appear, and as much as three hundred or more pounds of flowers can be collected from each tree. They have an unfortunate and disgusting smell of mice, and even after boiling with water retain the odour. They are eaten very extensively, especially in the Central Provinces (now Madhya Pradesh), for they contain when dried as much as 20 per cent of sugar. Europeans who have brought themselves to eat them are said to 'suffer afterwards'. Fermentation and distillation gave the spirit, which is variously described as resembling Irish whisky, Dutch gin, or as having a strong, smoky and rather foetid odour. Some 6 or 7 gallons of spirit are said to be obtainable from a hundredweight of dried flowers; if this is accurate, the spirits are certainly not as alcoholic as other arrack. At the time of the Phylloxera plague in France, dried mahua flowers were sent there for making into spirits for *vinage*. In order to purge the spirits of the tenacious mousy flavour, high rectification was necessary. This trade did not last long and was much easier to stop than the importation of raisins into France (see page 90). There is expectation of power alcohol being obtained in quantity from the mahua in the future.

Little date-wine is made into spirits, although the wild date (*Phoenix sylvestris*) is often tapped for *gur* and date-wine is made in many parts of India.

Other cereals than rice have been used for making spirits in India, and Sanskrit words have been current for many centuries for rice-spirit (*sura*), barley-spirit (*kohala*), and wheat-spirit (*madhulika*). *Kohala*, which may or may not have resembled whisky in flavour and aroma, has the distinction of passing into Arabic (*al kohl*) and thence into every other language (alcohol). It was originally derived from *kru* (earth) and *hala* (poison).

At one time a fair quantity of spirits derived from the *cashew-nut* (*Anacardium occidentale*) was made at Goa. After two distillations it had the reputation of being a 'useful stimulant', and sold at Rs. 1.8 the gallon (2*s*. 3*d*.) The sweet juice of nuts had been fermented elsewhere to make an alcoholic drink, but there appear to be no other records of distillation to make spirits from this source.

So far as alcoholic drinks are concerned, Mexico is an island. It makes a little wine, as mentioned on page 188, but as a beverage *pulque* is universally drunk (a constant and impudent challenge to the American soft-drinks industry), and as spirits *mezcal* and, to a much lesser extent, the more expensive *tequila*. These are all made from plants. Amongst the labouring classes of Mexico, pulque is what grape-wine is to France and tea to Britain. With maize, beans, and red pepper it forms the complete diet of the peasants. Pulque-drinking was well-established in antiquity. It was common in the days of the ancient Huaztecs, the tribe which originally inhabited Southern Mexico around the modern oil-port of Tampico, but when they were conquered by the Aztecs it was reserved for religious ceremonies. After the Spaniards overcame the Aztecs, they passed edicts to regulate the making and consumption of pulque; the natives promptly revolted, and the edicts were modified. In the eighteenth century, making pulque was a major industry: some two million gallons a year were consumed in Mexico City, and every day the Pulque Train (of ox-wagons) left Orizaba for the capital. Towards the end of the century there were 160 pulque factories in the country.

Nowadays pulque is made all over Central Mexico and less intensively in the rest of the country. The best is made in the plains around Apam, just to the north-east of Mexico City. Pulque quickly spoils and so must be made fairly near to the consumer. The plants used are species of agave, most commonly known as *maguey*, but also as *pita* (*A. salmiana*, Otto; *A. mexicana*, and others). It takes eight years to mature, and in practice this governs the economics of the industry, for only large landowners can afford the heavy tie-up of capital which a crop of this sort involves. It is the large haciendas which grow maguey. The plant has exceedingly deep roots and is a typical xerophyte, with its camel-like capacity for storing liquid against a dry spell. Except in the western states of Sinaloa and Nayarit, Mexico is a harsh arid country. It is not rainless, for fifteen to twenty inches fall, but in all but the three summer months water is very scarce because the soil does not retain it. Over a half of the country needs irrigation to cultivate any but xerophytes like the agaves, and only one-eighth of the area receives irrigation.

The maguey is a tall plant over twenty feet high with its flowers at the summit and thick fleshy leaves sprouting just above ground-level. It is in the stem within the crown of leaves that the liquid is stored, and in its eighth year the central stem is cut out of its collar of leaves and a cavity some twelve to eighteen inches across excavated in the stump. The cavity fills with sap at the rate of a gallon or more a day.

This is collected in skin bags and taken to the fermenting sheds. A single plant will give a ton of juice, but then the leaves wither and the plant dies.

The juice has a sweet acid taste, due to fructose and malic acid (see page 85). The protein is very high and there is also a considerable amount of gummy material. Fermentation is invariably carried out in large vats made of leather and it is to this fact that part of its characteristic taste is due. The odour is like that of sour butter, or, according to other accounts, putrid meat: this presumably depends on the age and treatment of the leather. Kept too long it turns to *madre pulque*, which is like sour beer. Pulque is said to have 'great powers of curing stomach complaints', but Latins are if anything even more credulous than Anglo-Saxons in these matters. Just recently it has been established that the fermentation is carried out partly by the milk-souring bacillus (*lactobacillus*) and this presumably accounts for the smell of sour butter. Another somewhat surprising fact about agave-juice, just discovered (at the University of New Mexico), is that there is a considerable proportion of sucrose, the sugar of the cane and the beet (in fact ordinary table-sugar), present. Pulque is not highly alcoholic and rarely exceeds 6 or 7 per cent alcohol. The malic acid content is rather higher in the pulque than in the unfermented juice. Pulque is often sweetened for drinking, or mixed with pineapple and sugar to form a sort of *bowle* called *pulque curado*.

Mescal (*mercal*, *mezcal*) is the popular spirit of the Mexican peon. It is made from the juice of the Dumpling cactus (*Laphophora williamsi*), which grows particularly in the states to the south-west of Mexico City, Jalisco, Sinaloa, and Michoacan, and just to the north of the capital, in Hidalgo. It is not only the juice, but also some of the fibrous heart-material, of the mescal agave which is fermented. Considering the ambient temperature, a long fermentation is given – several days – and then the alcoholic liquid is distilled in simple potstills with partial condensation in the still-head, similar to that in the bulbous partial condensers of the Charente (Plate 30). Only a single distillation is made and the product is usually colourless and, rather surprisingly, clear. It commonly runs about 45 to just over 50 per cent alcohol. It is not aged and has a unique 'herbaceous, weed-like taste'. The fusel-oil is a little on the high side, but analyses for the main constituents show no striking differences from those for ordinary brandies of mediocre quality. Part of the effect of mescal is due to the trace of mescaline it contains. Mescaline is an alkaloid which has been much publicized in the last decade or so because of the remarkable hallucinations it causes in those who take it. Mescal, and preparations of the Dumpling Cactus, have long been used in the religious rites of the Chiricahua Apache and other American Indians.

Tequila is the spirits of the Mexican middle classes. Another variety of agave is used to make it (*A. tequilana*), and, as in the case of mescal, some of the fibrous pulp of the plant is included in the fermentation mash, so as to utilize starch from the pulp in the production of the alcohol, as well as the sap-sugars. Some acid-cooking is employed (as in making grain-whisky) and fermentation occupies a week or two. The spirit is given two distillations from pot-stills, and the colourless spirit is then aged in casks (for the better qualities) or coloured with caramel to a pale brown. *Tequila* production centres around the town of Tequila in the eastern part of Jalisco state, that is, on the inland slopes of the Sierra Madre. The town has an altitude of 4,000 feet and is about 300 miles north-west of Mexico City. Tequila has the reputation of being very intoxicating, although it usually contains less than 50 per cent alcohol. It is sometimes sophisticated by the addition of a little neutral spirit to bring it up to 45 per cent or so, if it happens to be lower than this. It contains rather less congenerics than mescal, with which it is sometimes blended. Mr Sacheverell Sitwell says that, with orange-juice and chillies, it forms the drink 'devil's blood'.

The sap from some of the varieties of Mexican agave contains as much as 20 per cent sugar, but although agaves are now widely grown around the Mediterranean and elsewhere, nothing like this proportion occurs in the transplanted varieties. The agave was originally brought over the Atlantic in 1561, and in 1925 an account was published of French attempts to cultivate a high-sugar-containing agave in the North African and Asian colonies to use as raw material for power alcohol. These attempts appear to have been unsuccessful.

Tiquira is a Brazilian spirit made in the province of Maranhao, the coastal region east of the mouth of the Amazon, especially in the port of San Luis. It is made from tapioca roots, which contain much starch; this is malted and fermented, then distilled with unusually high rectification for tropical spirits (San Luis is 200 miles south of the equator) and is almost a neutral spirit. It is diluted to 45 per cent alcohol.

CHAPTER 16

MISCELLANEOUS DRINKS

Vermouth

Vermouth is of great antiquity, for ancient Palestinian records mention the addition of wormwood (*Artemisia absinthia*) to wines, and this is almost all that modern vermouth is. The problem of the re-invention of vermouth in modern times, attributed by the Germans to the Italians and by Italian writers to the Germans, is of rather trivial interest. Vermouth is a fortified herb wine and its constituents are wine, fortification spirit, sugar, and extracts of various herbs, with a little caramel for colouring. It was mentioned in Italian writings in 1773 and was being made about that time at Turin by Antonio Carpano.

It is not a wine which allows of any great delicacy of flavour, and this is implicit in the fact that wines of a most ordinary type are employed. There are two types of vermouth: Italian, which is sweet, and French, which is dry, though far from being as dry as an ordinary beverage wine. There is little between the percentage of alcohol in each, but the Italian contains four or five times as much sugar as the French.

Italian vermouth contains 15 or 16 per cent alcohol and rather more sugar than alcohol. The wine used is a white muscatel which is naturally rather sweet, but which has been fermented to give only a few per cent of alcohol, leaving most of the sugar undisturbed. A blend with other wines is used as a base for dissolving out the essential principles from the herbs. Some forty or fifty herbs are used, and it is perhaps unneccessary to mention that the composition of the herbal mixture is a 'closely guarded secret' which has been 'handed down for generations'. Wormwood is the principal, but calamus root, star-wort and centaury, forget-me-not and blessed thistle, elder-flowers and horehound, gentian, ginger, and coriander, as well as allspice and cinnamon are all used, besides others. It is important not to use too much nor to allow them to infuse too long, or the vermouth will be too strong and too astringent. Sometimes the extract is made not in wine but either in hot water or in a neutral brandy spirit. The amount of herbs used is in any case between one and four ounces to a gallon of wine-base. Fining is effected by means of isinglass as a rule. A short ageing in wood precedes filtration, bottling, and labelling.

In making French vermouth a more bitter taste is required and the balance of herbs is somewhat different: more wormwood is used and less coriander and cinnamon. The wine is dry and white. Most French vermouth is made in Marseilles from Picardy or Hérault wine which, it is arranged, shall be somewhat more acid than a beverage wine. In French isinglass is also used for fining, but a considerably longer ageing is necessary than is given to Italian wines.

Vermouth is made in several other countries, principally in Germany and the U.S.A., but also in Britain. In Holland and Germany, 'fruit vermouth' is made from fruit wines, usually from a fruit mixture which includes grapes. It is not unusual in all these countries to add some citric acid so as to prevent the wine tasting flabby. Vermouth substitutes are often sold under proprietary names; they are made from brandy, or some other spirit, water, sugar, and essential oils.

Proprietary aperitifs, whose names confront one in the most unlikely places in rural, urban, and suburban France, are generally based on vermouth, with additions such as quinine to give a sharper set to the appetite, or because they sell better thus. The French law of 1940 made it illegal to sell aperitifs with more than 16° (16 per cent) of alcohol in them.

Bitters are flavoured and slightly sweetened spirits. As bitters are to spirits, so is French vermouth to a fortified wine. An extract is made of an imposing list of herbs in spirits; after the maceration has continued for a week or more, the liquid is taken off and more spirits, together with a little sugar syrup and some water, are added. Colouring is done with caramel and cochineal. Bitters are sold under proprietary names such as 'Angostura', 'Amara', 'Campari', 'Fernet Branca', and so on. The composition of the herbal mixtures employed is not divulged.

Bitters are used to give a distinctive tang to cocktails which might otherwise taste too mellow.

Liqueurs

Liqueurs are sweetened and flavoured, and often coloured, spirits. They are drunk after a meal, with coffee. Liqueur brandy contains no sugar, however. It is a very fine brandy with nothing whatever added. As it has a truly magnificent aroma, it is traditionally drunk in huge glasses but in small quantities, so that when warmed in one's hands the aroma fills the glass, whence it is inhaled with profound reverence, unless the quality is very inferior. Liqueurs on the other hand are drunk from glasses no bigger than an egg-cup, without special genuflexion.

Neutral spirits are the basis of liqueurs and to add sugar-syrup to spirit is simple. It is the introduction of the flavour which gives some difficulty. For inferior liqueurs, a little essential oil is added to the alcohol, and then the sugar-syrup and dyestuff. This proceeding gives a crude flavour to the product, as one might imagine. The best liqueurs are made by steeping the mixture of dried herbs, which are to supply the flavour, in the spirit and then distilling the liquid off. The distillate is allowed to stand for a week or longer and then filtered. For liqueurs which are colourless, or to which the colouring matter is to be added subsequently, fining (see page 82) as for wines, with egg-white or gelatin, is employed. The best liqueurs are aged in oak casks. Quick-ageing, by heating and cooling to ice-temperature several times, is sometimes practised.

The essential oils extracted from some herbs will not stand the heating in the still and in that case simple infusion is employed, followed by straining and filtering. Generally speaking, liqueurs made by the infusion process are inferior to those prepared by distillation. Spirits containing aniseed, caraway, citronella, fennel, juniper, lavender, mint, orange, rose, thyme, and wormwood can all be distilled.

Many liqueurs are sold under proprietary names and almost all are made from secret recipes. Directions for simulating most of them are published in the well-known books of recipes (Henley's or Bennett's. See bibliography, page 309). Some liqueurs are made in monasteries (Benedictine, Chartreuse, and many Italian liqueurs), others by large manufacturers, especially near Bordeaux (Bardinet; Marie Brizard et Roger), and in Alsace and Anjou. The number of liqueurs made is legion, and it is possible to give only a note on a few well-known ones. (Carling, *The Complete Book of Drink*, includes a much fuller list.)

Absinthe: an unsweetened spirit flavoured with oil of wormwood (and also angelica, aniseed, cinnamon, cloves, etc.). After distillation, it is coloured with chlorophyll from nettles or spinach, and is then green, but on long storage it turns yellow. On addition of water it becomes opalescent because resins and oils are precipitated; the same effect is produced by sophisticating with gum benzoin, used in cheap absinthe. It is chiefly made in France (Lyons; Montpellier). All countries limit the amount of wormwood added, because of its toxic properties; Switzerland forbids the making of absinthe altogether.

Advocaat: a Dutch liqueur made by dissolving sugar and egg-yolk in spirit.

Alkermes: a Mediterranean liqueur. Orange-flower extract is added to the distillate from an infusion of nutmegs, cinnamon, cloves, etc., in brandy.

Allaseh: see Kümmel.

Anis, Anisette: a very popular South European liqueur made in Barcelona, Bordeaux, and Amsterdam. Coriander and fennel seeds as well as aniseed are used to prepare it. Usually green.

Aurum: an Italian dry liqueur.

Benedictine: a remarkably large number of herbs (all very secret) are used to make this amber-coloured liqueur, which has more delicacy than most.

Chartreuse: made at Voiron (near Grenoble) and at Tarragona, in two colours: green and yellow, properly drunk mixed. The green contains the more alcohol. White Chartreuse (*Melisse*) has not been made since 1900. One of the 'quality' liqueurs (see price-lists).

Cherry Brandy (Kirsch; Kirschwasser): normally sold sweetened in Britain and U.S.A. (see page 226). Sweetened with glycerine as well as sugar usually. Made in Alsace, Vosges, Switzerland, Germany, Yugoslavia, and Denmark in large quantities. (See Maraschino; Mirabelle.)

Cointreau: a popular, colourless, orange-flavoured liqueur.

Crème de Cacao: popular in France. Flavoured with vegetable extracts imported from Antilles, French Guiana, and Senegal. Chocolate flavour and aroma.

Crème de Menthe: one of the most popular of all. Flavour due to balm, cinnamon, ginger, peppermint, orris, and sage.

Curaçao: made originally in Amsterdam using the dried peel of unripe oranges from Dutch Guiana ('Curaçao apples'). Cinnamon and cloves are also added nowadays.

Drambuie: made in Edinburgh from whisky, honey, and Scottish herbs. Marketed since 1892 by Mr Mackinnon, descended from the Mackinnon to whom the recipe is said by legend to have been given by Prince Charles in 1745.

Framboise: a raspberry liqueur, made in Alsace.

Grand Marnier: an orange liqueur which claims to be unique in being based on fine cognac. A quality liqueur.

Kirsch: see Cherry Brandy.

Kümmel: a German and north European liqueur to which caraway seeds, orris, and fennel supply the flavour. *Allasch* is a very sweet type with bitter almonds, aniseed, etc., as additional flavouring.

Maraschino: Yugoslav cherry brandy made at Zadar in Dalmatia.

Mélisse: see Chartreuse.

Mirabelle: an Alsatian liqueur from wild cherries.

Prunelle: an Alsatian plum liqueur; also made at Angers.

Quetsch: another plum liqueur of Alsace.

Strega: reputedly the best Italian liqueur. Orange-flavoured.

Van der Hum: South African liqueur, the orange flavour of which is due to the peel of the Cape orange (*naartje*). Often drunk mixed with brandy (Brandyhum). 'Van der Hum' is equivalent to 'What's his name'.

Cocktails and Mixed Drinks

For anyone who likes mixed drinks, there is an infinite number to choose from. They vary. The older toddy and punch and shrub and negus are one thing, the modern cocktails another. Cocktails are short, usually sweet drinks, made originally to be drunk as aperitifs; they are all fairly high in alcohol. The older drinks were often drunk hot and are essentially convivial, for sipping comfortably and even meditatively.

Toddy is a mixture of hot spirits with sugar and boiling water and lemon. If the spirits are rum, it is a rum toddy, and so on, according to the spirits used. It has a high reputation, even among teetotallers, for curing a cold in the head, or for rendering its effects less distressing. Modern medical opinion favours the latter. In the U.S.A., toddy is often spiced spirits and water, with ice.

Punch, according to Sir George Watt, was invented by Anglo-Indians as early as 1658 or so. The only spirits were the native arrack, which was usually very raw. The word means 'five', from the number of ingredients (Hindustani, *panch;* Persian, *panj*). In India they were arak, sugar, lime-juice, spice, and water, but the recipe since then has become somewhat smeared and nowadays the mixture made on New Year's Eve and similar occasions usually contains rum, lemon, hot water, and sugar. Professor Saintsbury favours three parts of rum, two of brandy, one of lemon-juice, six of hot water, and sugar to taste. He adds that he 'never knew this mixture found fault with by respectable persons of any age, sex, or condition, from undergraduates to old ladies, at any hour between sunset and sunrise', and omits to mention what those persons who were not respectable could have had against it. In Germany wine punch (wine, rum, lemon-juice, sugar, and water) is popular.

Germany is well known for its *Bowlen*, which are mixtures of sparkling wine, or still wine and soda-water, with fruits such as peaches, strawberries, pineapple, and so on. They are to be highly recommended on hot afternoons in the Rhineland, so long as a short rest is taken afterwards. *Maibowle* contains no fruit but is ordinary wine scented and flavoured by the addition of sprigs of the common woodruff (*Asperula odorata*) gathered before the blossom appears (when the plant contains most coumarin, its odoriferous constituent). *Kalte Ente* ('cold duck') is the playful name given to a mixture of red and sparkling white wine. *Schorle*, or *Gespritzter*, is wine and soda-water: Byron's 'hock-and-seltzer'. (In France, watered wine is referred to as *Cru de Bercy*.)

The Cups, of which claret cup is the most well known, consist of wine and soda-water, with lemon or other fruit and sugar. The composition varies with the concoctor, who may at caprice add spirits, cucumber, borage, 'and what-not' (Professor Saintsbury). Saintsbury cup, invented solely by Professor Saintsbury, consists of sparkling Mosel and claret, with thick slices of pineapple and 'a lump of ice as big as a baby's head'.

Atholl Brose, says Sir Robert Bruce Lockhart, consists of equal quantities of honey and fine oatmeal, to which (malt) whisky is added. This is stirred until it froths, and is then bottled and corked tightly for two days.

Cocktails may be the development of the mint julep of the southern U.S.A. This was whisky and sugar with a little rum or brandy, well iced and decorated with sprigs of mint. Many cocktails belong to genera, like animals and plants. Thus there are the *Cobblers*, which consist of wine or whisky (or rum) with a little curaçao and brandy, iced and decorated with fruit or a sprig of mint. *Fizzes* are spirits (gin, brandy, or rum) with sugar, lemon-juice, and soda-water (or champagne). *Flips*, however, are wine or spirits with sugar and an egg, shaken well, strained, and served after powdering with nutmeg. A *Sling* is merely spirits and a few dashes of bitters, with soda-water, ice, and lemon-peel. *Sours* are spirits with sugar and lemon-juice, a slice of orange, and perhaps a cherry.

The basic cocktail is the martini. A dry martini has three dashes of bitters (angostura or orange) with ice, upon which are poured equal parts of French vermouth and dry gin. A sweet martini contains no bitters, and the sweet Italian vermouth instead of French (in fact it is identical with 'gin and it'.) Lemon-peel, and a cherry with the sweet, an olive with the dry, are added. Gin and vermouth are the basis of cocktails, although neither is present in a 'Sidecar', for instance. The fact is, a cocktail is pretty well anything you please, so long as it is strongly alcoholic. A minute selection is given here:

Black Velvet: ½ stout, ½ champagne.

Bronx: 1 gin, 1 French vermouth, 1 Italian vermouth; a little lemon-juice. Iced.

Champagne Cocktail: equal (small) parts of brandy, curaçao, maraschino, and Grand Marnier, a lump of sugar sprinkled with bitters; the glass is then filled with champagne, and iced.

John Collins: gin with the juice of two oranges and one lemon, and soda-water. Iced. (Substitution of other spirits for the gin gives other members of the Collins family.)

East Indian: equal parts of French vermouth and sherry, with a dash of orange bitters. Iced.

Gimlet: gin and lime-juice. Iced.

Hawaiian: 4 gin, 2 orange-juice, 1 curaçao. Iced.

Manhattan: 1 Italian vermouth, 3 rye whisky with a dash of bitters and a cherry. Iced.

Rickey Gin: same as Gimlet, or Gin and Lime.

Sidecar: 1 cointreau, 1 brandy (or gin), 1 lemon-juice. Iced.

Silver Streak: 1 kümmel, 1 gin. Iced.

White Lady: 1 cointreau, 1 lemon-juice, 2 gin. Iced. . . . and so on, *ad infinitum.*

Fruit Wines

If the fruit from which a wine has been made is not the grape, the appellation 'wine' is only a courtesy title. The thirst for alcohol, which appears to be deeply rooted in the human race, is so strong that if grape-wine is not available, other fruits are turned to account. In Northern Europe, especially in those parts which fall just outside the wine-belt, such as Poland, Northern Germany, and much of Russia, fruit wines are made in very large quantities. In Britain, it is only the farmer's wife or the cottager who takes any interest in their preparation.

Among all the fruits, only the grape contains sufficient sugar to carry out an unaided fermentation, to give a liquid which is pleasant to drink. It is therefore necessary to add sugar to the vat. It is probable, though not completely certain, that wines of really respectable quality need the agency of one of the special wine-yeasts and that brewer's yeast, which is a quite different strain of *Saccharomyces ellipsoideus*, is unsuitable. In remembering some of the nauseating brews one has drunk (and praised) among the country wines, one is apt to forget the few, the very few, wines of quite promising delicacy which have been encountered. Pasteur, seventy-five years ago, pointed out the importance of the yeast strain in forming the bouquet characteristic of each (grape) wine, and Kayser in 1924 confirmed and greatly amplified this. Selected yeasts are very widely used for making fruit wines in Eastern France, Belgium, Switzerland, Luxembourg, and Germany. In Britain quite recently, Mrs S. M. Tritton, a well-known oenological expert, has sponsored schemes for making fruit wines in Worcestershire and Herefordshire. Under licence from Mrs Tritton, some fruit-farmers in this area make a sherry-like wine from plums ('Sherrette') and wines from apples which may be sweet

('Sauternette') or dry. The important factor in Mrs Tritton's process appears to consist in the proper selection of yeasts. There seems no reason why fruit wines of very attractive taste and aroma should not be made, for wine made by fermenting pure sugar solutions with champagne yeast has something of the special champagne bouquet, as was discovered by Duclaux in 1900 and confirmed by Kayser twenty-three years later.

It is in Germany that fruit wines are most popular. The fruit-drink industry (*Zentralverband der Süssmost- und Obst-Getränke*) specifies that fruit wines shall have a certain minimum amount of alcohol and maximum acid. Fruit dessert wines are similarly specified, as are sparkling fruit wines and even fruit-vermouth wine. Commercial fruit wines are made from red-, white-, and black-currants, gooseberries, strawberries, blackberries, raspberries, whortleberries, elderberries, sloes, and several kinds of cherries. The alcohol content of these varies between 7 and 14 per cent. (The Z.S.O.G. minimum is 8 per cent for fruit wines except those from apples and pears.)

The fruit wines of Poland have been described (before 1939) as being high in alcohol and of good quality. In 1952, Poland suddenly admitted to making grape wine to the amount of over 8 million gallons, but no details are available. Romania had a high reputation for her fruit wines also, especially those from red- and white-currants made in Dobruja.

Russia makes a wide range of fruit wines, even including those from mountain-ash berries and rose-hips, which a Russian investigator describes as having a peculiar but pleasant taste. Imitations of grape-wines such as port are also described as being made from whortleberries.

Generally, the vinification methods employed for the fruit wines are very similar to those normally used for grape-wine. The juice is usually diluted, and this, as well as the addition of sugar, which is of course universal, renders it liable to bacterial attack. Sulphuring is practised, and it is necessary to be wary of the attentions of air-borne organisms if open vats are used. A mouse-like odour and corresponding taste easily result from carelessness.

The wines made from tropical fruits are innumerable but their preparation is local and scantily recorded. Banana wine of ten or twelve per cent alcohol content is widely made in Central Africa.

A NOTE ON WINE-GROWING
IN ENGLAND

Since grapes can be successfully grown out-of-doors in the South of England, one may naturally inquire if it is possible to make reasonably good wine from them. A few years ago one would have been satisfied at receiving such a reply as, 'wine of a sort can be made of course from any grapes, but English outdoor grapes won't give drinkable wine'.

However, in 1949 that well-known novelist and agricultural expert, Mr Edward Hyams, published *The Grape Vine in England*, and the reader, however sceptical, is forced to admit that by choosing the correct *cépage*, following Mr Hyams's instructions and heeding his warnings and hints, it is quite practicable to make your own wine from your own grapes, even if you have no greenhouse. In 1954, Mr G. Ordish wrote *Wine-Growing in England*, in which he recounted his own experiences. Meanwhile Mr Hyams edited the volume *Vineyards in England*, in which a number of other experts are assembled to stun the reader with even more irrefutable evidence.

Both Mr Hyams and Mr Ordish remind one that flourishing vineyards existed in Gloucestershire and further north in the late Middle Ages, and when they died out, it was not because the wine was poor or the climate had changed, so that there is no natural reason why they should not be revived.

No summary here can do justice to the case for growing one's own wine, and the interested reader is referred to the books already mentioned. Mr U. P. Hedrick's *Grapes and Wines from Home Vineyards* refers to U.S.A. practice, but is nevertheless extremely interesting and informative to the English *vigneron*, whom Mr Hyams would dub 'vinearoon'.

TABLE OF MEASURES

1 hectare is 2·47 acres; 1 are is 120 square yards.

1 hectolitre is 22 imperial gallons or about 26½ U.S. gallons.

1 hogshead contains 46 (imperial) gallons (nominally 276 bottles).

1 butt (sherry) contains 108 gallons.

1 pipe contains 115 gallons (port); 92 gallons (Madeira); 93 gallons (Marsala).

1 wine or spirit bottle holds about 0·75 litre, which is about one-sixth of a gallon. Normal serving gives six to eight glasses of table-wine from a bottle.

100 U.S. gallons are equal to 83⅓ imperial gallons.

1 hectolitre per hectare is equal to 8·9 gallons per acre.

For degrees proof in spirits, see page 212.

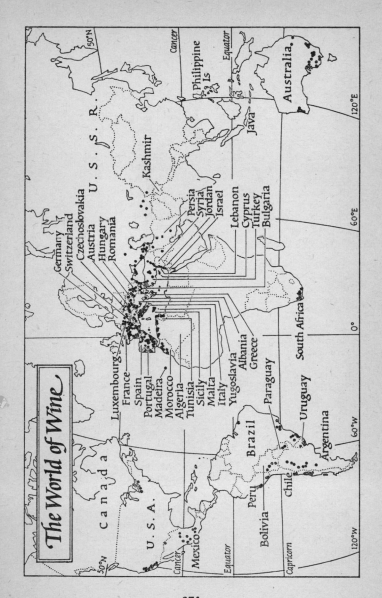

The World of Wine

MAP 2

WESTERN EUROPE

ALBANIA
- Elbasan c6.9
- Tirana c6.8
- Valona c6.10

AUSTRIA
- Dürnstein b6.3
- Eisenstadt b6.11
- Gumpoldskirchen b6.9
- Klosterneuberg b6.7
- Krems b6.4
- Neusiedler Lake b6.12
- Poysdorf b6.5
- Radkersburg (Radgona) b6.13
- Retz b6.2
- Salzburg b5.5
- Vienna b6.7
- Voslau b6.10
- Wachau b6.5

BULGARIA
- Pazardzhik c7.4
- Perushitsa c7.5
- Pleven c7.2
- Plovdiv c7.6
- Sofia c7.3
- Stara Zagora c8.1

CZECHOSLOVAKIA
- Brno b6.1
- Erz Gebirge a5.2
- Prague a5.3
- Riesengebirge a6.1

FRANCE
- Angers b2.2
- Arles c3.11
- Avignon c3.12
- Banyuls c3.5
- Beaune b3.5
- Béziers c3.7

FRANCE – *continued*
- Bordeaux c2.2
- Carcassonne c3.3
- Chablis b3.3
- Colmar b4.5
- Dijon b3.4
- Grenoble b4.12
- Lyons b3.7
- Marseilles c4.1
- Montpellier c3.9
- Mulhouse b4.6
- Nantes b2.1
- Narbonne c3.6
- Nice c4.3
- Nîmes c3.10
- Orange c3.13
- Paris b3.2
- Perpignan c3.4
- Rheims b3.1
- St-Émilion c2.1
- Saumur b2.3
- Sauternes c2.3
- Sète c3.8
- Strasbourg b4.4
- Tarbes c3.1
- Toulon c4.2
- Toulouse c3.2
- Tours b3.6
- Valence c3.14
- Vienne b3.8

GERMANY
- Augsburg b5.3
- Bingen b4.1
- Böhmer Wald b5.2
- Chemnitz a5.1
- Coblentz a4.1
- Dresden a5.4
- Frankfurt a.M. a4.2
- Freyburg a5.5
- Mainz b4.2
- Munich b5.4

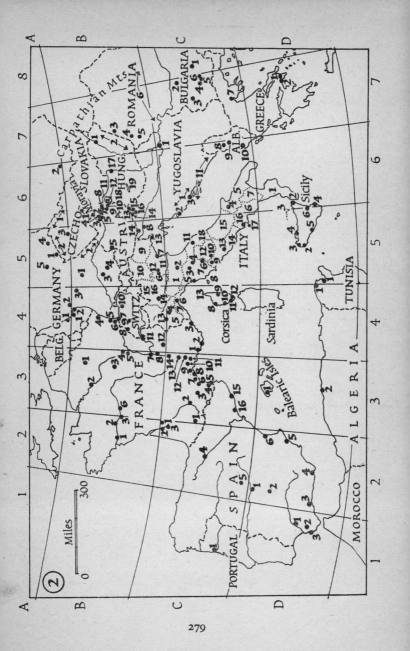

279

MAP 3

BORDEAUX AND THE CHARENTE

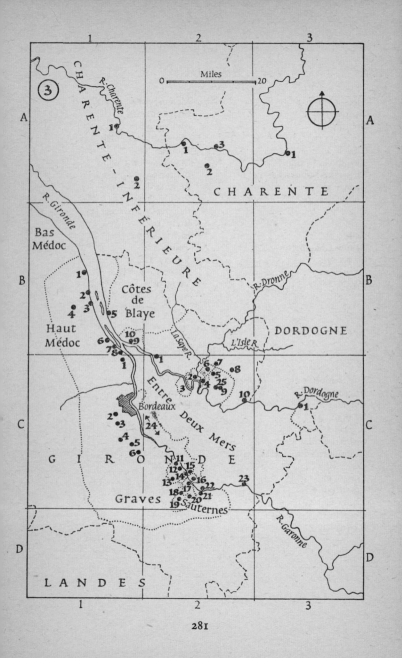

MAP 4

BURGUNDY

Aloxe-Corton 8
Beaune 9
Brouilly 31
Chagny 15
Chalon 20
Chambolle-Musigny 4
Chassagne-Montrachet 14
Chénas 26
Chiroubles 29
Dijon 1
Fixin 2
Fleurie 27
Gevrey-Chambertin 3
Givry 19
Juliénas 25
Mâcon 22
Mercurey 17
Meursault 12
Montagny 18
Monts du Beaujolais 32
Morgon 30
Moulin-à-Vent 28
Nuits-St-Georges 7
Pommard 10
Pouilly-Fuissé 23
Puligny-Montrachet 13
Rully 16
St-Amour 24
Tournus 21
Volnay 11
Vosne-Romanée 6
Vougeot 5

MAP 5

RHÔNE

Aigues-Mortes 25
Arles 24
Avignon 21
Beaucaire 23
Bollène 17
Château-Grillet 4
Châteauneuf-du-Pape 19
Condrieu 3
Cornas 10
Côte-Rotie 2
Crozes-Hermitage 6
Donzère 16
L'Hermitage 7
Montélimar 14
Orange 18
Privas 13
St-Péray 11
Serrière 5
Tain 8
Tarascon 22
Tavel 20
Tournon 9
Valence 12
Vienne 1
Viviers 15

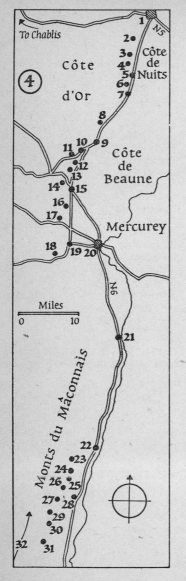

MAP 6

THE LOIRE VALLEY

Angers B2.2
Anjou B2
Amboise B3.8
Avranches A1.4
Azay-le-Rideau B3.3
Blois B4.2
Bourges B5.1
Bourgueil B3.1
Bourgneuf (en Mauges) B2.5
Brissac B2.7
Chalonnes B2.4
Chartres A4.1
Chaumes B2.14
Chinon B3.2
Châteaurault C3.1
Châteauroux C4.1
Durtal B2.1
Gennes B2.9
Laval A2.1
Le Mans A3.1
Loches B4.3
Montlouis B3.7
Montreuil B2.13

Mont-St-Michel A1.3
Nantes B1.1
Nevers C6.1
Orleans B4.4
Paramé A1.2
Poitiers C3.2
Pouilly B5.3
Rochefort-s/Loire B2.6
Rablay B2.12
Rennes A1.5
Rochecorbon B3.5
St Malo A1.1
Sancerre B5.2
Saumur B2.10
Savennières B2.3
Thouarcé B2.11
Touraine B3
Tours B3.4
Vauchrétien B2.8
Vendôme B4.1
Versailles A5.1
Vouvray B3.6

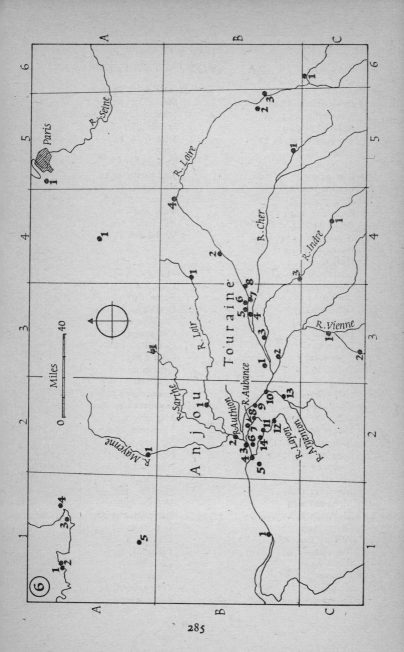

MAP 7
ALSACE, JURA, SAVOY, W. SWITZERLAND

FRANCE

Aix-les-Bains D2.2
Alberteville D3.3
Altkirch B4.5
Ammerschwihr A4.16
Annecy D3.2
Arbois C2.2
Barr A4.6
Beaune B1.1
Belfort B3.2
Bennwihr A4.13
Besançon B3.1
Bonneville C3.14
Bourg C2.7
Chalon C1.1
Chambéry D2.3
Chaumont A2.1
Chenin C2.1
Colmar A4.17
Conliège C2.4
Dambach A4.9
Dijon B2.1
Dôle B2.2
Épinal A3.1
Frangy C2.8
Gertwiller A4.8
Grenoble D2.4
Gübwiller B4.2
Heiligenstein A4.5
Kaysersberg A4.14
Lons-le-Saulnier C2.5
Lyons D1
Mâcon C1.2
Menetrux C2.6
Molsheim A4.3
Mulhouse B4.4
Ottrot A4.2
Poligny C2.3
Revermont C2.9
Rilsau A4.11
Riquewihr A4.12
Rouffach B4.1
St-Jean-de-Maurienne D3.4

FRANCE – *continued*

Ste-Odile A4.4
Selestat A4.10
Seyssel D2.1
Strasbourg A4
Thann B4.3
Thorens D3.1
Turckheim A4.15
Valence E1.1
Vienne D1.2
Ville A4.7
Villefranche D1.1
Wolxheim A4.1

SWITZERLAND

Basle B.4
Berne C4.1
Bex C4.5
Chablais C3
Commugny C3.5
Cortaillod C3.2
Côte C3.16
Geneva C3.4
Landeron B4.6
Lausanne C3.10
Lavaux C3.15
Martigny C4.6
Montreux C3.12
Morgues C3.9
Neuchâtel C3.1
Nyon C3.6
Rolle C3.7
St-Blaise B4.7
St-Prex C3.8
Sierre (Siders) C4.3
Sion C4.4
Thun C4.2
Valais C4
Vaud C3
Vévey C3.11
Villeneuve C3.13
Yverdon C3.3

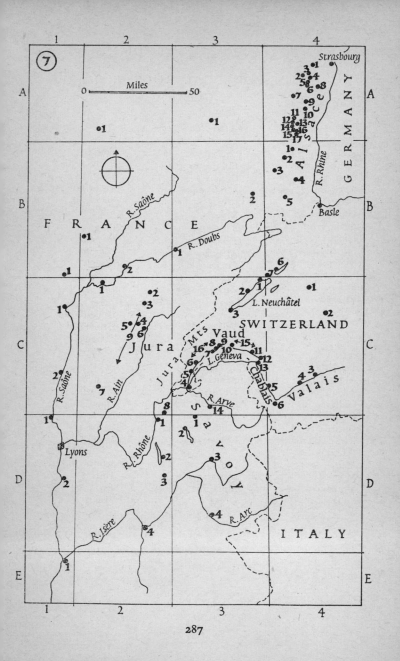

MAP 8

SPAIN, PORTUGAL, ROUSSILLON, LANGUEDOC

FRANCE
- Banyuls 1
- Béziers 10
- Carcassonne 6
- Cassis 7
- Collioure 2
- Corbières 4
- Frontignan 12
- Jurançon 17
- Limoux 5
- Minervois 9
- Montpellier 13
- Narbonne 8
- Pau 16
- Rivesaltes 3
- Sète 11
- Toulon 14
- Toulouse 15

SPAIN
Andalusia
- Almería 12
- Andujar 8
- Cádiz 1
- Cazalla 5
- Granada 11
- Jerez de la Frontera 3
- Lebrija 4
- Martos 10
- Montilla 7
- Moriles 6
- Sanlucar 2

SPAIN – *continued*
- Torredonjimeneo 9

Catalonia
- El Priorato 1
- Geróna 2
- Lérida 3
- Reus 4
- Sitges 5
- Tarragona 6

Extremadura
- Alcantara 1
- Garganta la Olla 2
- Jaraiz 3
- Zarzalamayor 4

León
- Ceclavin 1
- Valladolid 2

Murcia
- Yecla 1

New Castile
- Azofrin 4
- Canales 13
- Camarena 2
- Chinchon 9
- Ciudad Real 14
- Colmenar 10
- Esquivias 1
- La Membrilla 15
- Mascaraque 8
- Mora 7
- Orgaz 6

SPAIN – *continued*
- Sonseca 5
- Toledo 3
- Val de Peñas 16
- Villaminaya 12
- Yepes 11

Old Castile
- Avila 1
- Burgos 2
- Fuenmayor 3
- Logroño 4
- Rioja 5
- Santander 6

Valencia
- Alicante 1
- Benicarlo 2
- Liria 3
- Torrente 4

PORTUGAL
- Coimbra 9
- Monção 1
- Oporto 3
- Pinhão 5
- Regoa 4
- São João de Pesqueira 7
- Setubal 10
- Torre 8
- Tua 6
- Vianna 2

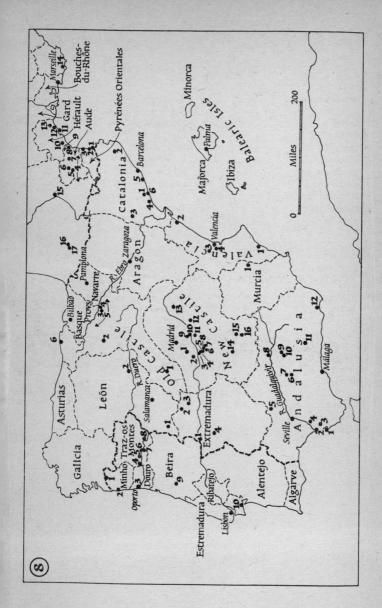

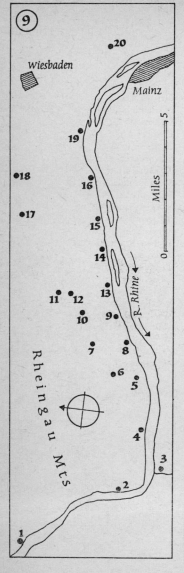

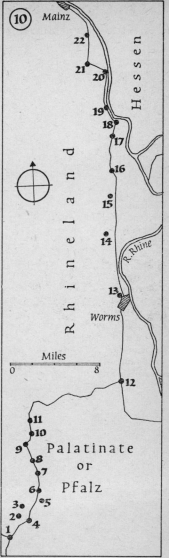

MAP 11

GERMANY: MOSEL, SAAR, RUWER, NAHE

Andernach A4.1
Assmannshausen B4.4
Bacharach B4.2
Bernkastel A3.1
Bingen B4.5
Bockelheim B3.4
Boos B3.3
Boppard A4.5
Brauneberg A2.12
Canzem A1.5
Casel A2.4
Cobern A4.3
Coblentz A4.4
Cochem (Kocheim) A3.11
Detzem A2.6
Dhron A2.9
Duchroth B3.5
Eitelsbach A2.2
Ems A4.6
Enkirch A3.9
Erden A3.6
Graach A3.2
Grünhaus A2.3
Hamm A1.6
Kinheim A3.7
Klüsserath A2.7
Kreuznach B3.7

Lorch B4.3
Mainz B4.7
Monzingen B3.1
Neuwied A4.2
Norheim B3.6
Ockfen A1.2
Piesport A2.10
Rüdesheim B4.6
Saarbrücken B1.2
Saarburg A1.1
Saargemunde B1.3
Saarlouis B1.1
St Goarshausen B4.1
Scharzhof A1.3
Sobernheim B3.2
Traben-Trarbach A3.8
Trier A2.1
Trittenheim A2.8
Urzig A3.5
Waldrach A2.5
Wehlen A3.3
Wiesbaden B4.8
Wiltringen A1.4
Wintrich A2.11
Zell A3.10
Zeltingen A3.4

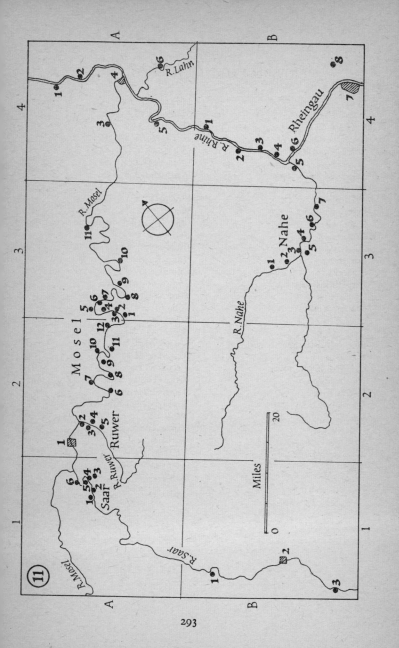

R.Mosel

R.Mosel

R.Lahn

R.Rhine

Rheingau

R.Mosel

Mosel

Ruwer

R.Ruwer

Saar

R.Saar

R.Nahe

Nahe

Miles

0   20

A

B

A

B

1   2   3   4

293

MAP 12

EASTERN EUROPE AND TURKEY

Alushta B3.2
Anapa B4.1
Anatolia C2.3
Ankara B3.6
Antep (Gaziantep) C4.3
Arad A1.2
Armenian S.S.R. B5.9
Athens C1.1
Azerbaijan S.S.R. B6.5
Balkan Mts B1.3
Batumi B5.6
Beirut D4.1
Bucharest B2.1
Burgas B2.5
Bursa B2.10
Carpathians A2.1
Cilicia C3.3
Constanţa B2.2
Çubuk B3.5
Dragasan B1.1
Edirne (Adrianople) B2.7
Elazig C4.2
Georgian S.S.R. B5.2
Hasandede C4.1
İsparta C3.1
İstanbul B2.9
Kalecik B3.7
Kilis C4.4
Krasnodar B4.2
Kura (river) B6.6
Kurdistan C5.1
Kutaisi B5.3
Lake Sevan B6.4

Limassol D3.1
Maikop B5.1
Napareuli B5.7
Nor Bayazet B5.11
Odessa A3.1
Oradea A1.1
Pazardzhik B1.5
Perushitsa B1.7
Piraeus C1.2
Pleven B1.2
Plovdiv (Philippopolis) B1.6
Poti B5.4
Rion (river) B5.12
Ruse (Ruscuk) B2.3
Salonika B1.8
Sevastopol B3.4
Smyrna (İzmir) C2.2
Sofia B1.4
Stara Zagora B2.6
Sudak B3.1
Tarsus C3.2
Tekirdag B2.8
Telavi B6.1
Tiflis (Tbilisi) B5.8
Timisoara A1.3
Transylvanian Alps A1.4
Troy C2.1
Tsinandali B6.2
Varna B2.4
Yalta B3.3
Yerevan B5.10
Zakataly B6.3

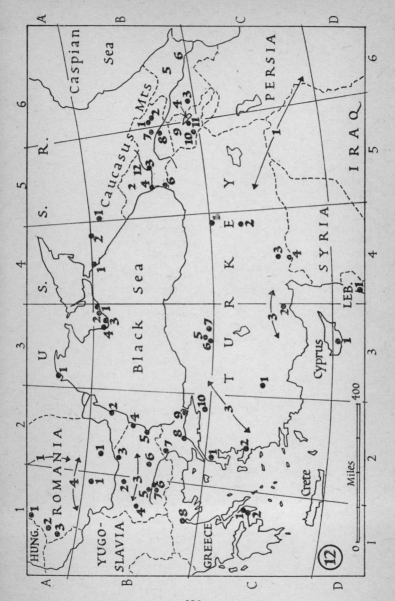

MAP 13

CENTRAL ASIA

Amritsar C4.1
Amu Darya (river) B3
Armenian S.S.R. B1.11
Astrakhan A1.1
Azerbaijan S.S.R. B1.16
Baghdad C1.1
Baku B1.17
Batumi B1.3
Bukhara B3.1
Dagestan B1.9
Derbent B1.10
Fergana B4.1
Georgian S.S.R. B1.4
Herat C3.1
Isfahan C2.1
Kabul C3.2
Kandahar C3.3
Kara-Kalpak A.S.S.R. B2.1
Kashgar B4.2
Kutaisi B1.2
Lahore C4.2
Napareuli B1.7
Nor Bayazet B1.12
Persepolis C2.2
Peshawar C4.3
Rion (river) B1.1
Samarkand B3.2
Sevan, Lake B1.14
Srinagar C4.4
Stalingrad A1.2
Syr Darya (river) B3
Tabriz B1.18
Tashkent B3.3
Tehran B2.2
Telavi B1.5
Tiflis (Tbilisi) B1.8
Tsinandali B1.6
Urmia, Lake B1.19
Yerevan B1.13
Zakataly B1.15

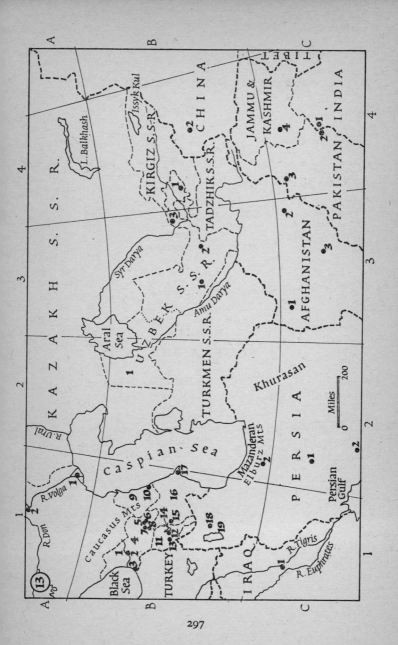

MAP 14

ALGERIA, TUNIS AND MOROCCO

TUNIS
  Bizerta A4.3
  Gabes B5.2
  Sfax B5.1
  Sousse A5.6
  Tunis A5.5

ALGERIA
  Algiers A3.4
  Bône A4.2
  Constantine A4.1
  Mascara A3.1
  Médéa A3.3
  Miliana A3.2
  Oran A2.1

MOROCCO
  Casablanca B1.3
  Fez B2.1
  Marrakesh B1.5
  Meknes B1.2
  Mogador B1.4
  Rabat B1.1

SICILY
  Agrigento A5.3
  Catania A5.4
  Marsala A5.2
  Trapani A5.1

MAP 15

SOUTH AFRICA

Bonnievale A2.2
Caledon B1.3
Calitz Dorp A2.5
Constantia B1.1
Drakenstein Mtns. A1.8
Ladismith A2.4
Langeberge A2.3
Malmesbury A1.2
Montagu A2.1
Oudtshoorn A3.1
Paarl A1.4

Port Elizabeth A4.1
Riversdale B2.2
Robertson A1.7
Somerset West B1.2
Stellenbosch A1.5
Swellendam B2.1
Tulbagh A1.1
Wellington A1.3
Wemmershoek Mountains A1.9
Worcester A1.6
Zwartberg A2.6

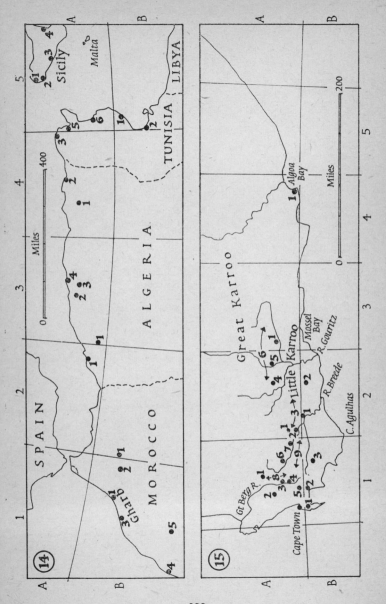

299

MAP 16

AUSTRALIA

QUEENSLAND
Roma 1

NEW SOUTH WALES
Albury 1
Corowa 2
Hunter River 3
Minchinbury 4
Parramatta 5

SOUTH AUSTRALIA
Berri 1
Clare 2
Coonawarra 9
Dorrien 4
McLaren Vale 3
Nuriootpa 5
Reynella 6

SOUTH AUSTRALIA – *continued*
Renmark 7
Waikerie 8

VICTORIA
Barnswartha 1
Chiltern 2
Cobram 3
Geelong 4
Great Western 5
Mildura 6
Rutherglen 7
Swan Hill 8

WEST AUSTRALIA
Dardanup 1
Gosnells 2
Northam 3
Swan 4
Toodyay 5
Wanneru 6

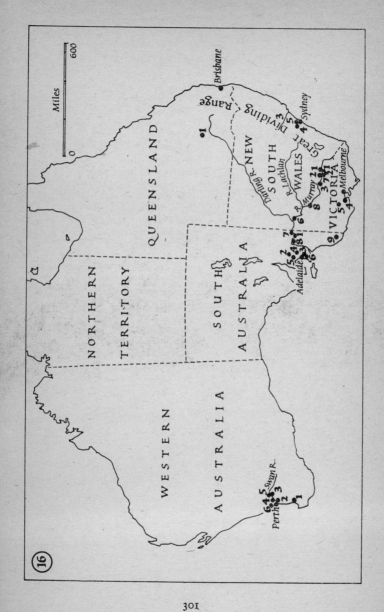

Miles

600

0

Brisbane

Great Dividing Range

Sydney

3
5 4

1

QUEENSLAND

NEW SOUTH WALES

Darling R.

R. Lachlan

2 1

VICTORIA

3 7 1
5
9

R. Murray

8

6

Melbourne

NORTHERN TERRITORY

SOUTH AUSTRALIA

7
2
5 4 3 1
Adelaide 6

WESTERN AUSTRALIA

5 Swan R.
4 3
6 4 2 1
Perth

⑯

MAP 17

NORTH AMERICA

Aguas Calientes C3.10
Apam D4.2
Ashtabula A5.3
Chihuahua C3.2
Ciudad Jaurez (Paso del Norte) B3.1
Conneaut A5.4
Durango (City) C3.5
Durango (State) C3.4
Fingers Lakes A6.6
Fresno B2.1
Grimsby A6.3
Hamilton A6.2
Hidalgo C4.1
Jalisco C3.12
Kings County B2.2
Kern County B2.4
Lake Erie A5.5
Lake Huron A5.7
Lake Michigan A5.6
Lake Ontario A6.7
Los Angeles B2.8
Mexico City D4.1
Michoacán D3.1
Mohave Desert B2.6
Monterrey C3.7

Napa B1.2
Nayarit C3.8
Niagara Falls A6.5
Orizaba D4.3
Parras C3.6
Peoria A5.1
Red Bluff A1.1
Sacramento River B1
Saint Helena B1.1
San Bernardino B2.7
Sandusky A5.2
San Francisco B1.4
San Joaquin River B1
Sierra Nevada B2.5
Sinaloa C3.3
Sonoma B1.3
Sonora C3.1
Stanislaus County B1.5
Tampico C4.2
Tepic C3.9
Tequila C3.11
Toronto A6.1
Tulare B2.3
Welland A6.4

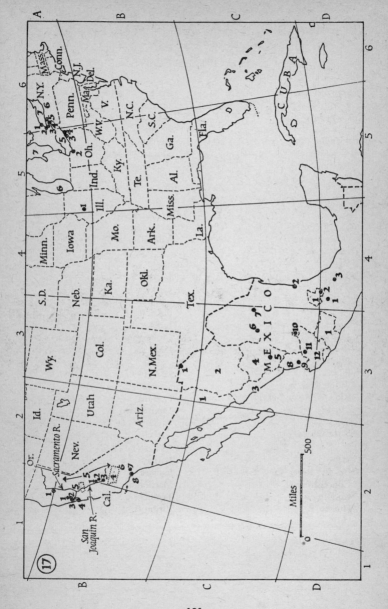

MAP 18

SOUTH AMERICA

ARGENTINA
Buenos Aires 8
Catamarca 2
Colonia Alvear Oeste 7
Mendoza 5
Neuquén 9
La Rioja 3
San Juan 4
San Rafael 6
Tucumán 1

BOLIVIA
Cochabamba 2
La Paz 1
Sucre 3
Tarija 4

BRAZIL
Alfredo Chaves 6
Caxias 7
Mairinque 5
Pelotas 10
Pôrto Alegre 8
Pinhal 3
Rio de Janeiro 2
Rio Grande do Sul 11
Santa Maria 9
São Luis 1
São Paulo 4

CHILE
Bió Bió River 12
Concepción 11
Coquimbo 3
Huasco 1

CHILE – *continued*
Linares 7
Los Angeles 10
Ñuble 9
Santiago 5
Talca 6
Talcahuano 8
Vallenar 2
Valparaíso 4

PARAGUAY
Asunción 1
Villa Rica 2

PERU
Callao 2
Chincha Is. 4
Ica 5
Ilo 7
Lima 1
Moquegua 6
Pisco 3

URUGUAY
Canelones 3
Colonia 2
Montevideo 4
Paysandú 1

WEST INDIES
Barbados 3
Jamaica 5
Martinique 2
Trinidad 4
Virgin Is. 1

BIBLIOGRAPHY

GENERAL

G. SAINTSBURY: *Notes on a Cellar-book* (London, 1920)

M. HEALY: *Stay Me With Flagons* (London, 1940)

> These two are also belles-lettres: diverting, idiosyncratic, incidentally informative.

A. L. SIMON: *A Wine Primer* (London, 1946; new edition, 1955)

A. L. SIMON: *Vintagewise* (London, 1945)

A. L. SIMON: *Bottlescrew Days* (London, 1926)

A. L. SIMON: *Wine and the Wine Trade* (London, 1921)

> Mr Simon is the acknowledged doyen of writers on wine in English. He has written a score of books on the subject, all of which are authoritatively informative. He has also edited *A Concise Encyclopædia of Gastronomy* (London, 1939–46), of which Volume 8 deals with wines and spirits, and a series of small handbooks on wines (*Burgundy, Claret, Champagne, Hocks and Moselles, Port, Sauternes, Sherry, South African, Rhône, Switzerland, Loire, Yugoslavia, Italy, Madeira, California,* and also one on *Brandy*); furthermore he edits the quarterly, *Wine and Food.*

P. MORTON SHAND: *A Book of Wine* (London, 1926)

P. MORTON SHAND: *A Book of French Wines* (London and New York, 1928)

P. MORTON SHAND: *A Book of Other Wines than French* (London and New York, 1929)

H. WARNER ALLEN: *Natural Red Wines* (London, 1951)

H. WARNER ALLEN: *White Wines and Cognac* (London, 1952)

> Mr Warner Allen has also written extensively and more discursively in several other books on wine.

A. SICHEL and others: *A Guide to Good Wine* (London and Edinburgh, 1952)

T. A. LAYTON: *Choose Your Wine* (London, 1949)

R. POSTGATE: *The Plain Man's Guide to Wine* (London, 1951)

> These three are admirable short accounts, to be strongly recommended. The first two are by members of the wine-trade; Mr Postgate is the well-known journalist and publicist: his *Good Food Guide* is famous.

O. MENDELSOHN: *The Earnest Drinker* (London, 1950)

F. C. LLOYD: *The Art and Technique of Wine* (London, 1936)

T. E. CARLING: *The Complete Book of Drink* (London, 1951)

F. SCHOONMAKER and T. MARVEL: *The Complete Wine Book* (London, 1935)

> Mr Schoonmaker is a well-known American expert and importer.

W. V. CRUESS: *Principles and Practice of WineMaking* (New York, 1946)
> Professor Cruess is in charge of oenological research at the University of California: see page 98.

L. GENEVOIS and J. RIBEREAU-GAYON: *Le Vin* (Paris, 1947)
> The authors are eminent oenologists of Bordeaux: see page 97.

E. VOGT: *Der Wein* (Stuttgart, 1952)
> Professor Vogt, one of the most famous of German experts, is Director of the State Wine Institute at Freiburg.

Larousse Gastronomique (Paris, 1938)

P. POUPON: *Pensées d'un Dégustateur* (Nuits St-Georges, 1957)

C. SELTMAN: *Wine in the Ancient World* (London, 1957)

JOURNALS

Wine and Food, quarterly (50 Grosvenor Gardens, London S.W.1)
Revue du Vin de France, quarterly (40 Avenue Junot, Paris 18)

CHAMPAGNE

G. CHAPPAZ: *Le Vignoble et le Vin de Champagne* (Paris, 1951)

FORTIFIED WINES

H. WARNER ALLEN: *Sherry and Port* (London, 1952)
W. J. TODD: *Port: How to Buy, Serve, Store and Drink It* (London, 1926)
R. CROFT-COOKE: *Sherry* (London, 1955)

FRENCH WINES

(See also P. M. Shand, under GENERAL).

A. LICHINE: *The Wines of France* (London, 1952)
J. M. SCOTT: *Vineyards of France* (London, 1950)
> Mr Scott's book is personal and impressionistic, with fine illustrations.

J. M. ROGER: *Les Vins de Bordeaux* (Paris, 1955)
C. COCKS and E. FERET: *Bordeaux et Ses Vins* (Bordeaux, 11th edition, 1949)
> Professor Roger's book is a succinct, authoritative modern monograph: the author is editor of *Revue du Vin de France*. Cocks details some three or four thousand vineyards.

P. POUPON and P. FORGEOT: *Les Vins de Bourgogne* (Paris, 1952)
> An authoritative and up-to-date monograph; Rodier's book is now out of print.

S. F. HALLGARTEN: *Alsace and its Wine Gardens* (London, 1957)
P. BREJOUX: *Les Vins de Loire* (Paris, 1957)

OTHER WINES

S. F. HALLGARTEN: *Wineland Rhineland* (London, 1951)

BIBLIOGRAPHY

G. LEONHARDT: *Weinfachbuch* (Leipzig, 1954)
> This contains valuable information on East European wine, but is very
> curt concerning those of other countries. (Russia, 12 pages; Italy, 2 pages.)

Der Wein (Leipzig, 1955)
> Translation, by B. Assmann, of articles from the Great Soviet Encyclo-
> pædia. The same remarks apply as to Leonhardt.

G. STEIN: *Reise durch den deutschen Weingarten* (München, 1956)

C. BODE: *The Wines of Italy* (London, 1956)

F. SCHOONMAKER: *Wines of Germany* (London & New York, 1957)

H. R. RUDD: *Hocks and Moselles* (London, 1935)

H. LANGENBACH: *Wines of Germany* (London, 1951–2)

W. JAMES: *Wine in Australia* (Melbourne, 1952)

SPIRITS: GENERAL

K. M. HERSTEIN and M. B. JACOBS: *Chemistry and Technology of Wines and
Liquors* (London and New York, 2nd edition, 1948)

BRANDY
(See also A. L. Simon, under GENERAL).

H. WARNER ALLEN: *White Wines and Cognac* (London, 1952)

R. DELAMAIN: *Histoire du Cognac* (Paris, 1936)

WHISKY

J. M. ROBB: *Scotch Whisky, a Guide* (London and Edinburgh, [1951])

SIR ROBERT BRUCE-LOCKHART: *Scotch* (London, 1951)

LIQUEURS

H. BENNETT: *The Chemical Formulary* (Volumes 1, 2, and 4) (New York
and London, 1933–1951)

Henley's 20th Century Formulas (New York, 1945, revised edition)

FRUIT WINES

A. L. SIMON: *English Wines and Cordials* (London, 1946)

M. AYLETT: *Country Wines* (London, 1953)

HOME GRAPE-WINE MAKING

G. ORDISH: *Wine-Growing in England* (London, 1954)

E. S. HYAMS: *The Grape Vine in England* (London, 1949)

E. S. HYAMS (editor): *Vineyards in England* (London, 1953)

U. P. HENDRICK: *Grapes and Wines from Home* [i.e. U.S.A.] *Vineyards*
(New York, 1945)

S. M. TRITTON: *Grape Growing and Wine Making* (Almondsbury, Glos.,
1951)

S. M. TRITTON: *Successful Wine Making* (Almondsbury, Glos., 1952)

INDEX